ROMANS

In the same series

MATTHEW – J. C. Ryle
JOHN – J. C. Ryle
EPHESIANS – Charles Hodge

The Classic New Testament Commentary

ROMANS

H. C. G. Moule

Edited by Philip Hillyer

Marshall Pickering
An Imprint of HarperCollinsPublishers

Marshall Pickering is an Imprint of
HarperCollins*Religious*
Part of HarperCollins*Publishers*
77–85 Fulham Palace Road, London W6 8JB

Originally published by Hodder & Stoughton, London, in 1894
Reprinted by Pickering and Inglis in 1900
This edition first published in Great Britain
in 1992 by Marshall Pickering

1 3 5 7 9 10 8 6 4 2

A catalogue record for this book is
available from the British Library

ISBN 0 551 02592-1

Phototypeset by Intype, London
Printed and bound in Great Britain by
HarperCollinsManufacturing Glasgow

PREFACE

The person who attempts to expound the Epistle to the Romans is little disposed to speak about his commentary when it is finished. Instead, he is occupied with an ever deeper reverence and wonder over the text which he has been permitted to handle, a text that is so full of a marvellous man, and above all so full of God.

But it seems necessary to say a few words about the style of the running translation of the epistle which is interwoven with this exposition. The writer is aware that the translation is often rough and formless. His defence is that it has been done to provide an explanation of details rather than a connected reading. He is also aware that some aspects of his translation are open to criticism, but they are only offered as suggestions. It is scarcely necessary to say that this commentary says little or nothing on questions of literary criticism that do not affect the exposition.

We may note here that some commentators argue that the aim of Romans is conciliation. They regard the great passage about Israel (9–11) as in some sense the heart of the epistle, and the doctrinal passages preceding this as all more or less meant to bear on the relations not only of the law and the gospel, but of the Jew and the Gentile as members of the one Christian Church. There is great value in this suggestion, but the argument can easily be pressed too far. It seems plain to the present writer that when the epistle is studied from within its deepest spiritual element, it shows us the apostle fully aware of the widest aspects of the life and work of the Church, but also, and yet more, occupied with the problem of the relation of the believing sinner to God. Paul never forgot the question of personal salvation when dealing with the question of Christian policy.

To return for a moment to this exposition, or rather to its setting; it may be thought that whether in imagining the dictation of the epistle to be begun and completed by St Paul within a single day we have not imagined something very difficult. But at worst it is not impossible, if the apostle's speech was as sustained as his thought.

It remains only to express the hope that these pages may encourage readers to turn to the actual text of Romans, if only by suggesting to them sometimes the words of St Augustine, 'To Paul I appeal from all interpreters of his writings.'

CONTENTS

CHAPTER 1

Time, Place, and Occasion

It is February, AD 58. In a room in the house of Gaius, a wealthy Corinthian Christian, Paul the Apostle, having at his side his secretary Tertius, addresses himself to write to the converts of the mission at Rome.

The great world meanwhile is rolling on its way. It is the fourth year of Nero; he is Consul for the third time, together with Valerius Messala; Poppaea has lately caught the unworthy prince in the net of her bad influence. Domitius Corbulo has just resumed the war with Parthia, and prepares to penetrate the highlands of Armenia. Within a few weeks, in the middle of spring, an Egyptian impostor is about to inflame Jerusalem with his Messianic claim, to lead four thousand fanatics into the desert, and to return to the city with a host of thirty thousand men, only to be totally routed by the legionaries of Felix. For himself, the apostle is about to end his three months' stay at Corinth; he has heard of plots against his life, and will prudently decline the more direct route from Cenchrea by sea, striking northward for Philippi, and thence over the Aegean to Troas. He must visit Jerusalem, if possible before May is over, for he has by him the Greek collections to deliver to the poor converts of Jerusalem. Then, dreaming of his further movements, he sees Rome, and thinks both with apprehension and longing hope about life and witness there.

A Greek Christian woman is about to visit the city, Phoebe, who had a ministry in the mission at Cenchrea. He must commend her to the Roman brethren, which prompts him to write a letter to them.

His thoughts have been turned for a long time to the capital city of the world. Not many months before, at Ephesus, when he had 'purposed in the Spirit' to visit Jerusalem, he had said, with an emphasis which his biographer remembered, 'I must also see Rome' (Acts 19.21). It was an '*I must*', in the sense of a divine decree, which had written this journey down in the plan of his life. He was assured too, by circumstantial and perhaps by supernatural signs, that he had 'now no more place in these parts' (Rom. 15.23)—that is, in the Eastern Roman world where he had so far worked. The Lord who previously had restricted Paul to a track which led him through Asia Minor to the Aegean, and across the Aegean to Europe (Acts 16), now prepared to guide him, though by paths which his servant did not know, from Eastern to Western Europe, and above all to Rome. Amongst these providential preparations was a growing occupation of the Apostle's thought with persons and interests in the Christian circle there. Here, as we have seen, was Phoebe, about to take ship for Italy. There, in the great capital, the beloved and faithful Aquila and Prisca were now resident again, no longer excluded by the edict of Claudius, and proving already, we may fairly conclude, the central influence in the mission, whose first days perhaps dated from Pentecost itself, when Roman 'strangers' (Acts 2.10) saw and heard the wonders and the message of that time. Other believers personally known to Paul also lived at Rome, drawn by unrecorded circumstances to the centre of the world. His 'well-beloved' Epaenetus was there; Mary, who had sometimes tried hard to help him; Andronicus, and Junias, and Herodion, his relatives; Amplias and Stachys, men very dear to him; Urbanus, who had worked for Christ at his side; Rufus, no ordinary Christian in his esteem, and Rufus' mother, who had once watched over Paul with a mother's love. All these rise before him as he thinks of Phoebe, and her arrival, and the faces and the hands which at his appeal would welcome her in the Lord, in the holy freemasonry of the early Christian fellowship.

Besides, he has been hearing about the actual state of that all-important mission. As 'all roads led to Rome', so all roads led from Rome, and there were Christian travellers everywhere (1.8) who could tell him how the gospel fared among Christians in the metropolis. As he heard of them, so he prayed for them, 'without ceasing' (1.9), and made definite and urgent request

too for himself, that his way might be opened to visit them at
last.

To pray for others, if the prayer is truly prayer, and based to
some extent on knowledge, is a sure way to deepen our interest
in them, and our sympathetic insight into their hearts and conditions. From the human side, nothing more than this news and
these prayers was needed to draw from St Paul a written message
to be placed in Phoebe's care. From this same human side again,
when he once addressed himself to write, there were circumstances of thought and action which would naturally shape his
message.

He stood amid circumstances that were most significant and
suggestive in matters of Christian *truth*. Quite recently his Judaist
rivals had invaded the congregations of Galatia, and had led the
impulsive converts there to abandon what seemed their firm
grasp on the truth of justification by faith alone. To St Paul this
was no mere battle of abstract definitions, nor a matter of merely
local importance. The success of the alien teachers in Galatia
showed him that the same plausible mischief-makers might win
their way, more or less quickly, anywhere. And what would such
success mean? It would mean the loss of the joy of the Lord, and
the strength of that joy, in the misguided churches. Justification
by faith meant nothing less than *Christ all in all*, literally all in
all, for sinful man's pardon and acceptance. It meant a profound
simplicity of complete personal reliance upon him in the face of
the fiery holiness of the eternal law. It meant a look out and up,
simultaneously intense and unanxious, from both the virtues and
the guilt of man, to the mighty merits of the Saviour. It was
precisely the foundation-fact of salvation, which guaranteed that
the process should be, from its beginning, not humanitarian but
divine. To discredit *that* was not merely to disturb the order of
a missionary community, it was to hurt the inner elements of the
Christian soul, contaminating the mountain springs of the peace
of God. Fresh as he was now from fighting this evil in Galatia,
St Paul would be sure to have it in his thoughts when he turned
to Rome; for there it was only too certain that his active enemies
would do their worst; probably they were at work already.

Secondly, he had been just engaged also with the problems of

Christian *life*, in the mission at Corinth. There the main trouble
was less of creed than of conduct. We find no great traces of an
energetic heretical propaganda in the Corinthian Epistles, but
rather a bias in the converts towards a strange license in outlook
and life. Perhaps this was even made more pronounced by a
popular logical assent to the truth of justification *taken alone*,
isolated from other associated truths, tempting the Corinthian to
dream that he might 'continue in sin that grace might abound'.
If such were his state of spiritual thought, he would encounter
(by his own fault) a positive moral danger in the supernatural
'gifts' which seem to have appeared with quite abnormal power
at Corinth about that time. An antinomian theory, in the presence of such exaltations, would lead a man easily to the idea
that he was too free and too rich in the supernatural order to be
the servant of common duties, and even of common morals. Thus
the apostle's soul would be full of the need of expounding to its
depths the vital harmony of the Lord's work *for* the believer and
the Lord's work *in* him; the co-ordination of a free acceptance
with both the requirement and the possibility of holiness. He
must show once for all how the justified are bound to be pure
and humble, and how they can so be, and what forms of practical
dutifulness their life must take. He must make it clear for ever
that the ransom which releases also purchases; that the Lord's
freeman is the Lord's property; that Christ's death on the cross,
reckoned as the death of the justified sinner, leads direct to his
living union with the Risen One, including a union of will with
will; so that the Christian life, if true to itself, *must* be a life of
loyalty to every obligation and relationship in human society
ordained by God. The Christian who is not attentive to others,
even where their mere prejudices and mistakes are in question,
is a Christian out of character. So is the Christian who is not a
scrupulously loyal citizen, recognizing civil order as the will of
God. So is the Christian who in any respect claims to live as he
pleases, instead of as the bondservant of his Redeemer should
live.

Thirdly, another question had been weighing on the apostle's
mind for years, but recently with a special force. It was the
mystery of Jewish unbelief. Who can estimate the pain and

greatness of that mystery in the mind of St Paul? His own conversion, while it taught him patience with his old associates, must have filled him also with some eager hopes for them. Every deep and self-evidencing manifestation of God in a man's soul suggests to him naturally the thought of the glorious things possible in the souls of others. Why should not the leading Pharisee, now converted, be the signal and means of the conversion of the Sanhedrin, and of the people? But the hard mystery of sin blocked such hopes, and more and more so as the years went on. Judaism outside the Church was stubborn, and energetically hostile. And within the Church, unhappily, it infiltrated secretly underground, and sprung up in an embittered opposition to the central truths. What did all this mean? Where would it end? Had Israel sinned, collectively, beyond pardon and repentance? Had God cast off his people? Did the conduct of the troublemakers of Galatia or the rioters at Corinth mean that all was over for the race of Abraham? The question was agony to Paul; and he sought his Lord's answer to it as a thing without which he could not live. His soul was full of that answer when he meditated on his Letter to Rome, and thought of the Judaists there, and also of the loving Jewish friends of his heart there who would read his message when it came.

This is how we dare to describe the possible outward and inward conditions under which the Epistle to the Romans was conceived and written. It is good to remember that these are only conjectures, although the epistle's outline and detail does support them. We do not forget again that the epistle, whatever the writer saw around him or felt within him, was, when produced, infinitely more than the product of Paul's mind and life; it was, and is, an oracle of God, a Scripture, a revelation of eternal facts and principles by which to live and die. This is how we approach it in this book; not just to analyse or explain, but to submit and to believe; taking it as not only Pauline but divine. But this does not make it any the less Pauline. And this means that both the thought and the circumstances of St Paul are to be traced and felt in it as truly, and as naturally, as if we had before us the letter of an Augustine, or a Luther, or a Pascal. He who chose the writers of the Holy Scriptures, many men scattered over many ages, used them each in his surroundings and in his character, yet so as to harmonize them all in the book which, while many, is one. He used them with divine sovereign skill. And that skilful use meant that he used their whole being, which he had made, and their whole circumstances, which he had ordered. They were truly his secretaries, I am not afraid to say that they were his pens. But God is such that he can use as his easy instrument not just a machine (which however complex and powerful, can never truly cause anything), but a human personality. He can take one, made in his own image and full of living thoughts, feelings and will that form things and cause them, and can throw it freely upon its task of thinking and expression—and behold, the product will be God's; his matter, his thought, his exposition, his word, 'living and abiding for ever'.

So we enter in spirit the Corinthian citizen's house, in the sunshine of the early Greek spring, and find our way invisible and unheard to where Tertius sits with his reed-pen and strips of papyrus, and where Paul is prepared to give him, word by word, sentence by sentence, this immortal message. Perhaps the corner of the room is heaped with hair-cloth from Cilicia, and the implements of the tent-maker. But the apostle is now the guest of Gaius, a man whose means enable him to be the host of the whole Church; so we may think instead that for the time this manual work is suspended. Do we seem to see the form and face of the person who is about to dictate his letter? There is some historical evidence for supposing that we find a small and much emaciated frame, and a face remarkable for its arched brows and wide forehead, and for the expressive mobility of the lips. We trace in looks, in manner and tone of speech, and even in unconscious attitude and action, signs of a mind that is rich in every faculty, a nature that is equally strong in energy and in sympathy, made both to govern and to win, to will and to love. The man is great and wonderful, a master soul, subtle, wise, and strong. Yet he strongly attracts us to his heart, like one who asks and will repay affection.

As we look on his face we think, with awe and gladness, that with those same thought-tired eyes (and are they not also troubled with disease?) he has literally seen, only twenty years ago, so he will quietly assure us, the risen and glorified Jesus. His work during those twenty years, his innumerable sufferings, above all, his spirit of perfect mental and moral sanity, yet of supernatural peace and love—all make his assurance absolutely trustworthy. He is a transfigured man since that vision of Jesus Christ, who now 'dwells in his heart by faith', and uses him as the medium of his will and work. And now listen. The Lord is speaking through his servant. The scribe is busy with his pen, as the message of Christ is uttered through the soul and from the lips of Paul.

CHAPTER 2

The Writer and His Readers (1.1–7)

V 1. *Paul, a bondservant of Jesus Christ.* So the man opens his Lord's
message with his own name. We may, if we please, leave it and
pass on, for to the letter-writer of that day it was as much a
matter of course to put one's name at the beginning of the letter
as it is to us to put it at the end. But then, as now, the name
was not a mere formality; certainly not in the communications
of a religious leader. It admitted personal responsibility. In a
letter destined to be read in public it set the man in the light
and glare of publicity, as truly as when he spoke in the Christian
assembly, or on the Areopagus, or from the steps of the castle
at Jerusalem. It tells us here, at the outset, that the messages we
are about to read are given to us as 'truth through personality';
they come through the mental and spiritual being of this wonderful and most real man. If we read his character aright in his
letters, we see in him a delicacy and dignity of thought which
would not make publicizing himself a light and easy thing. But
his feelings, with all else he has, have been given to Christ (who
never either rejects or spoils such gifts, while he accepts them);
and if it will the better win attention to the Lord that the servant
should stand out conspicuously, to point to him, it shall be done.

For he is indeed 'Jesus Christ's bondservant'; not just his ally,
subject, or friend. Recently, writing to the Galatian converts, he
has been justifying the glorious liberty of the Christian, set free
both from 'the curse of the law' and from the mastery of self.
But there too, at the close (6.17), he has dwelt on his own sacred
bondage; 'the brand of his Master, Jesus'. The freedom of the
gospel is one side of the shield whose other side is an uncon-
ditional bondservice to the liberating Lord. Our freedom is 'in
the Lord' alone; and to be 'in the Lord' is to belong to him, as

wholly as a healthy hand belongs, in its freedom, to the physical centre of life and will. To be a bondservant is terrible in the abstract. To be 'Jesus Christ's bondservant' is Paradise, in the concrete. Self-surrender, taken alone, is a plunge into a cold void. When it is surrender to 'the Son of God, who loved me, and gave Himself for me' (Gal. 2.20), it is the bright home-coming of the soul to the seat and sphere of life and power.

This bondservant of Christ is *called to be an Apostle*. It is a rare commission: to be a chosen witness of the resurrection, a divinely authorized bearer of the holy Name, a first founder and guide of the universal Church. Yet the apostleship, to St Paul, is just one aspect of bondservice. 'To every man is his work', given by the one sovereign will. In a Roman household one slave would water the garden, another keep accounts, another in the library would do skilled literary work; yet all equally would be 'not their own, but bought with a price'. So in the gospel, then, and now. All functions of Christians are equal expressions of the one will of him who has purchased them, and who 'calls'.

Meanwhile, this bondservant-apostle, because he is 'under authority', carries authority. His Master has spoken to him, that he may speak. He writes to the Romans as man, as friend, but also as the vessel chosen to bear the name of Jesus Christ (Acts 9.15).

Such is the sole essential work and purpose of his life. He is *separated to the gospel of God*; isolated from all other ruling aims to this. In some respects he is the least isolated of men; he is in contact all round with human life. Yet he is 'separated'. In Christ, and for Christ, he lives apart from even the worthiest personal ambitions. Richer than ever, since he 'was in Christ' (16.7), in all that makes man's nature wealthy, in power to know, to will, to love, he uses all his riches always for 'this one thing', to make men understand 'the gospel of God'. Such isolation, behind a thousand contacts, is still the Lord's call for his true followers.

'The gospel': The word is almost too familiar now, till the thing is too little understood. What is it? In its basic meaning it is the divine 'Good News'. It is the announcement of Jesus Christ, Son of God, Saviour of men, in whom God and man meet with joy. As we shall see in this epistle, that announcement is related to a string of commands and warnings, but neither are properly the gospel. The gospel saves from sin, and enables for holy conduct. But in itself it is just the pure message of redeeming Love.

It is 'the gospel of God'; that is, as the neighbouring sentences show, the gospel of the blessed Father. Its origin is in the Father's love, the eternal hill from which runs the eternal stream of the work of the Son and the power of the Spirit. 'God loved the world'; 'The Father sent the Son'. The stream leads us up to the mount. 'Hereby perceive we the love of God.' In the gospel, and in it alone, we have that certainty, 'God *is* Love'.

Now he enlarges a little in passing on this dear theme, the gospel of God. He whom it reveals as eternal Love was as true to himself in the preparation as in the event.

V 2. *He promised* his gospel *beforehand through his prophets in (the) holy Scriptures.* The sunrise of Christ was no abrupt, isolated and unintelligible phenomenon. It had been preceded 'Since the world began' (Luke 1.70), from the dawn of human history, by prophecy and much preparatory work. To think now only of the prediction, more or less explicit, and not of the preparation through God's general dealings with man—such had the prophecy been that, as the pagan histories tell us, 'the whole East' heaved with expectations of a Judaean world-rule about the time when, as a fact, Jesus came. He came, both to disappoint every merely popular hope and to satisfy simultaneously the concrete details and the spiritual significance of what had been long forecast. And he sent his messengers out to the world carrying as their text that old and varied literature which is yet one book; those holy writings (our own Old Testament) which were to them nothing less than the voice of the Holy Spirit. They always put the Lord, in their preaching, in contact with that prediction.

In this, as in other things, Christ's glorious figure is unique. There is no other person in human history, himself a moral miracle, heralded by a verifiable foreshadowing in a complex literature of previous centuries.

V 3. What was the essence of the vast prophecy, with its converging elements? It was *concerning his Son, Jesus Christ our Lord.* Whatever the prophets themselves knew, or did not know, of the inmost significance of their records and utterances, this is what it was. The Lord and the apostles do not commit us to believe that the old seers ever had a *full* conscious foresight, or even that in all they wrote of him they knew that it was of him they wrote; though they *had* insights above nature, and knew it, as when David 'in the Spirit called him Lord', and Abraham 'saw his day'. But they do commit us to believe, if we are truly their disciples, that the whole revelation through Israel did, in a quite unique way, concern the Son of God (see Luke 24.25–27; John 5.39, 46; Acts 3.21–25, 10.43, 28.23).

'Concerning his Son'. For St Paul, and for us, the fact is everything, for peace and life. This Jesus Christ is true man; that is certain. He is also, if we trust his life and word, true Son of God. He is on the one hand personally distinct from him whom he calls Father, and whom he loves, and who loves him with infinite love. On the other hand he is related to him in such a way that he fully possesses his nature, while he has that nature wholly from him. This is the teaching of the gospels and epistles; this is the universal Christian faith. Jesus Christ is God, is Divine, truly and fully. He is implicitly called by the incommunicable Name (compare John 12.41 with Isa. 6.7). He is openly called God in his own presence on earth (John 20.28). But what is, if possible, even more significant, because deeper below the surface—he is regarded as the eternally satisfying object of man's trust and love (*e.g.* Phil. 3.21, Eph. 3.19). Yet Jesus Christ is always preached as related as a Son to Another, so truly that the mutual love of the Two is freely used as example and motive for our love.

We can hardly make too much, in thought and teaching, of this divine Sonship. It is the very 'secret of God' (Col. 2.2), both as a light to guide our reason to the foot of the throne, and as a power upon the heart. 'He that hath the Son hath the Father'; 'He that hath seen me hath seen the Father'; 'He hath translated us into the kingdom of the Son of his love.'

Who was born of the seed of David, according to the flesh. So the New Testament begins (Matt. 1.1); so it almost closes (Rev. 22.6). St Paul, in later years, recalls the Lord's human pedigree again (2

Tim. 2.8): 'Remember that Jesus Christ *of the seed of David*, was raised from the dead'. In the latter passage the old apostle has entered the shadow of death; he feels with one hand for the rock of history, with the other for the pulse of eternal love. Here was the rock; the Lord of life was the child of history, son and heir of a historical king, and then, as such, the child of prophecy too. And this, against all surface appearances beforehand. The Davidic 'ground' (Isa. 53.2) had seemed to be dry as dust for generations, when the root of endless life sprang up in it.

'He was born' of David's seed. Literally, the Greek may be rendered, 'He became, He came to be'. Under either rendering we have the wonderful fact that he who in his higher nature eternally *is*, above time and including it, did in his other nature, by the door of 'becoming', enter time, and thus indeed 'fill all things'. This he did, and thus he is, 'according to the flesh'. 'Flesh' is, indeed, only a part of manhood. But a part can represent the whole; and 'flesh' is the part most opposed to the divine nature, with which here (and in 9.5) manhood is placed and in a sense contrasted.

V 4. And now, of this blessed Son of David, we hear further: *who was designated to be Son of God*; literally, 'defined as Son of God', shown to be such by infallible proof. Never for an hour had he ceased to be, in fact, Son of God. To the man healed of blindness from birth, Jesus had said (John 9.35), 'Dost thou believe on the Son of God?' But there was a time when he became openly and so to speak officially what he always is naturally; somewhat as a man born king is 'made' king by coronation. Historical act then affirmed independent fact, and as it were gathered it into a point for use. This affirmation took place *in power, according to the Spirit of Holiness, as a result of resurrection from the dead*. 'Sown in weakness', Jesus was indeed 'raised in' majestic, tranquil 'power'. Without an effort he stepped from out of the depth of death, from under the load of sin. It was no flickering life, crucified but not quite killed, creeping back in a convalescence mis-called resurrection; it was the rising of the sun. That it was indeed daylight, and not a day-dream, was shown not only in his mastery of matter, but in the transfiguration of his followers. No moral change was ever more complete and more invigorating than what his return worked in that large and various group, when they learnt to say, 'We have seen the Lord.' The man who wrote this epistle had 'seen him last of all' (1 Cor. 15.8). That was indeed a sight 'in power', which worked a transfiguration.

So the Son of the Father was affirmed to be what he is, made to be, for us his Church, the Son, in whom we are sons. And all this was, 'according to the Spirit of holiness'; according to the foreshadowing and foretelling of the Holy Spirit who, in the prophets, 'testified of the sufferings destined for the Christ, and of the glories that should follow' (1 Pet 1.11).

Now lastly (in the Greek), as if pausing for a solemn entrance, comes the whole blessed name; *even Jesus Christ our Lord*. Word by word the apostle dictates, and the scribe obeys. Jesus, the human name; Christ, the mystic title; our Lord, the term of royalty and loyalty which binds us to him, and him to us. Let those four words be ours for ever. If everything else vanishes from the memory, let this remain, 'the strength of our heart, and our portion for ever'.

V 5. *Through whom*, the apostle's voice goes on, *we received grace and apostleship*. The Son was the channel through which the Father's choice and call took effect. He 'grasped' Paul (Phil. 3.12), and joined him to himself, and in himself to the Father; and now through that union they will move Paul. They move him, to give him 'grace and apostleship'; that is, in effect, grace for apostleship, and apostleship as grace; the gift of the Lord's presence in him for the work, and the Lord's work as a spiritual gift. He often links the word 'grace' with his great mission in this way (for example, in Gal. 2.9, Eph. 3.2, 8, and perhaps Phil. 1.7). The enabling peace and power for service, and then the service itself, are equally to the Christian a free, loving, beatifying gift.

Unto obedience of faith among all the nations. This 'obedience of faith' is in fact faith in its aspect as submission. What is faith? It is personal trust, personal self-entrustment to a person. It 'gives up the case' to the Lord, as the one only possible giver of pardon and of purity. It is 'submission to the righteousness of

God' (10.3). Blessed is the man who obeys like this, stretching out empty and submissive arms to receive Jesus Christ.

'Among all the nations', 'all the Gentiles'. The words read easily to us, and pass perhaps half unnoticed, as a routine phrase. Not so to the ex-Pharisee who dictated them here. A few years before he would have held it highly unlawful to keep company with someone of another nation (Acts 10.2, 8). Now, in Christ, it is as if he had almost forgotten that it had been so. His whole heart, in Christ, is blended in personal love with hearts belonging to many nations; in spiritual affection he is ready for contact with all hearts. And now he, of all the apostles, is the teacher who by life and word is to bring this glorious catholicity home for ever to all believing souls, our own included. It is St Paul pre-eminently who has taught man, as man, in Christ, to love man; who has made Hebrew, European, Indian, Chinese, African, Eskimo, actually one in the conscious brotherhood of eternal life.

For his name's sake; for the sake of the Lord Jesus Christ revealed. The name is the self-unfolded person, known and understood. Paul had indeed come to know that name, and to pass it on was now his very life. He existed only to win for it more insight, more adoration, more love. The 'name' deserved his entire devotion. Does it not deserve our equally entire devotion now? Our lives will also be transfigured, in their own way, by taking for their motto, 'For his name's sake'.

V 6. Now he speaks directly of his Roman friends. *Among whom*, among these many nations, *you too are Jesus Christ's called ones*; men who belong to him, because 'called' by him. And what is 'called'? Compare the places where the word is used (or where related words are used) in the epistles, and you will find a particular meaning. 'Invited' is not an adequate paraphrase. The 'called' man is the man who has been invited *and has come*; who has obeyed the eternal welcome; to whom the voice of the Lord has been effective. See the word in the opening paragraphs of 1 Corinthians. There the gospel is heard, externally, by many indifferent or hostile hearts, who think it 'folly', or 'a stumbling block'. But among them are those who hear, understand, and truly believe. To them, 'Christ is God's power, and God's wisdom'. And they are 'the called'. The meaning in the epistles is different from that in the gospels, where the words 'chosen' and 'called' are contrasted: the called are many, the chosen few. There are many who hear externally, few who hear inwardly.

V 7. *To all who in Rome are God's beloved ones.* What a wonderful way of putting words together, what a wonderful possibility. On one side, the 'Beloved ones of God', as close to the eternal heart as it is possible to be, because 'in the Beloved'. On the other side, 'In Rome', in the capital of universal paganism, material power, iron empire, immeasurable worldliness, flagrant and indescribable sin. 'I know where thou dwellest', said the glorified Saviour to much-tried disciples at a later day; 'even where Satan has his throne' (Rev. 2.13). That throne was conspicuously present in the Rome of Nero. Yet faith, hope, and love could breathe there, when the Lord 'called'. They could do much more than breathe. This whole epistle shows that a deep and developed faith, a glorious hope, and the mighty love of a holy life were matters of fact in men and women who every day of the year saw the world as it went by in forum and basilica, in slave-chambers and in the halls of pleasure where they had to serve or to meet company. The atmosphere of heaven was carried down into that dark pool by the believing souls who were called to live there. They lived the heavenly life in Rome.

Read some vivid picture of Roman life, and think of this. What a deadly air for the renewed soul—deadly not only in its vice, but in its magnificence, and in its thought! But nothing is deadly to the Lord Jesus Christ. The soul's renewal means not only new ideas and likings, but an eternal presence, the indwelling of the Life itself. That Life could live at Rome; and therefore 'God's beloved ones in Rome' could live there also, while it was his will they should be there. The argument applies with even more reason to ourselves.

(His) called holy ones; they were 'called', in the sense we have seen, and now they were constituted 'holy ones', 'saints'. What does that word mean? Its usage gives us the thought of dedication to God, connection with him, separation to his service, his will. The 'saints' are those who belong to him, his personal property, for his ends. It is used generally in the Scriptures for *all* Christ-

ians, supposed to be true to their name. All, not just an inner circle, bear the title. It is not only a glorified aristocracy, but the ordinary believers; not the stars of the eternal sky but the flowers sown by the Lord in the common field; even in such a tract of that field as 'Caesar's household' was (Phil. 4.22).

So it was the apostle's habit to give the term 'saints' to whole communities; as if baptism always gave, or sealed, saintship. In a sense it did, and does. But then, this was, and is, on the assumption that title and possession agreed. The title left the individual still bound to examine himself, whether he was in the faith (2 Cor. 13.5).

These happy residents at Rome are now greeted and blessed in their Father's and Saviour's name; *Grace to you and peace, from God our Father and the Lord Jesus Christ.* What is 'grace'? There are two ideas involved, favour and gratuity. The grace of God is his favouring will and work for us, and in us. It is gratuitous, utterly and to the end unearned. Put differently (and remembering that his great gifts are only modes of himself, are in fact himself in will and action), grace is God for us, grace is God in us, sovereign, willing, kind. What is 'peace'? It is a holy rest within us and around us, which comes of a person's acceptance with God and abode in God; an 'all is well' in the heart, and in the believer's contact with circumstances, as he rests in his Father and his Redeemer. There is 'peace, perfect peace'; when feeling blame, in the middle of the crush of duties, in the cross-currents of human joy and sorrow, and in the mystery of death; because of the God of peace, who has made peace for us through the cross of his Son, and is peace in us, 'by the spirit which he hath given us'.

CHAPTER 3

Good Report of the Roman Church: Paul not ashamed of the Gospel 1.8–17

Paul has blessed the Roman Christians in the name of the Lord.
Now he hastens to tell them how he blesses God for them, and
how full his heart is of them. The gospel is warm all through
with life and love; this great message of doctrine and precept is
poured from a fountain full of personal affection.

V 8. *Now first I thank my God, through Jesus Christ, about you all.* It
is his delight to give thanks for all the good he knows of in his
brethren. Seven of his epistles open with such thanksgivings,
which simultaneously convey the commendations which love
rejoices to give, wherever possible, and trace all spiritual virtue
straight to its source, the Lord. Nor is it just to 'the Lord', here
but to '*my* God'; a phrase used in the New Testament only by
St Paul (except that one cry of Eli, Eli, by his dying Saviour).
It is the expression of an indescribable taking possession and
reverent intimacy. The believer grudges his God to no-one; he
rejoices with great joy over every soul that finds its wealth in
him. But at the centre of all joy and love is this: '*my* God'; 'Christ
Jesus *my* Lord'; 'who loved *me* and gave himself for *me*'. Is it
selfish? No, it is the language of a personality where Christ has
dethroned self in his own favour, but in which therefore reigns
now the highest happiness, the happiness which animates and
maintains a self-forgetful love of all. And this holy intimacy, with
its action in thanks and petition, is all the while 'through Jesus
Christ', the Mediator and Brother. The man knows God as '*my*
God', and deals with him as such, never out of that Beloved Son
who is equally one with the believer and with the Father, no
alien medium, but the living point of unity.

What moves his thanksgivings? *Because your faith is spoken of,* more literally, *is carried as tidings, over the whole world*. Go where he will, in Asia, in Macedonia, in Achaia, in Illyricum, he meets believing 'strangers from Rome', with spiritual news from the capital, gladly though seriously announcing, that at the great centre of this world eternal things are proving their power, and that the Roman mission is remarkable for its strength and simplicity of '*faith*', its humble reliance on the Lord Jesus Christ, and loving allegiance to him. Such news, wafted from point to point of early Christendom, was frequent then; we see another beautiful example of it where he tells the Thessalonians (I Thess. 1.8–10) how everywhere in his Greek tour he found the news of their conversion running in advance of him, to greet him at each arrival. What special importance would such intelligence bear when it was good news from Rome!

This constant good news from Rome makes him the more glad because it matches his incessant thought, prayer, and yearning over them.

V 9. *For God is my record, my witness*, of this; the God *whom I serve* with both adoration and obedience, *in my spirit, in the gospel of his Son*. The 'for' gives the connection we have just indicated; he rejoices to hear of their faith, for the Lord knows how much they are in his prayers. The divine Witness is the more instinctively appealed to, because these thoughts and prayers are for a mission Church, and the relations between St Paul and his God are above all missionary relations. He 'serves him in the gospel of his son', the gospel of the God who is known and believed in his Christ. He 'serves him in the gospel', that is, in the propagation of it (as in Rom. 1.1; 15.16, 19; Phil. 1.5, 12; 2.22). 'He serves him', in that great branch of ministry, 'in his spirit', with his whole love, will, and mind, working in communion with his Lord. And now to this eternal Friend and Witness he appeals to seal his assurance of unceasing prayers for them; *how without ceasing*, as a habit constantly in action, *I make mention of you*, calling them up by name, specifying before the Father Rome, and Aquila, and Andronicus, and Junias, and Persis, and Mary, and the whole circle, personally known or not, *in my prayers*; literally, *on occasion of my prayers*; whenever he found himself at prayer, statedly or as it were casually remembering and beseeching.

The prayers of St Paul are a study in themselves. See his own accounts of them, to the Corinthians, the Ephesians, the Philippians, the Colossians, the Thessalonians, and Philemon. Observe their topic; it is almost always the growth of grace in the saints, to their Master's glory. Observe now still more their manner; the frequency, the diligence, the resolution which grapples, wrestles, with the difficulties of prayer, so that in Colossians 2.1 he calls his prayer simply 'a great wrestling'. Learn here how to deal with God for those for whom you work, shepherd of souls, messenger of the Word, Christian man or woman who in any way are called to help other hearts in Christ.

V 10. In this case Paul's prayers have a very definite direction; he is *requesting, if somehow, now at length, my way shall be opened, in the will of God, to come to you.* It is a quite simple, quite natural petition. His inward harmony with the Lord's will never excludes the formation and expression of such requests, with the reverent 'if' of submissive reserve. The indifference of mystic pietism, which discourages specific petitions, is unknown to the apostles; 'in everything, with thanksgiving, they make their requests known unto God'. And they find such expression harmonized, in a holy experience, with a profound rest within this 'sweet beloved will of God'. Little did he here foresee how his way would be opened; that it would lie through the tumult in the Temple, the prisons of Jerusalem and Caesarea, and the cyclone of the Adrian sea. He had in mind a missionary journey to Spain, in which Rome was to be visited by the way.

V 11. His heart yearns for this Roman visit. We may almost translate the next clause, *For I am homesick for a sight of you* (see Phil 2.26; 2 Tim. 1.4). In this case the longing love however has a very practical purpose; *that I may impart to you some spiritual gift of grace, with a view to your establishment.* We take 'gift of grace' here in its widest sense (as in Rom. 1.15, 16, 23; 11.29) to mean God's gift of blessing in Christ. Paul pines to convey to them, as his Lord's messenger, some new development of spiritual light and joy; to expound the Christian way to them more perfectly; to open up to them such fuller and deeper insights into the riches of Christ that they, better using their possession of the Lord, might, as it were, gain new possessions in him, and might stand more boldly on the glorious certainties they held. And this was to be done as a servant, not a master.

V 12. For he goes on to say that the longed-for visit would be his gain as well as theirs; *that is, with a view to my concurrent encouragement among you, by our mutual faith, yours and mine together.* Shall we call this sentence a conciliatory and endearing example of tact? Yes, but it is also perfectly sincere. True tact is only the skill of sympathetic love, not the less genuine in its thought because that thought seeks to please and win. He is glad to show himself as his disciples' brotherly friend; but then he first is such, and enjoys the character, and has continually found and felt his own soul made glad and strong by the witness to the Lord given by less gifted believers, as he and they talked together. Does not every true teacher know this in his own experience? If we are not merely lecturers on Christianity but witnesses for Christ, we know what it is to recognize with deep thanksgivings the 'encouragement' we have had from the lips of those who perhaps believed long after we did, and have had far less outward advantages than we have. We have known and blessed the 'encouragement' carried to us by little believing children, and young men in their first faith, and poor old people counted ignorant in this world, illuminated in the Lord. 'Mutual faith', the pregnant phrase of the apostle, faith residing in each of both parties, and admitted by each to the other, is still a mighty power for Christian 'encouragement'.

V 13. *But I would not have you ignorant, brethren.* This is a characteristic term of expression with Paul (see Rom. 11.25; 1 Cor. 10.1; 12.1; 2 Cor. 1.8; 1 Thess. 4.13). He delights in confidence and information, and not least about his own plans bearing on his friends. *That often I purposed* (or better *have purposed) to come to you (but I have been hindered up till now) that I might have some fruit among you too, as actually among the other nations.* He cannot help giving more and more hint of his being drawn to them by love; nor yet of his desire for 'fruit', result, harvest and vintage for Christ, in the way of helping on Romans, as well as Asiatics, and Macedonians, and Achaians, to live a fuller life in him. This, we may infer from the whole epistle, would be the chief kind of 'fruit' he would be concerned with at Rome; but not the only one. For we shall see him at once go on to anticipate an evangelistic work at Rome, a speaking of the gospel message where there would be a temptation to be 'ashamed' of it. Edification of believers may be his main aim. But conversion of pagan souls to God cannot possibly be dissociated from it.

In passing we see (and can learn from it) that St Paul made many plans which came to nothing; he tells us this here without apology or misgiving. This means that he claims no omniscience that would make his resolutions and forecasts infallible. Tacitly, at least, he wrote 'If the Lord will' across them all, unless indeed there came a case where, as when he was guided out of Asia to Macedonia (Acts 16.6-10), direct abnormal or supernatural intimation was given him that such and not such was to be his path.

V 14. But now, he is not only 'homesick' for Rome, with a yearning love; he feels his obligation to Rome, with a wakeful conscience. *Alike to Greeks and to Barbarians, to wise men and to unthinking, I am in debt.* All mankind is on his heart. On the one hand were 'the Greeks'; that is to say, in the then popular meaning of the word, the peoples possessed of what we now call 'classical' civilization, Greek and Roman; an inner circle of these were 'the wise', the literati, the readers, writers, thinkers, in the curriculum of those literatures and philosophies. On the other hand were 'the Barbarians', the languages and tribes outside the Hellenic pale: and then, among them, or anywhere, 'the unthinking', the numberless masses whom the educated would despise or forget as utterly untrained in philosophy, unversed in the great topics of man and the world; the people of the field, the market, and the kitchen. To the apostle, because to his Lord, all these were now impartially his claimants, his creditors; he 'owed them' the gospel which had been trusted to him for them. Naturally, his will might be repelled alike by the frown or smile of the Greek, and by the coarse earthliness of the Barbarian. But supernaturally, in Christ, he loved both, and scrupulously remembered his duty to both. Such is the true missionary spirit still, in whatever region, under whatever conditions. The Christian and the Christian Church, delivered from the world, is still its debtor. Woe is to him, to it, if that debt is not paid, if the gospel is 'hidden in a napkin'.

V 15. Thus he is ready, and more than ready, to pay his debt to Rome. *So* (to render literally) *what relates to me is eager, to you too, to the men in Rome, to preach the gospel.* 'What relates to me'; there is an emphasis on 'me', as if to say that the hindrance, whatever it is, is not in him, but around him. The doors have been shut, but the man stands behind them, ready to enter when he may.

His eagerness is no light-heartedness, no carelessness of when or where. This wonderful missionary is too sensitive to facts and ideas, too rich in imagination, not to feel the peculiar, no the awful greatness, of a summons to Rome. He understands culture too well not to feel its possible obstacles. He has seen too much of both the real grandeur and the harsh force of the imperial power at its edge not to feel a genuine awe as he thinks of meeting that power at its gigantic centre. There is that in him which fears Rome. But he is therefore the very man to go there, for he understands the magnitude of the occasion, and he will the more deeply rely upon his Lord for peace and power.

Vv 16–17. Thus with a pointed fitness he tells himself and his friends, just here, that he is 'not ashamed of the gospel'. *For I am not ashamed*; I am ready even for Rome, for this terrible Rome. I have a message which, though Rome looks as if she must despise it, I know is not to be despised. *For I am not ashamed of the gospel; for it is God's power to salvation, for every one who believes, alike for Jew, (first,) and for Greek. For God's righteousness is in it unveiled, from faith on to faith; as it stands written. But the just man on faith shall live.*

These words state the great theme of the epistle. The epistle, therefore, is infinitely the best commentary on them, as we follow out its argument and hear its message. Here all we need to do is to note a point or two, and pass on.

First, we recollect that this gospel, this good news, is, in its essence, Jesus Christ. It is, supremely, 'he, not it'; person, not theory. Or rather, it is authentic and eternal theory in vital and eternal connection everywhere with a person. As such it is truly '*power*', in a sense as profoundly natural as it is divine. It is power, not only in the force of perfect principle, but in the energy of an eternal life, an almighty will, an infinite love.

Secondly, we observe that this message of power, which in essence is the Christ of God, starts with the 'righteousness of God'. His righteousness comes first, not his love. This phrase comes seven more times in this epistle (3.5, 21, 22, 23, 26; 10.3 twice). The key to its meaning is 3.26 where the 'righteousness of God', seen as it were in action, known by its effects, is that which secures 'that he shall be just and the justifier of the man who belongs to faith in Jesus'. It is that which makes wonderfully possible the mighty paradox that the Holy One, eternally truthful eternally rightful, infinitely 'law-abiding' in his jealousy for the law which is in fact his nature expressing itself in commands, nevertheless can and does say to man, in his guilt and loss of rights, 'I, your Judge, lawfully acquit you, lawfully accept you, lawfully embrace you.' In such a context we need not fear to explain this great phrase to mean the acceptance accorded by the Holy Judge to sinful man. Thus it stands practically equivalent to God's way of justifying the ungodly, his method for liberating his love while he glorifies and upholds his law. In effect, not as a translation but as an explanation, God's righteousness is God's justification.

Then again, we note the emphasis and the repetition here of the thought of faith. 'To every one that believeth'; 'From faith on to faith'; 'The just man on faith shall live'. Here, if anywhere, we shall find ample commentary in the epistle. Only let us remember from the first that in Romans, as everywhere in the New Testament, we shall see 'faith' used in its natural and human sense; we shall find that it means personal reliance. Faith, infinitely wonderful and mysterious from some points of view, is the simplest thing in the world from others. That sinners, conscious of their guilt, should be brought so to see their Judge's heart as to take his word of peace to mean what it says, is a miracle. But that they should trust his word, having seen his heart, is nature, illuminated and led by grace, but nature still. The 'faith' of Jesus Christ and the apostles is 'trust'. It is not a faculty for mystical intuitions. It is our taking the Trustworthy

at his word. It is the opening of a begging hand to receive the
gold of heaven; the opening of dying lips to receive the water of
life. It is that which makes an empty place for Jesus Christ to
fill, that he may be man's merit, peace, and power.

Hence the overwhelming prominence of faith in the gospel. It
matches the overwhelming, absolute, prominence of Jesus Christ.
Christ is all. Faith is man's acceptance to him as such. 'Justification by faith' is not acceptance because faith is a valuable
thing, a merit, a recommendation, or a virtue. It is acceptance
because of Jesus Christ, whom man, dropping all other hopes,
receives. It has absolutely nothing to do with earning the gift of
God, the water and the bread of God; it has all to do with taking
it, as we shall see as we proceed.

So the gospel 'unveils God's righteousness'; it draws the cur-
tains from his glorious secret. And as each fold is lifted, the glad
onlooker looks on 'from faith to faith'. He finds that this reliance
is to be his permanent part. He takes Jesus Christ by faith; he
holds him by faith; he uses him by faith; he lives and dies in
him by faith. That is to say, the believer is always received, held,
and used, by Christ.

Then lastly we note the quotation from the prophet, who, for
the apostle, is the instrument of the Holy Spirit. What Habakkuk
wrote is, for Paul, what God says, God's Word. The prophet
clearly finds his occasion and his first significance in the then
state of his country and his people. If we please, we may explain
the words as a patriot's contribution to the politics of Jerusalem,
and pass on. But if so, we take a road unknown to our Lord and
his apostles. To him, to them, the prophecies had more in them
than the prophets knew; and Habakkuk's appeal to Judah to
retain the Lord God among them in all his peace and power, by
trusting him, is known by St Paul to be an oracle about the work
of faith for all time. So he sees it in a message straight to the
soul which asks how, if Christ is God's righteousness, shall I, a
sinner, win Christ for me. 'Would you truly be *just* with God,
right with him as Judge, accepted by the Holy One? Take his
Son in the empty arms of mere trust, and he is yours for this
need, and for all.'

'I am not ashamed of the gospel.' So the apostle affirms, as he looks towards Rome. What is it about this gospel of God, and of his Son, which gives occasion for such a word? Why do we find, not here only, but elsewhere in the New Testament, contemplation of the possibility that the Christian may be ashamed of his creed, and of his Lord (see Luke 9.26; 2 Tim. 1.8, 12)?

This is paradoxical, when we come to think upon it. There is much about the purity of the gospel which might (and too often does) make an awe and dread of it seemingly reasonable. There is much about the mysteries that go with it which might seem to excuse an attitude, however mistaken, of reverent suspense. But what is there about this revelation of the heart of eternal Love, this record of a life equally divine and human, of a death as majestic as it is infinitely pathetic, and then of a resurrection out of death, to cause shame? Why, in view of this, should man be shy to avow his faith, and to let it be known that this is all in all to him, his life, his peace, his strength, his chief interest and occupation?

It seems to us that the answer is related to the words 'sin', 'pardon' and 'self-surrender'. The gospel reveals the eternal Love, but under conditions which remind man that he has done his worst to lose it. It tells him of a sublime and heavenly peace and strength; but it asks him, in order to receive them, to kneel down in the dust and take them, unmerited, for nothing. And it reminds them that he, delivered and endowed in this way, is by the same act the property of his deliverer; that not only the highest benefit of his nature is secured by his giving himself over to God, but the most relentless obligation lies on him to do so. He is not his own, but bought with a price.

Such views of the actual relation between man and God, even when accompanied, as they are in the gospel, with indications of man's true greatness that are found nowhere else, are deeply repellent to the soul that has not yet seen itself and God in the light of truth. And the human being who has seen this, and has submitted himself, the moment he looks beyond his own union with his Lord, is tempted to be reticent about a creed which he knows once repelled and angered him. Paul well remembered his old hatred and contempt; and he felt the temptations of that memory, when he presented Christ either to the Pharisee or to the Stoic, and now particularly when he thought of bearing witness to him at imperial, overwhelming Rome. But then he looked away from such thoughts to Jesus Christ and the temptation was trampled beneath his feet, and the gospel, everywhere, was upon his lips.

CHAPTER 4

Need for the Gospel:
God's Anger and Man's Sin (1.18–23)

We have, as it were, touched the heart of the apostle as he weighs the prospect of his Roman visit, and feels, almost simultaneously, the tender and powerful attraction, the solemn duty, and the strange desire to shrink from delivering his message. Now his lifted forehead, just lit up by the radiant truth of righteousness by faith, is shadowed suddenly. He is not ashamed of the gospel; he will speak it out, if necessary, in the presence of Caesar and his brilliant and cynical court. For there is a pressing need that he should thus 'despise the shame'. The very conditions in human life which bring out an instinctive tendency to be reticent about the gospel, are facts of dreadful urgency and peril. Man does not like to be exposed to himself, and to be summoned to the faith and surrender claimed by Christ. But man, whatever he likes or dislikes, is a sinner, exposed to the eyes of the All-Pure, and lying helpless, amidst all his dreams of pride, beneath the wrath of God. Such is the logic of this stern sequel to the affirmation, 'I am not ashamed' (1.16).

V 18. *For God's wrath is revealed, from heaven, upon all godlessness and unrighteousness of men who in unrighteousness hold down the truth.* 'God's wrath is revealed' chiefly in Scripture, but also in the mysterious and undeniable conscience, which is more truly part of man than his five senses. Conscience sees that there is an eternal difference between right and wrong, and feels, in the dark, the relation of that difference to a law, a lawgiver, and a doom. Conscience is aware of a fiery light beyond the veil. Revelation meets its wistful gaze, lifts the veil, and affirms the fact of the wrath of God, and of his coming judgment.

Let us not shun that 'revelation'. It is not the gospel. The

gospel, as we have seen, is in itself one pure warm light of life
and love. But then it can never be fully understood until, sooner
or later, we have seen something, and believed something, of the
truth of the anger of the Holy One. Let us utterly banish from
our idea of that anger every thought of impatience, of haste, of
what is abitrary, of what is in the faintest degree unjust, or
inequitable. It is the anger of him who never for a moment can
be untrue to himself; and he is love and light. But he is also, so
also says his Word, consuming fire (Heb. 10.31, 12.29); and it
is 'a fearful thing to fall into his hands'. Nowhere and never is
God not love, as the maker and preserver of his creatures. But
nowhere also and never is he not fire, as the judicial adversary
of evil, the antagonist of the will that chooses sin. Is there nothing
in God to fear? 'Yes,' says his Son (Luke 12.5), 'I say unto you,
fear him.'

At the present time there is a deep and almost universal
tendency to ignore the revelation of the wrath of God. No doubt
there have been times, and quarters, in the history of Christianity, when that revelation was thrown into disproportionate
prominence, and men shrank from Christ (as Luther tells us he
did in his youth) as from One who was nothing if not the
relentless Judge, a Being *from* whom, not *to* whom, the guilty
soul must fly. But the current reaction from such thoughts has
swung to such an extreme indeed, that the tendency of preaching
and teaching is practically to say that there is nothing in God
to be afraid of; that the words 'hope' and 'love' are enough to
neutralize the most awful murmurs of conscience, and to cancel
the plainest warnings of the loving Lord himself. Yet that Lord,
as we ponder his words in all the four gospels, so far from
speaking such 'peace' as this, seems to reserve it to himself,
rather than to his messengers, to utter the most formidable warnings. And the earliest literature which follows the New Testament
shows that few of his sayings had sunk deeper into his disciples'
souls than those which told them of the two ways and of the two
ends.

Let us go to him, the kind friend and teacher, to learn the true
attitude of thought towards him as 'the Judge, strong and
patient,' 'but who will in no wise clear the guilty' by unsaying

his commands and setting aside his threats. He undoubtedly will teach us, in this matter, no lessons of hard and narrow denunciation, nor encourage us to sit in judgment on the souls and minds of our brethren. But he will teach us to take deep and serious views for ourselves of both the pollution and also the guilt of sin. He will compel us to carry those views all through our personal theology and anthropology. He will make it both a duty and a possibility for us, in the right degree and manner, tenderly, humbly, governed by his Word, to let others know what our convictions are about the ways and the ends. In this, as in other ways, he will make his gospel to be to us not just a luxury or ornament of thought and life, like a decorous gilding on essential worldliness and the ways of self. He will unfold it as the soul's refuge and its home. From himself as Judge he will draw us in blessed flight to himself as propitiation and peace.

This wrath, holy, passionless, yet awfully personal, 'is revealed, from heaven'. That is to say, it is revealed as coming from heaven, when the righteous Judge 'shall be revealed from heaven taking vengeance' (2 Thess. 1.7, 8). 'Upon all godlessness and unrighteousness of men', upon every kind of violation of conscience, whether done against God or man; upon 'godlessness', which blasphemes, denies or ignores the Creator; upon 'unrighteousness', which perverts the claims of Creator or creature.

For the men in question 'hold down (not 'hold fast') the truth in unrighteousness'. The thought here is that man, fallen from the harmony with God in which manhood was made, but still keeping manhood, and therefore conscience, is never naturally ignorant of the difference between right and wrong, never naturally, innocently, unaware that he is accountable. On the other hand he is never fully willing, of himself, to do all he knows of right, all he knows he ought, all the demand of the righteous law above him. 'In unrighteousness', in a life which at best is not wholly and whole-heartedly with the will of God, 'he holds down the truth', silences the haunting fact that there is a claim he will not meet, a will he ought to love, but to which he prefers his own. He thrusts below his consciousness, or into a corner of it, the majesty of eternal right, always intimating the majesty of an eternal Righteous One, and keeps it there, that he may follow his own way. More or less, it wrestles with him for its proper place. And its even half-understood efforts may, and often do, exercise a deterrent force upon the energies of his self-will. But they do not dislodge it; he would rather have his way. With a force that is sometimes deliberate, sometimes impulsive, sometimes habitual, 'he holds down' the unwelcome monitor.

V 19. The moral responsibility incurred by such repression is deep. For man has always, by the very nature of the case, within him and around him, evidence for a personal righteous Power 'with whom he has to do'. *Because that which is known of God is manifest in them; for God manifested* (or rather, in practice *has manifested*) *it to them.* 'That which is known'; 'that which is knowable, that which may be known'. There is that about the Eternal which indeed neither is nor can be known, through the intelligence. All thoughtful Christians are agnostics in the sense that they gaze on the bright Ocean of Deity, and know that they do not know it in its fathomless but radiant depths, nor can explore its expanse which has no shore. They rest before absolute mystery with a repose as simple (if possible more simple) as that with which they contemplate the most familiar and intelligible event. But this is not not to know him. It leaves man quite as free to be sure that God is, to be as certain that he is personal, and is holy, as man is certain of his own consciousness and conscience.

That there is personality behind phenomena, and that this great personality is righteous, St Paul here affirms to be 'manifest', disclosed, visible, 'in men'. It is a fact present, however partially understood, in human consciousness. And more, this consciousness is itself part of the fact; indeed it is that part without which all others would be as nothing. To man without conscience—really, naturally, innocently without conscience—and without ideas of cause and effect, the whole majesty of the universe might be unfolded with a fulness beyond all our present experience; but it would say absolutely nothing of either personality or judgment. It is by the world within that we are able in the least degree to be aware of the world without. But having, naturally and permanently, the world of personality and of conscience within us, we are beings to whom God can, and *has manifested, the knowable about himself*, in his universe.

V 20. *For his things unseen, ever since the creation of the universe, are full in (man's) view, presented to (man's) mind by his things made — his ever-lasting power and Godlikeness together — so as to leave them inexcusable.* Since the ordered world came into existence, and since man's creation, as its observer and also as its integral part, there has been present to man's spirit — supposed true to its own creation — adequate testimony around him, taken along with that within him, to indicate the reality of a supreme and persistent Will, intending order, and thus making known its own correspondence to conscience, and expressing itself in 'things made' of such glory and wonder as to show the Maker's majesty as well as righteousness. What is that, what is he, to whom the splendours of the day and the night, the wonders of the forest and the sea, bear witness? He is not only righteous Judge but King eternal. He is not only charged with my guidance; He has unlimited rights over me. I am completely wrong if I am not in submissive harmony with him; if I do not surrender, and adore.

It has been like this, according to St Paul, 'ever since the creation of the universe' (and of man in it). And such everywhere is the theism of Scripture. It maintains, or rather it states as certainty, that man's knowledge of God began with his being as man. To see the Maker in his works is not, according to the Holy Scriptures, only the slow and difficult result of a long evolution which led through far lower forms of thought, the fetish, the nature-power, the tribal god, the national god, to the idea of a Supreme God. Scripture presents man as made in the image of the Supreme, and capable from the first of a true, however faint, understanding of him. It assures us that man's lower and distorted views of nature and of personal power behind it are degenerations, perversions, and results of a mysterious primeval dislocation of man from his harmony with God. The believer in the Holy Scriptures, in the sense in which our Lord and the apostles believed in them, will receive this view of the primeval history of theism as a true report of God's account of it. Remembering that it concerns an otherwise unknown moment of human spiritual history, he will not be disturbed by alleged evidence against it from lower down the stream.

Vv 21–22. So man, being what he is and seeing what he sees, is 'without excuse': *Because, knowing God, they did not glorify him as God, nor thank him, but proved futile in their ways of thinking, and their unintelligent heart was darkened. Asserting themselves for wise they turned fools, and transmuted the glory of the immortal God in a semblance of the likeness of mortal man, and of things winged, quadruped, and reptile.* Man, placed by God in his universe, and himself made in God's image, naturally and inevitably 'knew God'. Not necessarily in that inner sense of spiritual harmony and union which is (John 17.3) eternal life; but in the sense of a perception of his being and his character adequate, at its faintest, to make a moral claim. But somehow—a somehow which has to do with a revolt of man's will from God to self—that claim was, and is, disliked. Out of that dislike has sprung, in man's spiritual history, a reserve towards God, a tendency to question his purpose, character and existence; or otherwise, to degrade the conception of personality behind phenomena into forms which produce idolatry, as if phenomena were due to personalities no better and no greater than could be imaged by man or by beast, things of limit and of passion; at their greatest terrible, but not holy, ultimate, or One.

Man has spent on these unworthy ways of thinking a great deal of weak and dull reasoning and unintelligent imagination, but also some of the rarest and most splendid of the riches of his mind, made in the image of God. But all this thinking, because conditioned by a wrong attitude of his being as a whole, has had 'futile' results, and has been in the truest sense 'unintelligent', failing to see inferences correctly and as a whole. It has been a struggle 'in the dark'; a descent from the light into moral and mental 'folly'.

Was it not so, is it not so still? If man is indeed made in the image of the living Creator, a moral personality, and placed in the midst of 'God's world', then whatever process of thought leads man away from him has somewhere in it an inexcusable fallacy. It must mean that something in him which should be awake is asleep; or, still worse, something that should be nobly free to love and to adore is being repressed or 'held down' (1.18). Man only thinks as he should when he is in the right state. When he, made by and for the eternal Holy One, rests willingly in him, and lives for him. 'The fear of the Lord is', in the strictest fact, 'the beginning of wisdom'; for it is the attitude of man without which the creature cannot 'answer the idea' of the Creator, and therefore cannot truly follow out the law of its own being.

'Let him that glorieth, glory in this, that he understandeth and knoweth him' (Jer. 9.24) who necessarily and eternally transcends our ability to know and understand, yet can be known, can be touched, clasped, adored, as personal, eternal, almighty, holy Love.

CHAPTER 5

Man Given up to his own Way: The Heathen (1:24–32)

V 24. *Wherefore God gave them up, in the desires of their hearts, to uncleanness, so as to dishonour their bodies among themselves.*

There is a logical connection between unworthy thoughts of God and the development of the lowest forms of human wrong. 'The fool hath said in his heart, There is no God: – they are corrupt, and have done abominable works' (Ps. 14. 1). And the folly which does not deny God but debases the idea of him, always contributes to such corruption. It is so in the nature of the case. The individual atheist or polytheist may conceivably be a virtuous person, on the human standard; but if he is so it is not because of his creed. Let his creed become a real formative power in human society, and it will tend inevitably to moral disease and death. Is man really a moral personality, made in the image of a holy and almighty Maker? Then the inspiration of his moral life must be faithfulness to his God. Let man think of God as less than all, and he will think of himself less worthily; not less proudly perhaps, but less worthily, because he is not in his true and wonderful relation to the eternal Good. Wrong in himself will tend to seem less awful, and right less necessary and great. And nothing, literally nothing, from any region higher than himself – himself already lowered in his own thought from his true value – can ever come in to fill the blank where God should be, but is not. Man may worship himself, or may despise himself, when he has ceased to glorify God and thank him; but he cannot for one moment be what he was made to be, the son of God in the universe of God. To know God truly is to be saved from self-worship, and to be taught self-reverence; and it is the only way to those two secrets.

'God gave them up'. So Scripture says elsewhere (see Ps. 81.

12; Acts 7. 42; Rom. 1. 26, 28). It is a dreadful thought; but the inmost conscience, once awake, affirms the righteousness of the thing. From one point of view it is just the working out of a natural process, in which sin is simultaneously exposed and punished by its proper results, without the slightest injection, so to speak, of any force beyond its own terrible gravitation towards the sinner's misery. But from another point it is the personally allotted, and personally inflicted, retribution of him who hates sin with the antagonism of infinite personality. God has so constituted natural process that wrong leads to wretchedness; and he is in that process, and above it, always and for ever.

So he 'gave them up, in their desires of their hearts'; he left them there where they had placed themselves, 'in' the fatal region of self-will, self-indulgence; 'to uncleanness', described now with terrible explicitness in its full outcome, 'to dishonour their bodies', the intended temples of the Creator's presence, 'among themselves', or 'in themselves'; for the possible dishonour might be done either in a foul solitude, or in a fouler society.

V 25. *Seeing that they perverted the truth of God*, the eternal fact of his glory and claim, *in their lie*, so that it was travestied, misrepresented, lost, in the falsehood of polytheism and idols; *and worshipped and served the creature rather than the Creator, who is blessed for ever. Amen.* Paul casts this strong doxology into the thick air of false worship and foul life, as if to clear it with its holy echoing. For he is writing no mere discussion, no lecture on the origin and evolution of paganism. It is the story of a vast rebellion, told by one who, once himself a rebel, is now completely and for ever the absolute slave of the King whom he has 'seen in his beauty', and whom it is his joy to bless, and to claim blessing for him from his whole world for ever.

V 26a. As if invigorated by the blessing, he returns to denounce what God hates with still more terrible explicitness.

For this reason, because of their preference of the worse to the infinite Good, *God gave them up to passions of degradation*; he handed them over, self-bound, to the helpless slavery of lust; to 'passions', an eloquent word, which indicates how the man who will have his own way is all the while a 'sufferer', though by his own fault.

Should we avoid reading and translating the words which

follow? We will not comment and expound. May the presence
of God in our hearts, hearts which are otherwise as vulnerable
as those of the old pagan sinners, sweep all curiosity from our
minds and wills. But if it does so it will leave us the more able,
in humility, tears, and fear, to hear the facts of this stern judgment. It will call us to listen as those who are not sitting in
judgment on paganism, but standing beside the accused and
sentenced, to confess that we too share the fall, and stand, if we
stand, by grace alone. And we shall remember that if an apostle
uncovered the state of pagan morals in this way, he would have
been even less merciful, if possible, over similar symptoms still
lurking in modern Christendom, and found sometimes upon its
surface.

Now, as truly as then, man is awfully open to the worst
temptations the moment he trusts himself away from God. And
this needs indeed to be remembered in a stage of thought and
of society whose cynicism, and materialism, show similarities to
those last days of the old degenerate world in which St Paul
looked round him, and spoke out the things he saw.

Vv 26b–28. *For their females perverted the natural use to the unnatural.
So too the males, leaving the natural use of the female, burst out aflame
in their craving towards one another, males in males working out their
unseemliness – and duly getting in themselves that recompense of their error
which was owed them.*

*And as they did not approve of keeping God in their moral knowledge,
God gave them up to an abandoned mind.* That mind, taking the false
preconceptions of the Tempter, and reasoning from them to
establish the independence of self, led with terrible certainty and
success through evil thinking to evil doing; *to do the deeds which
are not becoming*, to expose the being made for God, in a naked
and foul unseemliness, to its friends and its foes.

Vv 29–32. They were *filled full of all unrighteousness, wickedness,
viciousness, greed; brimming with envy, murder, guile, ill-nature; whisper-
ers, defamers, repulsive to God, outragers, prideful, boastful, inventors of
evil, disobedient to parents, senseless, faithless, loveless, truceless, pitiless;
people who morally aware of God's ordinance, that they who practise such
things are worthy of death, not only do them, but assent and consent with
those who practise them.*

Here is a terrible accusation of human life, and of the human heart; especially because it is plainly meant to be, in a certain sense, inclusive or universal. We are not forced to think that the apostle charges every human being with sins against nature, as if the whole earth were actually one vast 'city of the plain' like Sodom or Gomorrah. We need not take him to mean that every descendant of Adam is actually an undutiful child, or actually untrustworthy in a bargain, or even actually a boaster, who claims praise or credit which he knows he does not deserve. We may be sure that on the whole, he is thinking here mainly of the then state of heathen society in its worst developments. Yet we shall see, as the epistle goes on, that all the while he is thinking not only of the sins of some men, but of the sin of man. He describes with this tremendous detail the varied symptoms of one disease – the corruption of man's heart; a disease that is present, and deadly, everywhere. It is limited in its manifestations by many circumstances and conditions, outward or within the man, but in itself it is quite unlimited in its dreadful possibilities. What man is, as fallen, corrupted, gone from God, is shown, in the teaching of St Paul, by what bad men are.

Do we rebel against the inference? Quite possibly. We have almost certainly done so, at one time or another. We look around at someone or other whose life should be respected or admired, although we cannot reasonably think that it is renewed in the scriptural sense. And we say, consciously or unconsciously, that that life stands clear outside this first chapter of Romans. Well, be it so in our thoughts; and let nothing stop us from being ready to recognize and honour right doing wherever we see it, both in the saints of God and in those who deny his very existence. But just now let us withdraw from all such looking outward, and calmly and quietly look in. Do we, do you, do I, stand outside this chapter? Are we definitely prepared to say that our own heart whatever our friend's heart may be, is such that under no change of circumstances could it, being what it is, conceivably develop the forms of evil condemned in this passage? Who, that knows himself, does not know that there lies in him indefinitely more than he can know of possible evil? Who has met all varieties of temptation, so that he can say, with even approximate truth, that he knows his own strength, and his own weakness, exactly as they are?

Experience shows that it is just when a man is nearest God for himself that he sees what, but for God, he would be; what, taken apart from God, he is, potentially if not in act. And it is in just such a mood that, reading this paragraph of Romans, he will beat his breast, and say, 'God, be merciful to me the sinner' (Luke 18. 13).

In doing this he will be meeting the very purpose of the writer of this passage. St Paul is full of the message of peace, holiness, and the Spirit. He is intent and eager to bring his reader into sight and possession of the fullness of the eternal mercy, revealed and secured in the Lord Jesus Christ, our sacrifice and life. But for this very purpose he works first to expose man to himself; to awaken him to the fact that he is before everything else a sinner; to reverse the Tempter's spell, and to let him see the fact of his guilt with open eyes.

'The gospel,' someone has said, 'can never be proved except to a bad conscience.' If 'bad' means 'awakened', the saying is profoundly true. With a conscience that is sound asleep we may discuss Christianity, whether to condemn it, or to praise it. We may see in it an uplifting programme for the human race. We may affirm, a thousand times, that from the belief that God became flesh there result boundless possibilities for humanity. But the gospel, 'the power of God unto salvation', will hardly be seen in its own prevailing self-evidence, as it is presented in this wonderful epistle, till the person studying it is first and foremost a penitent. The man must know for himself something of sin as condemnable guilt, and something of self as a thing in helpless yet responsible slavery, before he can so see Christ given for us, and risen for us, and seated at the right hand of God for us, as to say, 'There is now no condemnation; Who shall separate us from the love of God? I know whom I have believed.'

For there to be a proper view of Christ there needs to be a true view of self, that is to say, of sin.

CHAPTER 6

Human Guilt Universal: Paul Approaches the Conscience of the Jew (2.1–17)

We have appealed, for affirmation of St Paul's tremendous exposure of human sin, to a solemn and deliberate self-scrutiny, asking the person who doubts the justice of the picture to give up for the present any instinctive wish to clear others, while he thinks a little while solely of himself. But another and opposite class of mistake has to be reckoned with, and prevented; the tendency to an easy condemnation of others, in favour of oneself; 'God, I thank Thee that I am not as other men are' (Luke 18. 11). It is now, as it was of old, only too possible to read, or to hear, the most searching and most sweeping condemnation of human sin, and to feel a sort of false moral sympathy with the sentence, a feeling of righteous indignation against the wrong and the doers of it, and yet wholly to misunderstand the matter by thinking that the hearer is righteous though the world is wicked. Such a person listens as if he were allowed a seat beside the Judge's chair, as if he were a valued assessor of the court, and could listen with a serious yet untroubled approval to the speech before the sentence. In fact, he is an accomplice of his fallen fellows; he is a poor guilty man himself. Let him awake to himself, and to his sin, in time.

With such a reader or hearer in mind St Paul proceeds. We need not suppose that he writes as if such states of mind were to be expected in the Roman mission; though it was quite possible that this might be the attitude of some Christians there. More probably he speaks, as it were, in the presence of the Christians to persons whom at any moment any of them might meet, and particularly to that large element in religious life at Rome, the unconverted Jews. True, they would not read the epistle; but he could arm those who would read it against their objections and refusals, and show them how to reach the conscience of even the Pharisee of the Dispersion. He could show them how to seek his soul, by shaking him from his dream of sympathy with the Judge who all the while was about to sentence *him*.

It is plain that throughout this passage the apostle has the Jew in mind. He does not name him for a long while. He says many things which are as much for the Gentile sinner as for him. He dwells upon the universality of guilt indicated by the universality of conscience; a passage of awful significance for every human soul, quite apart from its place in the argument here. But all the while he keeps in view the case of the self-constituted judge of other men, the man who affects to be essentially better than they, to be, at least by comparison with them, good friends with the law of God. And the undertone of the whole passage is a warning to this man that his brighter light will prove his greater ruin if he does not use it. In fact, he has not used it, so it is his ruin already, the ruin of his claim to judge, to stand exempt, to have nothing to do with the criminal crowd at the bar.

All this points straight at the Jewish conscience. Paul longs to reach it, first for the unbeliever's own sake, that he might be led through the narrow pass of self-condemnation into the glorious freedom of faith and love. But also it was of first importance that the spiritual pride of the Jews should be conquered, or at least exposed, for the sake of the mission-converts already won. The first Christians, newly brought from paganism, must have regarded Jewish opinion with great attention and respect. Not only were their apostolic teachers Jews, and the scriptures of the prophets, to which those teachers always pointed, Jewish; but the weary Roman world of recent years had been disposed to own with more and more distinctness that if there were such a thing as a true voice from heaven to man it was to be heard among that unattractive yet impressive race which was seen everywhere, and yet refused to be 'reckoned among the nations'. The Gospels and the Acts show us plenty of instances of educated Romans drawn towards Israel and the covenant; and abundant parallels are given us by secular historians and satirists. It was

no slight trial to converts in their spiritual infancy to meet everywhere the question why the wise men of Jerusalem had slain
this Jewish prophet, Jesus, and why everywhere the synagogues
denounced his name and his disciples. The true answer would
be better understood if the bigot himself could be brought to say,
'God, be merciful to me the sinner.'

Vv 1–11. *Wherefore you are without excuse, O man, every man who
judges; when you judge the other party you pass judgment on yourself; for
you practise the same things, you who judge. For we know* – this is an
agreed point between us – *that God's judgment is truth-wise*, is a
reality, *upon those who practise such things. Now is this your calculation,
O man, you who judge those who practise such things, and do them yourself,
that you will escape God's judgment?* Do you feel that some byway
of privilege and indulgence will be kept open for you? *Or do you
despise the wealth of his kindness, and of his forbearance and longsuffering*
– despise it, by mistaking it for mere indulgence, or indifference –
*knowing not that God's kind ways lead you to repentance? No, true to
your own hardness, your own unrepentant heart, you are hoarding for
yourself a wrath* which will be felt *in the day of wrath*, the day *of
disclosure of* the *righteous judgment of God, who will requite each individual according to his works.* What will be that requital, and its
law? *To those who, on the line of perseverance in good work, seek glory,
and honour, and immortality,* he will requite *life eternal. But for those
who side with strife,* who take part with man, self and sin, against
the claims and grace of God, *and, while they disobey the truth of
conscience, obey unrighteousness,* yielding the will to wrong, *there shall
be wrath and fierce anger, trouble and bewilderment, inflicted on every soul
of man,* man *working out what is evil, alike Jew* – Jew first – *and
Greek. But glory, and honour, and peace shall be for every one who works
what is good, alike for Jew* – Jew first – *and Greek. For there is no
favouritism in God's court.*

Here Paul actually touches the Jew. He has named him twice,
and in both places recognizes the primacy in the history of
redemption which is really his. It is the primacy of the race
chosen to be the instrument of revelation and the birth-place of
God Incarnate. It was given sovereignly, not according to the
works, or the numbers, of the nation, but according to unknown
conditions in the mind of God. It carried with it genuine and

splendid advantages. It even gave the individual righteous Jew (so the language of verse 10 must imply) a certain special welcome to his Master's 'Well done, good and faithful'; not to the slightest disadvantage of the individual righteous 'Greek', but just such as among friends, kinship added to friendship makes attachment not more intimate but more interesting. Yes, the Jew has his priority or primacy, limited and qualified in many directions, but real and permanent in its place; this epistle (see chapter 11) is the great charter of it in the Christian Scriptures. But whatever the place of this primacy is, it has no place whatever in the question of the sinfulness of sin, unless indeed to make guilt deeper where light has been greater. The Jew has a great historical position in the plan of God. He has been granted as it were an official nearness to God in the working out of the world's redemption. But he is not one degree the less for this a poor sinner, fallen and guilty. He has not one moment for this to excuse, but all the more to condemn, himself. He is the last person in the world to judge others. Wherever God has placed him in history, he is to place himself, in repentance and faith, least and lowest at the foot of Messiah's cross.

What was and is true of the chosen nation is now and for ever true, by a deep moral parity, of all communities and of all persons who are in any sense privileged or advantaged by circumstance. It is true of the Christian Church, the Christian family, and the Christian person. Later in this second chapter we shall be led to some reflections on Church privilege. Let us reflect here, if only in passing, on the fact that privilege of other kinds must stand completely aside when it is a question of man's sin. No, 'there is no favouritism in God's court!' No one is acquitted there for his reputable connections, or for his possession of personal 'talents' given him only that he might work better for his Lord. These things have nothing to do with the law, which has everything to do with the accusation and the award.

Before we pass to another section of the passage, let us not forget the serious fact that here, in these opening pages of this great treatise on free salvation, this epistle which is about to unfold to us the divine paradox of the justification of the ungodly, we find this overwhelming emphasis laid upon 'perseverance in good work'. True, we are not to allow even it to confuse the grand simplicity of the gospel, which is to be explained soon. We are not to let ourselves think, for example, that verse 7 depicts a man deliberately aiming through a life of merit at an appropriate reward in heaven; so much glory, honour, and immortality for living as it would be sin not to live. St Paul does not write to contradict the parable of the unprofitable servant (Luke 17), any more than to reject in advance his own reasoning in Romans 4. The case he considers is one only to be realized where man has cast himself, without one plea of merit, at the feet of mercy, and then rises up to a walk and work of willing loyalty, covetous of the 'Well done, good and faithful', at its end, not because he is ambitious for himself, but because he is devoted to his God, and to God's will. And St Paul knows, and in due course will tell us, that this man has to thank God's mercy (and nothing else) for both the repentance and the loyalty (see Rom. 9. 16). But then, none the less, Paul does lay this emphasis, this indescribable stress, upon the 'perseverance in good work', as the actual march of the pilgrim who travels heavenward. True to the genius of Scripture (that is, to the mind of its Inspirer), he isolates a main truth for the time, and leaves us alone with it. Justification will come in order. But, so that it may come in its place and not out of it, he asks us first to consider right, wrong, judgment, and retribution, as if there were nothing else in the moral universe. He leads us to the fact of the permanence of the results of the soul's actions. He warns us that God is eternally in earnest when he promises and when he threatens; that he will see to it that time leaves its retributive mark for ever on eternity.

The whole passage, read by a soul aware of itself, and the holiness of the judge of men, will contribute from every sentence something to our conviction, repentance, dread of self, and persuasion that we must fly somehow from the judgment to the judge. But this is not to be unfolded yet.

It was, I believe, an instruction of John Wesley's to his evangelists, in unfolding their message, to speak first in general of the love of God; then, with all possible energy, and so as to search conscience to its depths, to preach the law of holiness;

and then, and not till then, to uplift the glories of the gospel of pardon, and of life. Intentionally or not, his directions follow the lines of the Epistle to the Romans.

But the apostle has by no means done with the Jew, and his hopes of heaven by pedigree and by creed. He returns to the impartiality of 'that day', the coming final crisis of human history, ever in his thoughts. He dwells now almost wholly on the impartiality of its severity, still concerned with the Pharisee's dream that somehow the law will be his friend, for Abraham's and Moses' sake.

V 12. *For all who sinned* (or, *all who have sinned, all who shall have sinned) not law-wise, even so, not law-wise, shall perish*, shall lose the soul; *and all who in* (or *under*) *law have sinned, by law shall be judged*, that is to say, in practice, *condemned*, found guilty.

V 13. *For not law's hearers are just in God's court*; no, *law's doers shall be justified*; for 'law' is never for a moment satisfied with applause, or approval; it always demands obedience.

Vv 14–15. *For whenever (the) nations*, nations *not having law, by nature* – as distinct from definite instruction – *do the things of the law*, when they act on the principles of it, observing in any measure the eternal difference of right and wrong, these men, though *not having law, are to themselves law; shewing as they do* – to one another, in moral intercourse – *the work of the law*, what is in fact its result where it is heard, a sense of the claims of right, *written in their hearts*, present to the intuitions of their nature; *while their conscience*, their sense of violated right, *bears concurrent witness*, each conscience agreeing with all; *and while, between each other*, in the interchanges of thought and discussion, *their reasonings accuse, or it may be defend*, their actions; in conversation, treatise or philosophic dialogue.

V 16. And all this makes one vast phenomenon, full of lessons of accountability, and warning of a coming judgment; *in the day when God shall judge the secret things of men*, even the secrets hid beneath the solemn robe of the formalist, *according to my gospel, by means of Jesus Christ*, to whom the Father 'hath committed all judgment, as he is the Son of Man' (John 5. 27). So he closes another solemn cadence with the blessed name. It is particularly appropriate here; for it was the name despised by the Pharisee, yet the name of him who was to judge him on the day of judgment.

The main meaning of the paragraph is plain. It is to enforce the fact of the equal accountability of the Jew and the Greek, from the point of view of law. The Jew, who is primarily in the apostle's thought, is reminded that his possession of *the* law, that is to say of the one specially revealed code not only of ritual but far more of morals, is no privilege that provides a recommendation, but a sacred responsibility. The Gentile meanwhile is shown, in passing but with the most serious purpose, to be by no means exempted from accountability simply for his lack of a revealed code of law. He possesses, as man, the moral consciousness without which the revealed code itself would be futile, for it would correspond to nothing. Made in the image of God, he has the mysterious sense which sees, feels, and deals with moral obligation. He is aware of the fact of duty. Not living up to what he is thus aware of, he is guilty.

Implicitly, all through the passage, human failure is taught side by side with human responsibility. Such a clause as that of verse 14, 'when they do by nature the things of the law', is certainly not to be pressed, in this context, to be an assertion that pagan morality ever actually satisfies the holy tests of the eternal Judge. It only asserts that the pagan acts as a moral being; that he knows what it is to obey, and to resist, the sense of duty.

What a stern, solemn, and merciful argument! Now from this side, now from that, it approaches the conscience of man, made for God and fallen from God. It strips the veil from his great sins; it lets in the sun of holiness upon his more religious sins; it speaks in his dull ears the words 'judgment', 'day', 'tribulation', 'wrath', 'bewilderment', 'perishing'. But it does all this so that man, convicted, may ask in earnest what he shall do with conscience and his Judge, and may discover with joy that his Judge himself has 'found a ransom', and personally acts to set him free.

CHAPTER 7

Jewish Responsibility and Guilt (2. 17–29)

'The Jew, first, and also the Greek'; this has been the essence of the apostle's thought so far. He has had the Jew for some while in his chief thought, but he has returned again and again in passing to the Gentile. Now he faces the Pharisee explicitly and openly, before he passes from this long exposure of human sin to the revelation of the glorious remedy.

Vv 17–20. *But if you*, you emphatically, the reader or hearer now in mind, you who perhaps have excused yourself from considering your own case by this last mention of the responsibility of the non-Jewish world; *if you bear the name of Jew*, whether or not you possess the corresponding spiritual reality; *and repose yourself upon the law*, as if the possession of that awful revelation of duty was your protection, not your sentence; *and glory in God*, as if he were your private property, the decoration of your national position, whereas the knowledge of him is given you in trust for the world; *and know the will*, his will, the supreme will; *and put the touchstone to things which differ*, like someone skilled in moral problems *schooled out of the law*, under continuous training by principles and instructions which the law supplies; (*if*) *you are sure that you, yourself*, whoever else, *are a leader of blind men, a light of those who are in the dark, an educator of the thoughtless, a teacher of beginners, possessing, in the law, the outline*, the system, *of real knowledge and truth* (the outline indeed, but not the power and life related to it) – if this is your estimate of your position and capacities, I turn it upon yourself.

Vv 21–22. Think and answer – *You therefore, your neighbour's teacher, do you not teach yourself? You, who proclaim, Thou shalt not steal, do you steal? You, who say, Thou shalt not commit adultery, do you commit it? You, who abominate the idols*, pretending to loathe their very surroundings, *do you plunder temples*, entering the polluted precincts readily enough for purposes which are at least equally polluting? Vv 23–24. *You who glory in the law*, as the security of your race, *do you, by your violation of the law, disgrace your God?* 'For the name of our God is, because of you, railed at among the heathen', as it stands written, in Ezekiel's message (36. 20) to the ungodly Israel of the ancient Dispersion – a message true of the later Dispersion also.

We need not overstrain the emphasis of the apostle's stern attack. Certainly not every non-Christian Jew of the first century was an adulterer, a thief, a plunderer. When a few years later (Acts 28.17) St Paul gathered round him the Jews of Rome, and spent a long day in discussing the prophecies with them, he appealed to them with a noble frankness which in some sense evidently expected a response in kind. But it is certain that the Jews of the Roman Dispersion had a poor general reputation for truth and honour. And in any case St Paul knew well that there is a deeply natural connection between unhallowed religious bigotry and that innermost failure of self-control which leaves man only too open to the worst temptations. Whatever feeds gross personal pride promotes a swift and deadly decay of moral fibre. Did this man pride himself on Abraham's blood, and his own rabbinic lore and skill, and scorn both the Gentile 'sinner' and 'the people of the land', the rank and file of his own race? Then he was the very man to be led helpless by the Tempter. In fact, there are rabbinic sayings of a later period which represent beyond reasonable doubt the spirit if not the letter of the worst watchwords of the Jews of St Paul's time: 'Circumcision is equivalent to all the commandments of the law'; 'To live in Palestine is equal to the commandments'; 'He that has his abode in Palestine is sure of eternal life.' The man who could even for a moment entertain such a creed was ready (however unconsciously) for anything, if tempted.

So it is now, very far beyond the limits of the Jewish Dispersion of our time. Now as then, for the person who is outwardly Christian as well as for the one who is outwardly Jewish, there is no surer path to spiritual degeneracy than spiritual pride. What are the slogans which have succeeded those of the rabbinic leaders who encountered St Paul? Are they words or thoughts of self-congratulation because of the historic orthodoxy of your creed? Because of the scriptural purity of your theory of salvation? Because of the distinguished history of your national Church, older than the nation which it has so largely welded and developed? Because of the patient courage with which your Church (called a denomination or sect by some people) has faced contempt or exclusion from society? Because of your loyalty to order? Because of your loyalty to freedom? Take heed. The best, corrupted, becomes inevitably the worst. In religion, there is only one completely safe 'glorying'. It is when the believer can say from the soul, with open eyes, and therefore with a deeply humbled heart, 'God forbid that I should glory, save in the cross of our Lord Jesus Christ, whereby the world is crucified unto me, and I unto the world' (Gal. 6. 14). All other 'glorying is not good'. Be thankful for every genuine privilege. But for Christ's sake, and for your own soul's sake, do not, even in the inner secret of your soul, value yourself by them. It is disease, it is disaster, to do so.

And shall not we of the Christian Dispersion take to heart also what Ezekiel and St Paul say about the blasphemies, the abuse of our God, caused by the sins of those who bear his name? Who does not know that, in every non-Christian region, the missionary's plea for Christ is always best listened to where the pagan or the Muslim, is not presented with the Christianity of treaty-ports, and other places where European life is to be seen lived without restraint? The stumbling-block may be the drunken sailor, or the unchaste merchant, civilian, soldier, or traveller. Or it may be just the man who, belonging to a race supposed to be Christian, merely ignores the Christian's holy book, and day, and house, and avoids all appearance of fellowship with his countrymen who have come to live beside him that they may preach Christ where he is not known. Or it may be the government, supposedly Christian, which, among all its noble benefits to the vast races it holds in sway, allows them to know, to think, at least to suspect, that there are cases where it cares more for revenue than for righteousness. In all these cases the Christian Dispersion gives occasion for abuse of the Christian's God: and the reckoning at the day of judgment will be serious.

But shall the Christians of the Christendom at home be exempt from the charge? Let us who name the blessed name with even the least emphasis of faith and loyalty, among the masses who only passively, so to speak, are Christian, who profess nothing, though they are, or are supposed to be, baptized – let us, in the world which understands not a little of what we ought to be, and watches us so closely, and so legitimately – let us take home this message, sent first to the old inconsistent Israel. Do we, professing godliness, show the mind of Christ in our secular business? Do we, on the whole, give others cause to expect that a Christian, as such, is a man to trust in business, in friendship? Is the conviction quietly forced upon them that a Christian's temper and speech are not like other people's? That the Christian minister habitually lives high above self-seeking? That the Christian tradesman faithfully remembers his customers' just interests, and is true in all his dealings? That the Christian servant, and the Christian master, are both exceptionally mindful of each other's rights, and easy-going about their own? That the Christian's time, and his money, are to a remarkable degree applied to the good of others, for Christ's sake? This is what the members of the Christian society, in the inner sense of the word Christian, are expected to be in what we all understand by 'the world'. If they are so, God be thanked. If they are not so – who shall measure the guilt? Who shall adequately estimate the dishonour done in this way to Christ?

But Paul has more to say about the position of the Jew. He would not even seem to forget the greatness of the God-given privilege of Israel; and he will use that privilege once more as a cry to conscience.

V 25. *For circumcision indeed profits you, if you carry law into practice*; in that case circumcision is for you God's seal upon God's own promises to the true sons of Abraham's blood and faith. Are you someone who practises the holy code whose summary and essence is love to God and love to man? Can you look your Lord in the face and say not, 'I have satisfied all thy demands; pay me that thou owest', but, 'Thou knowest that I love thee, and therefore oh how I love thy law'? Then you are truly a child of the covenant, through his grace; and the seal of the covenant speaks to you the certainties of its blessing. *But if you are a transgressor of law, your circumcision is turned uncircumcision*; the divine seal is nothing to you, for you are not the rightful holder of the deed of covenant which it seals.

V 26. *If therefore the uncircumcision*, the Gentile world, in some individual instance, *carefully keeps the ordinances of the law*, reverently remembers the love owed to God and to man, *shall not his uncircumcision*, the uncircumcision of the man in question, *be counted as if circumcision*? Shall he not be treated as a lawful recipient of covenant blessings even though the seal upon the document of promise is, not at all by his fault, missing?

V 27. *And thus shall not this hereditary uncircumcision*, this Gentile born and bred, *fulfilling the law* of love and duty, *judge you, who by means of letter and circumcision are – law's transgressor*, using as you do in practice use the terms, the letter, of the covenant, and the rite which is its seal, as means to violate its inner meaning, and claiming, in the pride of privilege, blessings promised only to self-forgetting love?

Vv 28–29. *For not the (Jew) in the visible* sphere *is a Jew; nor is circumcision in the visible* sphere, *in the flesh, circumcision. No, but the Jew in the hidden* sphere; *and circumcision of heart, in Spirit, not letter;* circumcision in the sense of a work on the soul, carried out by God's Spirit, not in that of a legal claim that is supposed to rest upon a routine of prescribed observances. *His praise*, the praise of such a Jew, the Jew in this hidden sense, thus circumcised in heart, *does not come from men, but does come from God*. Men may, and very likely will, give him anything but praise; they will not like him the better for his deep divergence from their standard and their spirit. But the Lord knows him, and loves him, and prepares for him his own welcome; 'Well done, good and faithful'.

Here is a far-reaching passage, like the previous paragraphs. Its immediate bearing needs only brief comment and explanation. We need do little more than wonder at the moral miracle of words like these written by one who, a few years before, was spending all the energy of his mighty will on the defence of ultra-Judaism. The miracle lies not only in the vastness of the man's change of view, but in the manner of it. It is not only that he denounces Pharisaism, but he denounces it in a tone entirely free from its spirit, which he might easily have carried into the opposite camp. What he meets it with is the assertion of truths as pure and peaceable as they are eternal; the truths of the supreme and ultimate importance of the right attitude of man's heart towards God, and of the relentless connection between such an attitude and a life of unselfish love towards man. Here is one great instance of that wider spiritual phenomenon, the transfiguration of the first followers of the Lord Jesus from what they had been to what under his risen power they became. We see in them men whose convictions and hopes have undergone an incalculable revolution; yet it is a revolution which disorders nothing. Rather, it has taken fanaticism for ever out of their thoughts and purposes. It has softened their whole souls towards man, as well as drawn them into an unimagined intimacy with God. It has taught them to live above the world; yet it has brought them into the most practical and affectionate relations with every claim upon them in the world around them. 'Your life is hid with Christ in God'; 'Honour all men'; 'He that loveth not, knoweth not God'.

But the significance of this particular passage is truly far-reaching, permanent, and universal. As before, so here, the apostle warns us (not only the Jew of that distant day) against the fatal but easy error of perverting privilege into pride, forgetting that every gift of God is a 'talent' with which the man is to trade for his Lord, and for his Lord alone. But also, more explicitly here, he warns us against the subtle tendency of man's heart to substitute, in religion, the outward for the inward, the mechanical for the spiritual, the symbol for the thing. Who can read this passage without reflections on the privileges and seals of membership of the Christian Church? Who may not take from it a warning not to misplace the divine gifts of order, and sacrament? Here is a great Hebrew teacher dealing with the primary sacrament of Judaism, which is valued so highly in the Old Testament. But when he has to consider the case of one who has received the physical ordinance apart from the right spiritual attitude, he speaks of the ordinance in terms which a hasty reader might think slighting. He does not slight it. He says it 'profits', and he is going soon to say more on the same subject. For him it is nothing less than God's own seal on God's own word, assuring the individual, as if with a literal divine touch, that all is true for him, as he claims grace in humble faith. But then he considers the case of one who, not through contempt but by force of circumstance, has never received the holy seal, yet believes, loves, and obeys. And he lays it down that the Lord of the covenant will honour that man's humble claim as surely as if he brought the covenant-document ready sealed in his hand. Not that even for him the seal, if it may be had, will be nothing; it will undoubtedly be divine still, and will be sought as God's own gift, his seal after the event. But the principle remains that the ritual seal and the spiritual reality are separable; and that the greater thing, the thing of absolute and ultimate necessity between the soul and God, is the spiritual reality; and that where that is present there God accepts.

It was the temptation of Israel of old to put circumcision in the place of faith, love, and holiness, instead of in its right place, as the divine seal upon the covenant of grace, the covenant to be claimed and used by faith. It is the temptation of some Christians now to put the sacred order of the Church, and particularly its divine sacraments, the holy bath and the holy meal, in the place of spiritual renewal, and spiritual communion, rather than in their right place as divine seals on the covenant which guarantees both to faith. For us, as for our spiritual ancestors, this paragraph of the great argument is therefore altogether relevant. As has been said, 'Faith is greater than water'. And the thought is in perfect unison with St Paul's principle of reasoning here. We should value reverence, and use the ordinances of our Master with the devotion we feel we would have if we saw him dip his hand in the font, or stretch it out to break the bread, and hallow it, and give it, at the table. But let us be quite certain, for our own souls' warning, that it remains true – in the sense of this passage – that 'he is not a Christian which is one outwardly, neither is that baptism, or communion, which is outward; but he is a Christian which is one inwardly, and baptism and communion are those of the heart, in the Spirit, not in the letter.'

The God-given externals of Christian order and ordinance are truly sacred. But there are degrees of greatness in the world of sacred things. And the direct moral work of God upon the soul of man is greater than his sacramental work done through man's body.

CHAPTER 8

Jewish Claims: No Hope in Human Merit (3.1–20)

As the apostle dictates, there comes into his mind a figure often seen by his eyes, the rabbinic disputant. Keen, subtle, unscrupulous, both eagerly in earnest yet ready to use any argument for victory, how often that opponent had crossed his path, in Syria, in Asia Minor, in Macedonia, in Achaia! He is present now to his consciousness, within the quiet house of Gaius; and his questions come thick and fast, following on this urgent appeal to his, alas, almost impenetrable conscience.

V 1. *'What then is the advantage of the Jew? Or what is the profit of circumcision?' 'If some did not believe, what of that? Will their faithlessness cancel God's good faith?' 'But if our unrighteousness sets off God's righteousness, would God be unjust, bringing his wrath to bear?'*

We group the questions together in this way, to make it clearer that we enter here, at this opening of the third chapter, upon a brief controversial dialogue; perhaps the almost word for word record of many an actual dialogue. The Jew, pressed hard with moral proofs of his responsibility, must often have turned in this way upon his pursuer, or rather have tried to escape from him in the subtleties of a false appeal to the faithfulness of God.

And first he meets the apostle's stern assertion that circumcision without spiritual reality will not save. He asks, where then is the advantage of Jewish descent? What is the good of circumcision? It is a mode of reply not unknown in discussions on Christian ordinances; 'What then is the good of belonging to a historic church at all? What do you give the divine sacraments to do?'

V 2. The apostle answers his questioner at once; *Much, in every way; first, because they were entrusted with the oracles of God.* 'First', as if there were more to say in detail. At least something of what is here left unsaid is said later, in Romans 9.4–5, where he recounts the long catalogue of Israel's spiritual and historical splendours. But here he places first of these wonderful treasures this, that Israel was 'entrusted with the oracles of God', the utterances of God, his unique message to man 'through his prophets, in the Holy Scriptures'. Yes, here was something which gave to the Jew an advantage without which the others would either have had no existence, or no significance. He was the trustee of revelation. In his care was lodged the book by which man was to live and die; through which he was to know far more about God and about himself than he could learn from all other informants put together. He, his people, his Church, were the witness and keeper of Scripture. And therefore to be born of Israel, and ritually entered into the covenant of Israel, was to be born into the light of revelation, and committed to the care of the witnesses and keepers of the light.

To insist upon this immense privilege is vital to St Paul's purpose here. For it is a privilege which clearly carries an awful responsibility with it. What would be the guilt of the soul, and of the community, to whom those oracles were – not given as property, but *entrusted* – and who did not do the things they said?

Again the message passes on to the Israel of the Christian Church. 'What advantage has the Christian? What profit is there in baptism?' 'Much, in every way; first, because to the Church is entrusted the light of revelation.' To be born in it, to be baptized in it, is to be born into the sunshine of revelation, and laid on the heart and care of the community which witnesses to the genuineness of its oracles and sees to their preservation and their spread. Great is the talent. Great is the accountability.

V 3. But the rabbinic objector goes on. *For if some did not believe*, what of that? *Will their faithlessness cancel God's good faith?* These oracles of God promise endless glories to Israel, to Israel as a community, a body. Shall not that promise hold good for the whole mass, though some have rejected the Promiser? Will not the unbelieving Jew, after all, find his way to eternal life for his part and lot in the covenant community? 'Will God's faith', his good faith, his promised word, be reduced to empty sounds by the bad Israelite's sin?

V 4. *Away with the thought*, the apostle answers. Anything is more possible than that God should lie. *No, let God prove true, and every man prove liar; as it stands written* (Ps. 51.4), *'That thou mightest be justified in thy words, and mightest overcome when thou impleadest* or *goes to law'*. He quotes the Psalmist in the deep self-accusation, where he takes part against himself, and finds himself completely guilty and, in the loyalty of the renewed and now awakened soul, is jealous to vindicate the justice of the God who condemns him. The whole of Scripture contains no more impassioned, yet no more profound and deliberate, statement of the eternal truth that God is always in the right or he would be no God at all; that it is better, and more reasonable, to doubt anything than to doubt his righteousness.

V 5. But again the objector, intent not on God's glory but on his own position, takes up the word. *But if our unrighteousness exhibits, sets off, God's righteousness*, if our sin gives occasion to grace to abound, if our guilt lets the generosity of God's way of acceptance stand out the more wonderful by contrast – *what shall we say? Would God be unjust, bringing his wrath to bear* on us, when our pardon would illustrate his free grace?

We struggle, in our paraphrase, to bring out the meaning of this difficult passage. The apostle seems to be caught between the wish to represent the objector's thought, and the dread of one really irreverent word. He throws the man's last question into a form which, grammatically, expects a 'no' when the drift of the thought would lead us up to a shocking 'yes'. And then at once he passes to his answer. *I speak as man*, humanly; as if this question of balanced rights and wrongs were one between man and man, not between man and eternal God. Such talk, even for argument's sake, is impossible for the renewed soul except when absolutely necessary.

V 6. *Away with the thought* that he would not be righteous, in his punishment of any given sin. *Since how shall God judge the world?* How, on such conditions, shall we rest on the ultimate fact that he is the universal Judge? If he could not, righteously, punish a deliberate sin because pardon, under certain conditions, illustrates his glory, then he could not punish any sin at all. But he *is* the Judge; he *does* bring wrath to bear!

Vv 7–8. Now Paul takes up the objector on his own ground, takes it to its conclusion, and then rejects it. *For if God's truth, in the matter of my lie, has abounded*, has come more fully out, *to his glory, why am I too called to judgment as a sinner? And* why *not* say, *as the slander against us goes, and as some assert that we do say, 'Let us do the ill that the good may come'?* So they assert of us. But *their doom is just*, – the doom of those who would say such a thing, finding shelter for a lie under the throne of God.

No doubt he speaks from a bitter and frequent experience when he takes this particular case, and with a solemn irony claims exemption for himself from the liar's sentence of death. It is plain that the charge of untruth was, for some reason or other, often thrown at St Paul; we see this in the marked urgency with which, from time to time, he asserts his truthfulness (see 9. 1; Gal. 1. 20). Perhaps the varied sympathies of his heart gave innocent occasion sometimes for the charge. The man who could be 'all things to all men' (1 Cor. 9. 22), taking with a genuine insight their point of view, and saying things which showed that he took it, would be very likely to be judged by narrower minds as untruthful. And the very boldness of his teaching might give further occasion, equally innocent; as he asserted at different times, with equal emphasis, opposite sides of truth. But these rather subtle excuses for false witness against this great master of holy sincerity would not be necessary where genuine malice was at work. No man is so truthful that he cannot be charged with falsehood; and no charge is so likely to injure even where it only pretends to strike. And of course the mighty paradox of justification lent itself easily to the distortions, as well as to the contradictions, of sinners. 'Let us do evil that good may come' no doubt represented the report which prejudice and bigotry would regularly carry away and spread after every discussion and argument about free forgiveness. People still say: 'If this is true, we may live as we like; if this is true, then the worst sinner makes the best saint.' Later in the epistle we shall see the unwilling evidence which such distortions bear to the nature of the maligned doctrine; but here the allusion is too passing to bring this out.

'Whose doom is just'. What a witness is this to the undeniable truthfulness of the gospel! This brief statement rejects all argument that the end justifies the means. The temptation for the Christian to think otherwise has been a strong one, almost from the first. So we now find whole systems of reasoning developed whose aim seems to be to go as near to the edge of untruthfulness in religion as possible, if not beyond it.

But the New Testament sweeps the entire idea of the pious fraud away, with this short thunder-peal, 'Their doom is just'. It will hear of no holiness that leaves out truthfulness; no word, no deed, no habit, that even with the purest purpose gives a false picture of the God of reality and truth.

If we read correctly Acts 24. 20, 21, with Acts 23.6, we see St Paul himself once, under pressure of circumstances, betrayed into an ambiguous statement, and then, publicly and soon, expressing his regret. 'I am a Pharisee, and a Pharisee's son; about the hope and resurrection of the dead I am called in question.' True, true in fact, but not the whole truth, not the complete account of his attitude towards the Pharisee. Therefore, a week later, he confesses, does he not, that in this one thing there was 'evil in him, while he stood before the council'. Happy the Christian, happy the Christian in public life, immersed in management and discussion, whose memory is as clear about truth-telling, and whose conscience is as sensitive!

V 9. *What then? are we superior?* Say *not* so *at all*. Who are the 'we' here, and with whom are 'we' compared? There are two possibilities. 'We' may be 'we Jews'; as if Paul placed himself in instinctive sympathy, by the side of the compatriot whose objections he has just fought, and gathered up here into a final assertion all he has said before of the (at least) equal guilt of the Jew beside the Greek. Or 'we' may be 'we Christians', taken for the moment as men apart from Christ; it may be a rejection of the thought that he has been speaking from a pedestal, or from a tribunal. As if he said, 'Do not think that I, or my friends in Christ, would say to the world, Jewish or Gentile, that we are holier than you. No; we speak not from the bench, but from the bar. Apart from him who is our peace and life, we are "in the same condemnation". It is exactly because we are in it that we

turn and say to you, "Do not ye fear God?" ' On the whole, this
latter reference seems truer to the context.

*For we have already charged Jews and Greeks, all of them, with being
under sin;* or more exactly *with being brought under sin,* giving us the
thought that the race has fallen from a good estate into an evil
one.

Vv 10–18. *As it stands written, that there is not even one man righteous;
there is not a man who understands, not a man who seeks his God. All
have left the road; they have turned worthless together. There is not a man
who does what is good, there is not, even so many as one. A grave set open
is their throat,*breathing out the stench of polluted words; *with their
tongues they have deceived; asps' venom is under their lips; (men) whose
mouth is brimming with curse and bitterness. Swift are their feet to shed
blood; ruin and misery* for their victims *are in their ways; and the way
of peace they never knew. There is no such thing as fear of God before
their eyes.*

Here is a patchwork of Old Testament oracles, from the Psalms
(6. 9, 10. 7, 14. 1–3, 36. 1, 140. 3), from the Proverbs (1. 16),
and from Isaiah (54. 7). All in the first instance depict and
denounce classes of sins and sinners in Israelite society; and we
may wonder at first sight how their evidence convicts all men
everywhere of sin. But we need not only accept that somehow it
must be so, because 'it stands written' here; we may see, in part,
how it is so. These special charges against certain sorts of human
lives stand in the same book which levels the general charge
against the human heart that it is 'deceitful above all things,
hopelessly diseased' (Jer. 17. 9), and incapable of knowing all
its own corruption. The crudest surface phenomena of sin are
thus never isolated from the underlying epidemic of the human
race. The actual evil of men shows the potential evil of man. The
tiger-strokes of open wickedness show the tiger-nature, which
is always present, even where its possessor least suspects it.
Circumstances infinitely vary, and among them those internal
circumstances which we call special tastes and dispositions. But
everywhere amidst them all is the human heart, made upright
in its creation, self-wrecked into moral wrongness when it turned
itself from God. That it *is* turned from him, not to him, appears
when its direction is tested by the collision between his claim

and its will. And in this turning away from the Holy One, who claims the whole heart, there lies at least the potential of 'all unrighteousness'.

Long after this, as his glorious rest drew near, St Paul wrote again of the human heart, to 'his true son' Titus (3.3). He reminds him of the wonder of that saving grace which he so fully unfolds in this epistle; how, 'not according to our works', the 'God who loves man' had saved Titus, and saved Paul. And what had he saved them from? From a state in which they were 'disobedient, deceived, the slaves of divers lusts and pleasures, living in malice and envy, hateful, hating one another'. What, the loyal and hard working Titus, the chaste, the upright, the unutterably earnest Paul? Is not the picture greatly, lamentably exaggerated, a burst of religious rhetoric? The French Protestant pastor Adolphe Monod tells us that he once thought it must be so. But years passed, and he saw deeper into himself, seeing deeper into the holiness of God; and the truthfulness of that passage grew upon him.

In the same way, Robert Browning confesses in one of his poems that, amidst a thousand doubts and difficulties, his mind was anchored to faith in Christianity by the fact of its doctrine of sin.

V 19. *Now we know that whatever things the law says, it speaks them to those in the law*, those within its range, its dominion; *that every mouth may be stopped, and all the world may prove guilty with regard to God.* 'The law'; that is to say, here, the Old Testament revelation. This not only contains the moral code of Moses and the prophets, but has one great aim throughout, to prepare man for Christ by exposing him to himself, in his shame and need. It shows him in a thousand ways that 'he cannot serve the Lord' (Jos. 24. 19), so that in that same Lord he may take refuge from both his guilt and his lack of power. And this it does for 'those in the law'; that is to say here, primarily, for the Jews. Yet they, surely, are not alone on Paul's mind. We have seen already how 'the law' is, after all, only the more full and direct statement of 'law'; so that the Gentile as well as the Jew has to do with the light, and with the responsibility, of a knowledge of the will of God. While the chain of stern quotations we have just handled lies heaviest

on Israel, it binds the world. It 'shuts every mouth'. It drags
man in guilty before God.

'That every mouth may be stopped'. The harsh or muffled
voices of self-defence, of self-assertion, are hushed at last, as with
Job of old (Job 40. 4). He leaves speech to God, and learns at
last to listen. What shall he hear? A scolding, or an eternal
rejection? No, something far different, and better, and more
wonderful. But there must first be silence on man's part, if it is
to be heard. 'Hear – and your souls shall live.'

So the great argument pauses, gathered up into a statement
which both concentrates what has gone before, and prepares us
for a glorious sequel. Shut your mouth, O man, and listen now:
V 20. *Because by means of works of law there shall be justified no flesh
in his presence; for by means of law comes – moral knowledge of sin.*

CHAPTER 9

The One Way of Divine Acceptance (3.21–31)

So then there is silence on earth, that man may hear the 'still, small voice', 'the sound of stillness' (1 Ki. 19.12), from the heavens. 'The law' has spoken, with its heart-shaking thunder. It has driven in upon the soul of man, from many sides, that one fact—guilt; the eternity of the claim of righteousness, the absoluteness of the holy will of God, and, in contrast, the failure of the human race to meet that claim and do that will. It has told man, in effect, that he is 'depraved', that is to say, morally distorted. He is 'totally depraved', that is, the distortion has affected his whole being, so that he can supply on his own part no power which will restore him to harmony with God. And the law has nothing more to say to him, except that this condition is not only deplorable, but guilty, accountable, condemnable; and that his own conscience is also a witness that it is so. He is a sinner. To be a sinner is before all things to be a law-breaker. It is other things besides. It is to be morally diseased, and in need of surgery and medicine. It is to be morally unhappy, and an object of compassion. But first of all it is to be morally guilty, and in urgent need of justification, of a reversal of sentence, of satisfactory settlement with the offended (and eternal) law of God.

That law, having spoken its relentless conditions, and having announced the just sentence of death, stands stern and silent beside the now silent offender. It is not its job to relieve his fears, to allay his grief, to pay his debts. Its awful, merciful business is say 'Thou shalt not sin', and 'The wages of sin is death'. It summons conscience to attention, and tells it in its now hearing ear far more than it had realized before of the horror and the doom of sin; and then it leaves conscience to take up the message and alarm the whole inner world with the certainty of guilt and judgment.

Is it a merely abstract picture? Or do our hearts, the writer's and the reader's, bear any witness to its living truthfulness? God knows that these things are no curiosities of the past. We are not studying an interesting phase of early Christian thought. We are reading a living record of the experiences of innumerable lives which are lived on earth today. There is such a thing indeed in our time as conviction of sin. There is such a thing now as a human soul, struck dumb amidst its defences, doubts and denials, by the speech and then the silence of the law of God. There is such a thing now as a real man, strong and sound in thought, healthy in every faculty, used to looking facts of daily life in the face, yet broken down in the indescribable conviction that he is a poor, guilty, lost sinner, and that his overwhelming need is—not now, not just now—the solution of problems of being, but the assurance that his sin is forgiven. He must be justified, or he dies. The God of the law must somehow say he has no quarrel with him, or he dies a death which he sees, as by an intuition unique to conviction of sin, to be in its proper nature a death without hope, without end.

Is this 'somehow' possible?

Listen, guilty and silent soul, to a sound which is audible now. In the turmoil of either secular indifference or blind self-justification you could not hear it; at best you heard a meaningless murmur. But listen now; it is clear, and it speaks to you. The earthquake, the wind, the fire, have passed; and you are indeed awake. Now comes 'the sound of stillness' in its turn.

Vv 21–24. *But now, apart from law, God's righteousness stands displayed, attested by the law and the prophets; but*—though attested by them, in the Scriptures which all along, in word and example, promise better things to come, and above all a Blessed One to come—*(it is) God's righteousness, through faith in Jesus Christ,* prepared *for all and bestowed upon all who believe in him. For there is no distinction; for all have sinned, and fall short of the glory of God, being justified giftwise, by his grace, through the redemption,* the ransom-rescue, *which is in Christ Jesus.*

V 25. Yes, it is always in him, the Lord of saving merit, and so is to be found in him alone; *whom God presented*, put forward, *as propitiation, through faith in his blood*, his blood of death, of sacrifice, of the altar; *so as to demonstrate*, to explain, to clear up, *his righteousness*, his way of acceptance and its method. The Father 'presented' the Son so as to show that his grace meant no conniving, no indulgence without a lawful reason. He 'presented' him because of *his passing-by of sins done before*; because an explanation was needed for the fact that, while he proclaimed his law, and had not yet revealed his gospel, he did nevertheless bear with sinners, reprieving them, *in the forbearance of God*, in the ages when he was seen to 'hold back' his wrath, but did not yet disclose the reason why.

V 26. *It was with a view*, he says again, *to this demonstration of his righteousness in the present period*, the season of the revealed gospel; *that he may be*, in our view, as well as in divine fact, both *just*, true to his eternal law, *and justifier of him who belongs to faith in Jesus*.

This is the voice from heaven, audible when the sinner's mouth is shut, while his ears are opened by the touch of God. Without that spiritual introduction to them, very likely they will seem either just an interesting fact in the history of religious thought, or a series of disputable assertions. Read them when convicted of sin; in other words, bring to them your whole being, stirred from above to its moral depths, and you will not be indifferent to them or oppose them. They will meet your deep need, as the key meets the lock. Every sentence, every link of reasoning, every affirmation of fact, will be precious to you beyond all words. And you will never *fully* understand them except then, or in the life which has such experience among its memories.

'But now'; the happy 'now' of present fact, of waking certainty. It is no daydream. Look, and see; touch, and feel. Turn the blessed page again; 'It stands written.' There is indeed a 'righteousness of God', a settled way of mercy which is as holy as it is kind, an acceptance as good in eternal law as in eternal love. It is 'attested by the law and the prophets'; countless lines of prediction and foreshadowing meet upon it, to contradict for ever the fear of illusion or delusion. Here is no accidental meeting, but the long-laid plan of God. See its cause, the beloved Son of the Father. The law-giver is the Christ-giver; he has 'set him forth', he has provided in him an expiation which does not persuade him to have mercy, for he is eternal love already, but liberates his love along the line of a wonderfully satisfied holiness, and explains that liberation (to the contrite) so as supremely to win their worship and their love to the Father and the Son. Behold the Christ of God; behold the blood of Christ. In the gospel, he is everywhere, it is everywhere; but what is your delight to find him, and it, here at the start of your life of blessing? Looking upon the crucified, you understand the joy with which, age after age, men have spoken of a death which is their life, of a cross which is their crown and glory. You are in no mood, here and now, to disparage the doctrine of the atoning blood; to place it in the background of your Christianity. You cannot now think well of any gospel that does not say, 'First of all, Christ died for our sins, according to the Scriptures' (1 Cor. 15.3). You are a sinner, and you know it; 'guilty before God'; and for you as a sinner such the propitiation governs your whole view of man, God, life, and heaven. For you, whatever may be the case for others, redemption cannot be thought of, apart from its first precious element, 'remission of sins', justification of the guilty. The all-blessed God, with all his attributes, his character, is seen by you evermore as 'just, yet the justifier of him that believeth in Jesus'. He shines on you through the Word, and in your heart's experience. But all those others are affected for you by this, that he is the God of a holy justification; that he is the God who has accepted you, the guilty one, in Christ. All your thoughts of him are formed and developed at the foot of the cross.

How precious to you now are the words which once, perhaps, were worse than insipid, 'faith', 'justification', 'the righteousness of God'! In the discovery of your need, and of Christ as the all-in-all to meet it, you see the little need of exposition the place and power of 'faith'. It means, you see it now, simply your reception of Christ. It is not virtue; it has no connection with merit. But it is necessary. The meaning of 'justification' is now to you no philosophical riddle. Like all the great words of scriptural theology it carries with it in divine things the meaning it bears in common things, only for a new and noble application; you see this with joy, by the insight of awakened conscience. He who 'justifies' you does exactly what the word always means. He does not educate you, or inspire you, up to acceptability. He pronounces you acceptable, satisfactory, at peace with law. And this he does for Another's sake; on account of the merit of Another, who has done and suffered so as to win an eternal welcome for himself and everything that is his, and therefore for all who are found in him, and therefore for you who have fled to him, believing. So you receive with joy and wonder 'the righteousness of God', his way to bid you, so deeply guilty in yourself, welcome without fear to your Judge. You are 'righteous', that is to say, satisfactory to the law. How? Because you are transfigured into a moral perfectness of the kind that could constitute a claim? No, but because Jesus Christ died, and you, receiving him, are found in him.

'There is no difference'. Once, perhaps, you resented that word, if you paused to note it. Now you take all its meaning to heart. Whatever otherwise your difference may be from the most disgraceful and notorious breakers of the law of God, you know now that there is none in this respect—that you are as hopelessly, whether or not as distantly, remote as they are from 'the glory of God'. His moral 'glory', the absolute perfectness of his character, with its inherent demand that you must perfectly correspond to him in order so to be at peace with him—you are indeed short of this. The prostitute, the liar, the murderer, are short of it; but so are you. Perhaps they stand at the bottom of a mine, and you on the crest of an Alp; but you are as little able to touch the stars as they. So you thankfully give yourself up, side by side with them, if they will but come too, to be carried to the height of divine acceptance, by the gift of God, 'justified gift-wise by his grace'.

V 27. *Where then is our boasting? It is shut out. By means of what law? Of works? No, but by means of faith's law*, the institute, the ordinance, which lays it upon us not to deserve, but to confide. And who can analyse or describe the joy and rest of the soul from which at last is 'shut out' the foul inflation of a religious 'boast'? We have praised ourselves, we have valued ourselves, on one

thing or another supposed to make us worthy of the Eternal. We
may perhaps have had some plausible pretexts for doing so; or
we may have 'boasted' (such boastings are not unknown) of
nothing better than being a little less ungodly, or a little more
manly, than someone else. But this is over now for ever. And
great is the rest and gladness of sitting down at our Redeemer's
feet, while the door is shut and the key is turned upon our self-
congratulation. There is no holiness without that 'exclusion'; and
there is no happiness where there is no holiness.

V 28. *For we reckon*, we conclude, we gather up our facts and
reasons thus, *that man is justified by faith, apart from*, irrespective
of, *works of law*. In other words, the cause of merit lies wholly in
Christ, and wholly outside conduct. We have seen, implicitly, in
the passage above, verses 10–18, what is meant here by 'works
of law' or by 'works of the law'. The thought is not of prescribed
ritual, but of moral rule. The law-breakers of verses 10–18 are
men who commit violent deeds, and speak foul words, and fail
to do what is good. So the law-keeper is the man whose conduct
in such respects is right. And the 'works of the law' are such
deeds accordingly. So here 'we conclude' that the justification of
fallen man takes place, in relation to the merit which obtains it,
irrespective of doing right. In relation to merit it is respective
only to Christ. In relation to personal reception it is respective
only to the acceptance of the meriting Christ, that is to say, with
faith in him.

Then come two brief questions and their answers, spoken
almost as if a rabbinic objector was involved again.

Vv 29–30. *Is God the Jews' God only? Not of the nations too? Yes, of
the nations too; assuming that God is one*, the same person in both
cases; *who will justify circumcision on the principle of faith, and uncircumcision by means of faith*. He takes the fact now discovered, that faith,
that is to say, Christ received, is the condition of justification for
all mankind; and he reasons back to the fact (so amply attested
by the law and the prophets, from Genesis onwards) that the
true God is equally the God of all. There is probably an inference
here that the fence of privilege drawn for ages round Israel was
meant ultimately for the whole world's blessing, and not to hold
Israel in a selfish isolation.

V 31. *We cancel law, then, by this faith of ours?* We open the door, then, to moral licence? We abolish code and command, then, when we ask not for conduct, but for faith? *Away with the thought; no, we establish law*; we go the very way to give a new sacredness to its every command, and to disclose a new power for the fulfilment of them all, as will be argued later.

CHAPTER 10

Abraham and David (4.1–12)

The Jewish disputant is present still in the apostle's thought. Hardly surprising, for no question was more pressing on the Jewish mind than that of acceptance; thus far, truly, the teaching and discipline of the Old Testament had not been in vain. And St Paul had not only, in his Christian apostleship, debated that problem countless times with rabbis; he had been himself a rabbi, and knew by experience both the misgivings of such a person's conscience, and the tricks of his reasoning.

So now there rises before him the great name of Abraham, as a familiar watchword of the argument about acceptance. He has been contending for an absolutely inclusive verdict of 'guilty' against man, against every man. He has been shutting with all his might the doors of thought against human 'boasting', against the least claim of man to have merited his acceptance. Can he carry this principle into quite impartial issues? Can he, a Jew in presence of Jews, apply it without apology or reserve, to Abraham, whom even we Gentiles honour as so close to the ideal man, portrayed as walking and talking with God himself? Was not at least Abraham accepted because he was morally worthy of acceptance? And if Abraham, then surely, in abstract possibility, others also.

On the other hand, if this was not the case with Abraham, the inference for others is clear. The unique title 'Friend of God' seems to exclude altogether the question of a legal acceptance. Who thinks of his friend as one whose relation to him needs to be good in law at all? The friend stands as it were behind or above law. He holds a relation implying personal sympathies, identity of interests, contact of thought and will, not an anxious previous settlement of claims, and remission of liabilities. If then the friend of the eternal Judge proves, nevertheless, to have needed justification, and to have received it by the channel not of his personal worth but of the grace of God, there will be little hesitation about other people's need, and the sole way by which they shall find it met.

In approaching this great example St Paul is about to illustrate all the main points of his inspired argument. By the way, by implication, he gives us the all-important fact that even an Abraham, even 'the Friend', did need justification somehow. The eternal Holy One is such that no man can walk by his side and live, no, not in the path of inmost 'friendship', without an acceptance before his face as he is Judge. Then again, such is God, that even an Abraham found this acceptance not by merit but by faith; not by presenting himself, but by renouncing himself, and taking God for all; by pleading not, 'I am worthy', but, 'Thou art faithful'. It is to be shown that Abraham's justification was such that it gave him not the least ground for self-congratulation; it was not in the least degree based on merit. A promise of sovereign kindness, connected with the redemption of himself, and of the world, was made to him. He was not morally worthy of such a promise, if only because he was not morally perfect. And he was, humanly speaking, physically incapable of it. But God offered himself freely to Abraham, in his promise; and Abraham opened the empty arms of personal reliance to receive the unearned gift. Had he stayed first to earn it he would have shut it out; he would have closed his arms. Rightly renouncing himself, because seeing and trusting his gracious God, the sight of whose holy glory annihilates the idea of man's claims, he opened his arms, and the God of peace filled the emptiness. The man received his God's approval, because he put nothing of his own in the way.

From one point of view, the all-important viewpoint here, it did not matter what Abraham's conduct had been. As a fact, he was already devout when the incident of Genesis 15 occurred. But he was also actually a sinner; *that* is made quite plain by Genesis 12, the chapter that records his call. And potentially, according to Scripture, he was a great sinner; for he was an instance of the human heart. But this, while it made up Abraham's urgent need of acceptance, was not in the least a barrier to it, when he turned from himself, in the great crisis of absolute faith, and accepted God in his promise.

The principle of the acceptance of 'the Friend' was identical to that which underlies the acceptance of the worst sinner. As St Paul will soon remind us, David in the guilt of his murderous adultery, and Abraham in his worshipping obedience, stand upon the same level here. Actually or potentially, each is a great sinner. Each turns from himself, unworthy, to God in his promise. And the promise is his, not because his hand is full of merit, but because it is empty of himself.

It is true that Abraham's justification, unlike David's, is not explicitly connected in the narrative with a moral crisis of his soul. He is not depicted, in Genesis 15, as a conscious penitent, flying from justice to the Judge. But is there not a deep suggestion that something not unlike this did then pass over him, and through him? That short assertion, that 'he trusted the Lord, and he counted it to him for righteousness', is an anomaly in the story, if it has not a spiritual depth hidden in it. Why, just then and there, should we be told this about his acceptance with God? Is it not because the vastness of the promise had made the man see in contrast the absolute failure of a corresponding merit in himself? Job (43.1–6) was brought to self-despairing penitence not by the fires of the law but by the glories of creation. Was not Abraham brought to the same consciousness, whatever form it may have taken in his character and period, by the greater glories of the promise? Surely it was there and then that he learnt that secret of self-rejection in favour of God which is the other side of all true faith, and which came out long years afterwards, in its mighty issues of 'work', when he laid Isaac on the altar.

It is true, again, that Abraham's faith, his justifying reliance, is not connected in the narrative with any clear expectation of an atoning sacrifice. But here we dare to say first, that probably Abraham knew much more about the Coming One than modern criticism will commonly allow. 'He rejoiced to see my day; and he saw it, and was glad' (John 8.56). And secondly, the faith which justifies, though what it touches in fact is the blessed propitiation, or rather God in the propitiation, does not always imply a clear knowledge of the whole 'reason of the hope'. But it does imply a true submission to all that the believer knows of the revelation of that reason. But he may (by circumstances) know very little of it, and yet be a believer. The saint who prayed (Ps. 143.2) 'Enter not into judgement with thy servant, O Lord, for in thy sight shall no man living be justified', cast himself upon a God who, being absolutely holy, yet can somehow, just as he is, justify the sinner. Perhaps he knew much of the reason of atonement, as it lies in God's mind, and as it is explained and demonstrated, in the cross. But perhaps he did not. What he did was to cast himself up to the full light he had, 'without one plea', upon his Judge, as a man awfully conscious of his need, and trusting only in a sovereign mercy, which must also be a righteous, a law-honouring mercy, because it is the mercy of the Righteous Lord.

Let us not be misunderstood, meanwhile, as if such words meant that a definite creed of the atoning work of Christ is not possible, or is not precious. This epistle will help us to such a creed, and so will Galatians, Hebrews, Isaiah, Leviticus, and the whole Scripture. 'Prophets and kings desired to see the things we see, and did not see them' (Luke 10.24). But that is no reason why we should not adore the mercy that has unveiled to us the cross and the blessed Lamb.

But it is time to come to the apostle's words as they stand.

V 1. *What then shall we say that Abraham has found*—'has found', the perfect tense of a lasting and always significant fact—'has found', in his great discovery of divine peace—*our forefather, according to the flesh?* 'According to the flesh'; that is to say, 'in respect of self', 'in the region of his own works and merits'.

V 2. *For if Abraham was justified as a result of works, he has a boast*; he has a right to self-congratulation. Yes, such is the principle indicated here; if man merits, man is entitled to self-congratulation. May we not say, in passing, that the common instinctive sense of the moral inappropriateness of self-congratulation, above all in spiritual things, is one among many witnesses to the truth of our justification by faith only? But St Paul goes on; *Ah, but not towards God*; not when even an Abraham looks him in the face, and sees himself in that light. As if to say, 'If he earned justification, he might have boasted rightly; but "rightful boasting", when man sees God, is an unthinkable thing; therefore his justification was given, not earned.'

Vv 3–5. *For what says the Scripture*, the passage, the great text (Gen. 15.6)? *'Now Abraham believed God, and it was reckoned to him as righteousness.' Now to the man who works, his reward*, what he has earned *is not reckoned grace-wise*, as a gift of generosity, *but debt-wise; it is to the man who does not work, but believes*, confides, *in him who justifies the ungodly one, that 'his faith is reckoned as righteousness'*. 'The ungodly one'; as if to bring out by an extreme case the glory of the wonderful paradox. 'The ungodly', means not just the sinner, but the open, defiant sinner. Every human heart is capable of such sinfulness, for 'the heart is deceitful above all things'. In this respect, as we have seen, even an Abraham is potentially a great sinner. But there are indeed 'sinners and sinners' in the experiences of life; and St Paul is ready now with a conspicuous example of the justification of one who was truly, at one miserable period, by his own fault, 'an ungodly one'.

The faithful record of the Scriptures shows us David, the chosen, the faithful, the man of spiritual experiences, acting out his lustful look in adultery, and half covering his adultery with the most base of constructive murders, and then, for long months, refusing to repent. Yet David was justified: 'I have sinned against the Lord'; 'The Lord also hath put away thy sin'. He turned from his awfully ruined self to God, and at once he received forgiveness. Then, and to the last, he was punished. But then and there he was unreservedly justified, and with a justification which made him sing a loud blessing.

Vv 6–8. *Just as David too speaks his felicitation of the man* (and it was himself) *to whom God reckons righteousness irrespective of works, 'Happy they whose iniquities have been remitted, and whose sins have been covered; happy the man to whom the Lord will not reckon sin'* (Ps. 32. 1, 2). Wonderful words, in the context of the experience out of which they spring! A human soul which has greatly transgressed, and which knows it well, and knows too that to the end it will suffer a sore discipline because of it, as an example and humiliation, nevertheless knows its pardon, and knows it as an indescribable happiness. The iniquity has been 'lifted'; the sin has been 'covered', has been struck out of the book of 'reckoning' written by the Judge. The penitent will never forgive himself; in this very Psalm he tears from his sin all the covering woven by his own heart. But his God has forgiven him, has reckoned him as one who has not sinned, so far as access to him and peace with him are concerned. And so his song of shame and penitence begins with a blessing, and ends with a cry of joy.

We pause to note the exposition implied here of the phrase, 'to reckon righteousness'. It is to treat the man as one whose account is clear. 'Happy the man to whom the Lord will not reckon sin.' In the phrase itself, 'to reckon righteousness' (as in its Latin equivalent, 'to inpute righteousness'), the question, 'What clears the account?' is not answered. Suppose the impossible case of a record kept absolutely clear by the man's own sinless goodness; then the 'reckoned', the 'imputed, righteousness' would mean the law's contentment with him on his own merits. But the context of human sin fixes the actual reference to an 'imputation' which means that the awfully defective record is treated, for a divinely valid reason, as if it were, what it is not, good. The man is at peace with his Judge, though he has sinned, because the Judge has joined him to himself, and taken up his liability, and answered for it to his own law. The man is dealt with as righteous, being a sinner, for his glorious Redeemer's sake. It is pardon, but more than pardon. It is no mere indulgent dismissal; it is a welcome as of the worthy to the embrace of the Holy One.

Such is the justification of God. We shall need to remember it through the whole course of the epistle. To make 'justification' a mere synonym for 'pardon' is always inadequate. Justification is the contemplation and treatment of the penitent sinner, found in Christ, as righteous, as satisfactory to the law, not merely as one whom the law lets go. Is this a fiction? Not at all. It is vitally linked to two great spiritual facts. One is, that the sinner's friend has himself dealt, in the sinner's interests, with the law, honouring its holy claim to the uttermost under the human conditions which he freely undertook. The other is that he has mysteriously, but really, joined the sinner to himself, in faith, by the Spirit; joined him to himself as limb, branch, and bride.

Christ and his disciples are really one in the order of spiritual life. And so the community between him and them is real, the community of their debt on the one side, of his merit on the other.

Now the question comes up again, never far from St Paul's thought and life, what these facts of justification have to do with Gentile sinners. Here is David blessing God for his unmerited acceptance, an acceptance by the way wholly unconnected with the ritual of sacrifice. Here above all is Abraham, 'justified in consequence of faith'. But David was a child of the covenant of circumcision. And Abraham was the father of that covenant. Do not their justifications speak only to those who stand, with them, inside that charmed circle? Was not Abraham justified by faith plus circumcision? Did not the faith act only because he was already one of the privileged?

V 9. *This felicitation therefore*, this cry of 'Happy are the freely justified', *is it upon the circumcision, or upon the uncircumcision? For we say that to Abraham*, with an emphasis on 'Abraham', *his faith was reckoned as righteousness.* The question, he means, is legitimate, 'for' Abraham is not at first sight a case in point for the justification of the outside world, the non-privileged races of man.

V 10. But consider: *How then was it reckoned? To Abraham in circumcision or in uncircumcision? Not in circumcision, but in uncircumcision*; fourteen years at least had to pass before the covenant rite came in.

Vv 11–12. *And he received the sign of circumcision* (with a stress upon 'sign', as if to say that the 'thing', the reality signed, was his already), *as a seal on the righteousness of the faith that was in his uncircumcision*, a seal on the acceptance which he received, before all formal privilege, in that bare hand of faith. And all this was so, and was recorded so, with a purpose of far-reaching significance: *that he might be father*, example, representative, *of all who believe not withstanding uncircumcision, that to them righteousness should be reckoned; and father of circumcision*, example and representative within its circle also, *for those who do not merely belong to circumcision, but for those who also step in the track of the uncircumcision-faith of our father Abraham.*

So privilege had nothing to do with acceptance, except to

countersign the grant of an absolutely free grace. The seal did nothing whatever to make the covenant. It only verified the fact, and guaranteed the good faith of the giver. The patriarchal sacrament, like the Christian sacraments, was 'a sure testimony and effectual sign of God's grace and good will'. But the grace and the good will come not through the sacrament as through a channel, but straight from God to the man who took God at his word. He received them through faith. The rite did not come between the man and his accepting Lord, but as it were, was present at the side to assure him with a physical associated fact that all was true.

CHAPTER 11

Abraham Again (4.13–25)

Again we approach the name of Abraham, Friend of God, father of the faithful. We have seen him justified by faith, personally accepted because he turned completely to the sovereign Promiser. We see him now in some of the glorious results of that acceptance; 'heir of the world', 'father of many nations'. And here too all is of grace, all comes through faith. Neither works nor merit, ancestral or ritual privilege, obtained the mighty promise for Abraham; it was his because he 'believed God'.

We see him as he steps out from his tent to look at the stars. The lonely old man who stands gazing there, perhaps side by side with his divine Friend revealed in human form, is told to try to count. And then he hears the promise, 'So shall thy seed be'.

It was then and there that he received justification by faith. It was then and there also that, by faith, as a man uncovenanted, unworthy, but called upon to take what God gave, he received the promise that he should be 'heir of the world'.

'Heir of the world'! Did this mean, of the universe itself? Perhaps it did, for Christ was to be the claimant of the promise in due time (see Matt. 13.37, 38); and under his feet all things, literally all, are set already by right, and shall be hereafter set in fact. But the more limited, and probably in this place the fitter, reference is vast enough; a reference to the world of earth, and of man upon it. In his 'seed', the childless man was to be king of men, monarch of the continents and oceans. To him, in his seed, 'the utmost parts of the earth' were given 'for his possession'. Not just his little clan nor even his direct descendants, however numerous, but 'all nations', 'all kindreds of the earth', were 'to call him blessed', and to be blessed in him, as their patriarchal chief, their head in covenant with God. We do not yet see everything of this astonishing promise fulfilled. But we do see already significant and irrevocable steps taken towards that result.

No secular conscious programme has had to do with this. Causes entirely beyond the reach of human combination have been, as a fact, combined; the world has been opened to the Abrahamic message just as the Church has been awakened to a deeper understanding of her glorious mission. For here too is the finger of God; not only in the history of the world, but in the life of the Church and of the Christian. For a long century now, in the most living centres of Christendom, there has been waking and rising a mighty revived consciousness of the glory of the gospel of the cross, and of the Spirit; of the grace of Christ, and also of his claim. And now, after many a gloomy forecast of unbelieving and apprehensive thought, there are more men and women ready to go to the ends of the earth with the message of the Son of Abraham, than in all time before.

Contrast these results—leaving out of sight the mighty future—with the starry night when the wandering Friend of God was asked to believe the incredible, and was justified by faith, and was invested through faith with the world's crown. Is not God in the fulfilment? Was he not in the promise? We are ourselves a part of the fulfilment; we are one of the 'many nations' of whom Abraham was then made the father.

Abraham's reliance, at that time of crisis, merited nothing, but received everything. He took in the first place acceptance with God, and then with it he took inexhaustible riches of privilege and blessing; above all, the blessing of being made a blessing. So now, in view of that hour of promise, and of these ages of fulfilment, we see our own path of peace in its divine simplicity. We read, as if written on the heavens in stars, the words, 'justified by faith'. And we understand already, what the epistle will soon fully reveal to us, how for us, as for Abraham, untold further blessings are contained in the gift of our acceptance.

Let us turn again to the text.

Vv 13–15. *For not through law came the promise to Abraham, or to his seed, of his being the world's heir, but through faith's righteousness;*

through the acceptance received by uncovenanted, unprivileged faith. *For if those who belong to law inherit* Abraham's promise, *faith is ipso facto void, and the promise is ipso facto annulled. For wrath is what the law works out*; it is only *where law is not that transgression is not either.* This is as much as to say, that to suspend eternal blessing, the blessing which in its nature can deal only with ideal conditions, upon man's obedience to law, is to bar fatally the hope of a fulfilment. Why? Not because the law is not holy; not because disobedience is not guilty; as if man were ever, for a moment, automatically compelled to disobey. But because as a fact man is a fallen being, however he became so, and whatever is his guilt as such. He is fallen, and has no true self-restoring power. If then he is to be blessed, the work must begin in spite of himself. It must come from outside, it must come unearned, it must be of grace, through faith.

Vv 16–17. *Therefore it is on* (literally, 'out of') *faith, in order to be grace-wise, to make secure the promise, to all the seed, not only to that which belongs to the law, but to that which belongs to the faith of Abraham,* to the 'seed' whose claim is no less and no more than Abraham's faith; *who is father of all us, as it stands written* (Gen. 17.5), '*Father of many nations have I appointed thee — in the sight of the God whom he believed, who vivifies the dead, and calls,* addresses, deals with, *things not-being as being.* 'In the sight of God': as if to say, that it matters little what Abraham is for 'us all' in the sight of man, in the sight and estimate of the Pharisee. The eternal Justifier and Promiser dealt with Abraham, and in him with the world, before the birth of the law which the Pharisee has perverted into his stronghold of privilege and isolation. He took care that the mighty transaction should take place not actually only, but significantly, in the open field and beneath the stars. It was to affect not one tribe, but all the nations. It was to secure blessings which were not to be demanded by the privileged, but taken by the needy. And so Abraham the great representative believer was called to believe before law, before legal sacrament, and under every personal circumstance of humiliation and discouragement.

Vv 18–22. *Who, past hope, on hope, believed*; stepping from the dead hope of nature to the bare hope of the promise, *so that he became father of many nations; according to what stands spoken, 'So shall thy seed be.'* And, because he failed not in his faith, he did not notice his own *body, already turned to death, near a century old as he now was, and the death-state of the womb of Sarah. No, on the promise of God*—he did not *waver by his unbelief, but received strength by his faith, giving glory to God*, the 'glory' of dealing with him as being what he is, almighty and all-true, and *fully persuaded that what he has promised he is able actually to do. Wherefore actually it was reckoned to him as righteousness.* Not because such a 'giving to God the glory' which is only his eternal due was in the least degree morally meritorious. If it were so, Abraham 'would have whereof to glory'. The 'wherefore' is concerned with the whole record, the whole transaction. Here was a man who took the right way to receive God's blessing. He put nothing between the Promiser and himself. He treated the Promiser as what he is, all-sufficient and all-faithful. He opened his empty hand in that belief, and so, because the hand was empty, the blessing was put in it.

Vv 23–25. *Now it was not written only on his account, that it was reckoned to him, but also on account of us, to whom it is sure to be reckoned,* in the fixed intention of the divine Justifier, as each successive applicant comes to receive; *believing as we do on the Raiser-up of Jesus our Lord from the dead; who was delivered up on account of our transgressions, and was raised up on account of our justification.*

Here the great argument pauses. More and more, as we have followed it, it has disengaged itself from the obstructions of the opponent, and advanced to a positive and rejoicing assertion of the joys and wealth of the believer. We have left far behind the persistent objections which ask, now whether there is any hope for man outside legalism, now whether within legalism there can be any danger even for deliberate unholiness, and again whether the gospel of free acceptance does not cancel the law of duty. We have left the Pharisee for Abraham, and have stood beside him to look and listen. He, in the simplicity of a soul which has seen itself and seen the Lord, and so has not one word or thought about personal privilege, claim, or even fitness, receives a perfect acceptance in the hand of faith, and finds that the acceptance carries with it a promise of unimaginable power and blessing. And now from Abraham the apostle turns to 'us', 'us all' , 'us also'. His thoughts are no longer upon adversaries and objections, but on the company of the faithful, on those who are one with Abraham, and with each other, in their happy willingness to come, without a dream of merit, and take from God his mighty peace in the name of Christ. He finds himself not in synagogue or in philosophical school, debating, but in the assembly of believers, teaching, unfolding in peace the wealth of grace. He speaks to congratulate, to adore.

Let us join him there in spirit, and sit down with Aquila, Priscilla, and the rest, and in our turn remember that 'it was written for us also'. Quite surely, and with a fullness of blessing which we can never completely grasp, to us also 'faith is sure to be reckoned as righteousness, believing as we do on the Raiser-up of Jesus our Lord, ours also, from the dead'. To us, as to them, the Father presents himself as the Raiser-up of the Son. He is known by us in that act. It gives us his own warrant for a boundless trust in his character, purposes, and unreserved intention to accept the sinner who comes to his feet in the name of his crucified and risen Son. He asks us—not to forget that he is the Judge, who cannot for a moment pretend ignorance of the situation. But he asks us to believe, to see, that he, being the Judge, and also the law-giver, has dealt with his own law, in a way that satisfies it, that satisfies himself. He asks us to under-stand that he now is sure to justify, to accept, to find not guilty, to find the sinner who believes righteous and satisfactory. He comes to us, he, this eternal Father of our Lord, to assure us, in the resurrection, that he has sought and found a ransom; that he has not been forced to have mercy, a mercy behind which there may therefore lurk a gloomy reserve, but has himself 'set forth' the beloved Propitiation, and then accepted him (not it, but him) with the acceptance of not just his word but his deed. He is the God of peace. How do we know it? We thought he was the God of judgment and doom. Yes, but he has 'brought the great Shepherd from the dead, in the blood of the everlasting covenant' (Heb. 13.20). Then, O eternal Father of our Lord, we will believe you; we will believe in you. Truly, in this glorious respect, though you are consuming fire, there is nothing in you to dread.

'Who was delivered up because of our transgressions'. So the

Father dealt with the Son, who gave himself. 'It pleased the Lord to bruise him'; 'He spared not his own Son.' 'Because of our transgressions': to meet the fact that we had gone astray. Was our self-will, pride, falsehood, impurity, indifference and resistance to God, to be met in this way? Was it to be met at all, and not just abandoned to its own horrible results? Was it eternally necessary that, if met, it must be met in this way, by nothing less than the delivering up of Jesus our Lord? Yes. There is no doubt that if a milder means would have met our guilt, the Father would not have 'delivered up' the Son. The cross was nothing if not absolutely indispensable. There is that in sin, and in God, which made it eternally necessary that—if man was to be justified—the Son of God must not only live but die, and not only die but die in this way, delivered up, given over to be done to death, like those who commit great sin.

Deep in the heart of the divine doctrine of atonement lies this element of it, the 'because of our transgressions'; the necessity of Golgotha, due to our sins. The forgiveness, acquittal, or acceptance, was not a matter for a divine pronouncement. It was a matter not between God and creation, which to him is a little thing, but between God and his law, that is to say, himself as eternal Judge. And this, to the Eternal, is not a little thing. So the solution called for no little thing, but for the atoning death of Christ, for the laying by the Father on the Son of the iniquities of us all, that we might open our arms and receive from the Father the merits of the Son.

'And was raised up because of our justification', because our acceptance had been won, by his deliverance up. Such is the simplest explanation of the grammar and meaning. The Lord's resurrection appears as, so to speak, the mighty sequel, and also the demonstration, warrant, and proclamation of his acceptance as the propitiation, and therefore of our acceptance in him. For indeed it was our justification, when he paid our penalty. True, the acceptance does not fall to the individual till he believes, and so receives. The gift is not put into the hand till it is open, and empty. But the gift has been bought ready for the recipient long before he kneels to receive it.

A little while before he wrote to Rome, St Paul had written to

Corinth, and the same truth was in his heart then, though it came out only in passing. 'If Christ is not risen, idle is your faith; you are yet in your sins' (1 Cor. 15.17). That is to say, as the context undoubtedly shows, you are still in the guilt of your sins; you are still unjustified. 'In your sins' cannot possibly there refer to the moral condition of the converts; for as a matter of fact, which no doctrine could deny, the Corinthians were 'changed men'. 'In your sins' refers therefore to guilt, to law, to acceptance. And it bids them look to the atonement as the objective requirement for that, and to the resurrection as the one possible, and the only necessary, guarantee to faith that the atonement had achieved its end.

'Who was delivered up; who was raised up'. When? About twenty-five years before Paul sat dictating this sentence in the house of Gaius. There were at that moment at least three hundred known living people (1 Cor. 15.6), who had literally seen and heard the Risen Christ. From one point of view, all was eternal, spiritual, invisible. From another point of view our salvation was as concrete and historical as the battle of Actium, or the death of Socrates. And what was done, remains done.

CHAPTER 12

Peace, Love, and Joy
For the Justified (5.1–11)

We reached a pause in the apostle's thought at the end of Romans 4. We may imagine that there is also a pause in his dictation to Tertius, a silence in which they both meditate and worship: The Lord delivered up; his people justified; the Lord risen again, alive for evermore—here was matter for love, joy, and wonder.

But the letter must continue, and the argument be developed. It has now already expounded the tremendous need of justifying mercy. It has shown how faith always and only, is the way to appropriate that mercy—the way of God's will, and manifestly also in its own nature the way of deepest fitness. We have been allowed to see faith in action, in Abraham, who by faith, absolutely, without the least advantage of traditional privilege, received justification, with the great blessings that came with it. Lastly we have heard St Paul dictate to Tertius, for the Romans and for us, those summarizing words (4.25) in which we now have God's own certificate of the triumphant efficacy of the atoning work of Christ, which sustains the promise in order that the promise may sustain us in believing.

We are now to approach the glorious theme of the life of the justified. This is to be seen not only as a state whose basis is the reconciliation of the law, and whose gate and walls are the covenant promise. It is to appear as a state warmed with eternal love; illuminated with the prospect of glory. In it the man, knit up with Christ his Head, his Bridegroom, his all, yields himself with joy to the God who has received him. In the living power of the heavenly Spirit, who perpetually delivers him from himself, he obeys, prays, works, and suffers, in a freedom which is only not yet that of heaven, and in which he is maintained to the end by the One who has planned his full personal salvation from eternity to eternity.

It has sometimes been the temptation of Christians to regard the truth and exposition of justification as if there were a certain hardness and dryness about it; as if it were a topic more for study than for life. But there is no basis for that view in Romans. For Paul certainly does not discuss it drily; he certainly lays deep the foundations of law and atonement, but he does it like a man who is not drawing the plan of a shelter, but calling his reader from the storm into what is not only a shelter but a home. And again he does not discuss it in isolation. He devotes his fullest, largest, and most loving expositions on its intense and living connection with associated truths. He is about now to take us into the sanctuary of the life of the accepted, the life of union, of surrender, the life of the Holy Spirit.

Vv 1–2. *Justified therefore on terms of faith, we have peace towards our God,* we possess in regard of him the quietness and assurance of acceptance, *through our Lord Jesus Christ,* thus delivered up, and raised up, for us; *through whom we have actually found our introduction,* our free admission, *by our faith, into this grace,* this unearned acceptance for Another's sake, *in which we stand,* instead of falling ruined, sentenced, at the judgment. *And we exult,* not with the sinful 'boasting' of the legalist, *but in hope* (literally, 'on hope', as in resting on the promised sight) *of the glory of our God,* the light of the heavenly vision and fruition of our justifier, and the splendour of an eternal service of him in that fruition.

Vv 3–5. *Nor only so, but we exult too in our tribulations,* with a better fortitude than the Stoic's artificial serenity, *knowing that the tribulation works out, develops, patient persistency,* as it gives proof after proof of the power of God in our weakness, and thus generates the habit of reliance; *and then the patient persistency* develops *proof,* bring out in experience, as a proved fact, that through Christ we are not what we were; *and then the proof* develops *hope,* solid and definite expectation of continuing grace and final glory, and, in particular, of the Lord's return; *and the hope does not shame,* does not disappoint; it is a sure and steadfast hope, for it is the hope of those who now know that they are objects of eternal Love; *because the love of our God has been poured out in our hearts*; his love to us has been as it were diffused through our consciousness, poured out in a glad experience like rain from a cloud, like floods from a rising spring, *through the Holy Spirit that was given to us.*

Here is the first explicit mention in the apostle's argument (disregarding 1.4), of the Holy Spirit. Up to now the occasion for mention has hardly arisen. Attention has been mainly upon the personal guilt of the sinner, and the objective fact of the atonement, and the exercise of faith, of trust in God, as a genuine personal act of man. With a definite purpose, we may reverently think, the discussion of faith has so far been kept clear of the thought of anything lying behind faith, of any 'grace' giving faith. For whether or not faith is the gift of God, it is most certainly the act of man; no-one should assert this more decidedly than those who hold (as we do) that Ephesians 2.8 *does* teach that where there is saving faith, it is there because God has given it. But how does he give it? Not, surely, by implanting a new faculty, but by opening the soul to God in Christ so that the divine magnet effectually draws the man to a willing rest and reliance upon such a God. But the man does this, as an act, himself. He trusts God as genuinely, as personally, as much with his own faculty of trust, as he trusts a man whom he sees to be quite trustworthy and precisely fit to meet an urgent need. Thus it is often the work of the evangelist and the teacher to insist upon the duty rather than the grace of faith; to bid men rather thank God for faith when they have believed than wait for the feeling of inspiration before believing. And is this not what St Paul does here? At this point of his argument, and not before, he reminds the believer that his possession and peace, happiness and hope, has been attained and realized not, ultimately, through himself but through the working of the Eternal Spirit. The insight into mercy, into a propitiation provided by divine love, and so into the holy secret of the divine love itself, has been given him by the Holy Spirit, who has taken of the things of Christ, and shown them to him, and secretly handled his 'heart' so that the fact of the love of God is a part of experience at last. The man has been told of his great need, and of the sure and open shelter, and has stepped through its peaceful gate in the act of trusting the message and the will of God. Now he is asked to look round, to look

back, and bless the hand which, when he was outside, opened
his eyes to see, and guided his will to choose.

What a looking back it is! Let us trace it from the first words
of this paragraph again. First, here is the sure fact of our acceptance, and the reason of it, and the method. Our justification is
no arbitrary matter, whose lack of a cause suggests an illusion,
or a precarious peace. Note the word 'therefore'. It rests upon
something previous in the logical chain of divine facts, 'Jesus our
Lord was given up because of our transgressions, and was raised
up because of our justification' (4.25). We assented to that fact;
we have accepted him, only and altogether, in this work of his.
Therefore we are justified, placed by an act of divine love, working in the line of divine law, among those whom the Judge
accepts, that he may embrace them as Father. Then, in this
possession of the 'peace' of our acceptance, thus led in through
the gate of the promise, with the footstep of faith, we find inside
our shelter far more than merely safety. We look up from inside
the blessed walls, sprinkled with atoning blood, and we see above
them the hope of glory, invisible outside. And we turn to our
present life within them and we find resources provided there for
a present as well as a future joy. We address ourselves to the
discipline of the place; for it has its discipline; the shelter is
home, but it is also school; and we find, when we begin to try
it, that the discipline is full of joy. It brings out into a joyful
consciousness the power we now have, in him who has accepted
us, in him who is our Acceptance, to suffer and to serve in love.
Our life has become a life not just of peace but of the hope which
animates peace, and makes it flow like a river. From hour to
hour we enjoy the never-disappointing hope of 'grace for grace',
new grace for the next new need; and beyond it, and above it,
the certainties of the hope of glory. To drop our metaphor of the
shelter sanctuary for that of the pilgrimage, we find ourselves on
a steep and rocky pathway, but always mounting into purer air,
and so as to show us nobler views. And at the summit the
pathway will be continued, and transfigured, into the golden
street of heaven.

The Holy Spirit has led us into all this. He has been at the
heart of the whole internal process. He made the thunder of the

law clear to our conscience. He gave us faith by revealing Christ. And, in Christ, he has 'poured out in our hearts the love of God'.

For now the apostle picks on the phrase 'the love of God', and we see in its pure glory no vague abstraction, but the face and the work of Jesus Christ. Paul's argument continues, 'For Christ, when we still were weak'. He has set justification before us in its majestic lawfulness. But he has now to expand its mighty love, of which the Holy Spirit has made us conscious in our hearts. We are to see in the atonement not only a guarantee that we have a valid title to a just acceptance. We are to see in it the love of the Father and the Son, so that not just our security but our bliss may be full.

V 6. *For Christ, we still being weak* (a gentle euphemism for our utter powerlessness, our guilty inability to meet the sinless claim of the law of God) *in season*, in the fullness of time, when the ages of rule and failure had done their work, and man had learnt something useful of the lesson of self-despair, *for the ungodly—died*. 'For the ungodly', 'concerning them', 'with reference to them', that is to say, in this context of saving mercy, 'in their interests, for their rescue, as their propitiation'. 'The ungodly', or, more literally still, without the article, 'ungodly ones'; a general and inclusive designation for those for whom he died. We saw the word used above (4.5) with a certain limitation, as of the worst among the sinful. But here, surely, with a solemn paradox, it covers the whole field of the fall. The ungodly here are not just the flagrant and disreputable; they are all who are not in harmony with God; the potential as well as the actual doers of serious sin. For them 'Christ died': not 'lived', let us remember, but 'died'. It was a question not of example, nor of persuasion, nor even of statements of divine compassion. It was a question of law and guilt; and it was to be met only by the death sentence and the death-fact; such death as he died of whom, a little while before, Paul had written to the converts of Galatia (Gal. 3.13) 'Christ bought us out from the curse of the law, when he became a curse for us.' All the emphasis of the sentence lies here on those last words, 'for ungodly ones—he died'.

Vv 7–8. The sequel shows this to us; he proceeds: *For scarcely*, with difficulty, and in rare instances, *for a just man will one die*;

'scarcely', he will not say 'never' *for the good man*, the man answering in some degree the ideal of gracious and not only of legal goodness, perhaps *someone actually ventures to die. But God commends*, as by a glorious contrast; *his love*, 'his' as above all current human love, 'his own love', *towards us, because while we were still sinners*, and as such repulsive to the Holy One, *Christ for us did die*.

We are not to read this passage as if it were a statistical assertion about the facts of human love and its possible sacrifices. The moral argument will not be affected if we are able, as we shall be, to bring up cases where an unrenewed man has given his life to save the life of one, or of many, to whom he is not emotionally or naturally attracted. All that is necessary to St Paul's tender plea for the love of God is the certain fact that the cases of death even on behalf of one who morally deserves a great sacrifice are relatively very, very few. The thought of merit is the ruling thought in the context. Paul works to bring out the sovereign Lovingkindness, which went even to the length and depth of death, by reminding us that, whatever moved it, it was not moved, even in the lowest imaginable degree, by any merit or fitness in us. And yet we were sought, and saved. He who planned and provided salvation, was the eternal lawgiver and Judge. He who loved us is himself eternal Right, to whom all our wrong is unutterably repellent. What then is he as Love, who, being also Right, does not stop until he has given his Son to the death of the atonement?

So we have indeed a basis to 'believe the love of God' (1 John 4.16). Yes, to believe it. We look within us, and it is incredible. If we have really seen ourselves, we have seen ground for a sorrowful conviction that he who is eternal Right must view us with aversion. But if we have really seen Christ, we have seen ground for—not feeling at all, it may be, at this moment, but— believing that God is love, and loves us. What is it to believe him? It is to take him at his word; to act not upon our internal consciousness but upon his promise. We look at the cross, or rather, we look at the crucified Lord Jesus in his resurrection; we read at his feet these words of his apostle; and we go away to take God at his assurance that we, unlovely, are beloved.

As a dying French saint said, as she gave a last embrace to

her daughter, 'My child, I have loved you because of what you are; my heavenly Father, to whom I go, has loved me in spite of myself.'

Vv 9–11. And how does the divine reasoning continue? 'From glory to glory', from acceptance by the Holy One, who is Love, to present and endless preservation in his Beloved One. *Therefore much more, justified now in his blood,* as it were 'in' its washing, or again 'within' its circle of sprinkling as it marks the precincts of our inviolable sanctuary, *we shall be kept safe through him,* who now lives to administer the blessings of his death, *from the wrath,* the wrath of God, in its present imminence over the head of the unreconciled, and in its final fall 'in that day'. *For if, being enemies,* with no initial love to him who is Love, no, when we were hostile to his claims, and as such subject to the hostility of his law, *we were reconciled to our God through the death of his Son* (God coming to judicial peace with us, and we brought to submissive peace with him), *much more, being reconciled, we shall be kept safe in his life,* in the life of the Risen One who now lives for us, and in us, and we in him. *Nor only so, but we* shall be kept *exulting too in our God through our Lord Jesus Christ, through whom now we have received this reconciliation.*

Here, by anticipation, Paul indicates already the mighty results of the act of justification, in our life of union with the Lord who died for us, and lived again. This will be more fully unfolded in Romans 6; but he cannot completely put it aside so long. As he has advanced from the law-aspect of our acceptance to its love-aspect, so now with this latter he also gives us the life-aspect, our vital incorporation with our Redeemer, our part and lot in his resurrection-life (a subject that is more fully expounded in Colossians and Ephesians). 'Kept safe in his life', not 'by' his life, but 'in' his life. We are livingly knit to him the Living One. From one point of view we are the accused, wonderfully transformed, by the Judge's provision, into welcomed and honoured friends of the law and the lawgiver. From another point of view we are the dead wonderfully brought to life and put into a spiritual connection with the mighty life of our lifegiving Redeemer. The aspects are perfectly distinct. They belong to different orders of thought. Yet they are in the closest and most genuine relation. The justifying sacrifice procures the possibility of our regeneration into the life of Christ. Our union by faith with the Lord who died and lives brings us into a real share in his justifying merits. And our share in those merits, our 'acceptance in the Beloved', assures us again of the permanence of the mighty Love which will maintain us in our part and lot 'in his life'. This is the view of the matter which is before us here.

So the apostle meets our need on every side. He shows us the holy law satisfied for us. He shows us the eternal love freely given to us. He shows us the Lord's own life clasped around us, imparted to us: 'our life is hid in God with Christ, who is our Life' (Col. 3. 3,4). Shall we not 'exult in God through him'?

And now we are to learn something of the great covenant-headship, in which we and Christ are one.

CHAPTER 13

Christ and Adam (5.12–21)

We approach a paragraph of the epistle full of mystery. It leads us back to primal man, to the Adam of the beginning of Scripture, to his encounter with the suggestion to follow himself rather than his Maker, to his sin, and then to the results of that sin in his race. We shall find those results given in terms which certainly we should not have devised by reasoning from cause to effect. We shall find the apostle teaching, or rather stating, for he writes as to those who know, that mankind inherits from primal man, tried and fallen, not only taint but guilt, not only moral hurt but legal fault.

Scripture nowhere undertakes to tell us about everything it contains. It undertakes to tell us truth, and to tell it from God. It undertakes to give us pure light, 'to bring life and immortality out into the light' (2 Tim. 1. 10). But it reminds us that we know in part, and that even prophecy, even the inspired message, is 'in part' (I Cor. 13. 9). It illuminates immensely much, but it leaves yet more to be seen hereafter. It does not yet light up the whole sky and the whole landscape. It sheds its glory upon our Guide, and upon our path.

This fact is well worth remembering here. This passage tells us, with the voice of the apostle's Lord, great facts about our own race, and its relations to its primeval Head, which show that every individual man has a profound moral and judicial link with the first man. It does not tell us how those mysterious but solid facts fit into the whole plan of God's creative wisdom and moral government. The lamp shines on the edges of a deep ditch beside the road; it does not shine like the sun over the whole landscape.

As with other mysteries which will meet us later, so with this;

we approach it like those who 'know in part', and who know that the apostolic prophet, by no fault of inspiration, but by the limits of the case, 'prophesies in part'. Thus with reverence, and free from the wish to explain away, yet without anxiety lest God should be proved unrighteous, we listen as Paul dictates, and receive his witness about our fall and our guilt in that mysterious First Father.

We also remember that this paragraph deals only incidentally with Adam; its main theme is Christ. Adam is the illustration; Christ is the subject. We are to be shown in Adam, by contrast, some of 'the unsearchable riches of Christ'. This is why our main attention is called not to the brief outline of the mystery of the fall, but to the assertions of the related splendour of the redemption.

St Paul is about to conclude his exposition of the 'way of acceptance', and to pass to its connection with the 'way of holiness'. And he shows us here last, in the matter of justification, this fragment from 'the bottoms of the mountains' – the union of the justified with their redeeming Lord as race with Head; the link in that respect between them and him which makes his righteous act of such infinite value to them. In the previous paragraph, as we have seen, he has gravitated toward the deeper regions of the blessed subject; he has indicated our connection with the Lord's life as well as with his merit. Now, returning to the thought of the merit, he still tends to the depths of truth, and Christ our righteousness is lifted before our eyes from those pure depths as not just the propitiation, but the propitiation who is also our Covenant-Head, our Second Adam, holding his mighty merits for a new race, bound up with himself in the bond of a real unity.

Paul 'prophesies in part', meanwhile, even in respect of this element of his message. As we saw a few verses earlier, the fullest explanations of our union with the Lord Christ in his life were reserved by St Paul's Master for other letters. In the present passage we have not, what probably we should have had if the epistle had been written five years later, a definite statement of the deep, necessary and significant connection between our union with Christ in his covenant and our union with him in his life.

It is not quite absent from this passage, if we read verses 17 and 18 correctly; but it is not prominent.

Vv 12–14. *On this account*, on account of the aspects of our justification and reconciliation 'through our Lord Jesus Christ' which he has just presented, it is *just as through one man sin entered into the world*, the world of man, *and, through sin, death and so to all men death travelled*, penetrated, pervaded, *inasmuch as all sinned*; the race sinning in its head, the nature in its representative bearer. The facts of human life and death show that sin did thus pervade the race, as to liability, and as to penalty: *For until law came sin was in the world*; it was present all along, in the ages previous to the giving of the law. *But sin is not imputed*, is not put down as debt for penalty, *where law does not exist*, where in no sense is there statute to be obeyed or broken, whether it was clearly expressed, or not. *But death became king, from Adam down to Moses, even over those who did not sin on the model of the transgression of Adam – who is* (in the present tense of the plan of God) *pattern of the Coming One*.

He argues from the fact of death, and from its universality, which implies a universality of liability, of guilt. According to the Scriptures, death is essentially penal in the case of man, who was created not to die but to live. How that purpose would have been fulfilled if he had not sinned against God, we do not know. We need not think that the fulfilment would have violated any natural process; higher processes might have governed the case, in perfect harmony with the surroundings of earthly life, till perhaps that life was transfigured, as by a necessary development, into the heavenly and immortal. But, however, the record does connect, for man, the fact of death with the fact of sin. And the fact of death is universal, and so has been from the first. And so it includes generations most remote from the knowledge of a revealed code of law. And it includes individuals incapable of a conscious act of sin like Adam's; it includes unbelievers, infants, and the mentally defective. Therefore wherever there is human nature, since Adam fell, there is sin, in its form of guilt. And therefore, in some sense which perhaps only God himself fully knows, but which we can follow a little way, all men offended in the First Man. The guilt contracted by him is possessed also by them. And thus is he 'the pattern of the Coming One' or the 'Second Adam' or 'Second Man' of I Corinthians 15.45, 47.

V 15. *But not as the transgression, so the gracious gift. For if, by the transgression of the one, the many*, the many affected by it, *died, much rather did the grace of God*, his kind action, *and the gift*, the grant of our acceptance, *in the grace of the one Man, Jesus Christ* ('in his grace', because involved in his kind action, in his redeeming work), *abound unto the many* whom it, whom he, affected.

We observe here some of the phrases in detail. 'The One'; 'the One Man': – 'the one', in each case, is related to 'the many' involved, in bane or in blessing respectively. 'The One Man': – the Second Adam is described, not the First. As to the First, it goes without saying that he is man. As to the Second, it is infinitely wonderful, and of eternal significance, that he, as truly, as completely, is one with us, is Man of men. 'Much rather did the grace, and the gift, abound': – the thought here is that while the dreadful sequel of the fall was solemnly permitted, as good in law, the sequel of the divine counter-work was gladly advanced by the Lord's willing love, and was brought to an altogether unmerited effect, in the present and eternal blessing of the justified. 'The many', mentioned twice in this verse, are the whole group which, in each case, stands related to the respective representative. It is the whole race in the case of the fall; it is the 'many brethren' of the Second Adam in the case of the reconciliation. The question is not one of numerical comparison between the two, but of the numerousness of each group in relation to the oneness of its covenant Head. What the numerousness of the 'many brethren' will be we know – and we do not know; for it will be 'a great multitude, which no one can number'. But that is not in the question here. The emphasis lies not on the compared numbers, but on the extent of the blessing which overflows upon 'the many' from the justifying work of the One.

Paul proceeds, developing the thought. From the act of each representative, from Adam's fall and Christ's atonement, there followed results of dominion and royalty. But what was the contrast of the cases! In the fall, the sin of the One brought upon 'the many' judgment, sentence, and the reign of death over them. In the atonement, the righteousness of the One brought upon 'the many' an 'abundance', an overflow, a generous and loving acceptance, and the power of eternal life, and royal rule over sin and death. We follow out the apostle's wording:

Vv 16–17. *And not as through the one who sinned*, who fell, *so is the gift*; our acceptance in our Second Head does not follow the law of mere and strict retribution which appears in our fall in our first Head. (*For*, he adds in emphatic parenthesis, *the judgment* stemmed, *from one* transgression, *in condemnation*, in sentence of death; *but the gracious gift* stemmed, *from many transgressions* – not indeed as if earned by them, as if caused by them, but as occasioned by them; for this wonderful process of mercy found in our sins, as well as in our fall, a reason for the cross – *in a deed of justification*.) *For if in one transgression*, 'in' it, as the effect is involved in its cause, *death came to reign through the one* offender, *much rather those who are receiving*, in their successive cases and generations, *that abundance of the grace* just spoken of (v 15), *and of the free gift of righteousness*, of acceptance, *shall, in life*, eternal life, begun now, to end never, *reign* over their former tyrants *through the One*, their glorious One, *Jesus Christ*.

And now he sums up the whole in one comprehensive inference and affirmation. The fundamental thought is the whole mercy for the all due to the one work of the One. It is illustrated by the one and the many of the fall, but still so as to throw the real weight of every word not upon the fall but upon the acceptance. Here, as throughout this paragraph, we should be greatly mistaken if we thought that the illustration and the object illustrated were to be pressed, detail by detail, into one mould. For example, we are certainly not to take him to mean that Adam's 'many' are not only fallen in him, but actually guilty, therefore Christ's 'many' are not only accepted in him, but actually and personally worthy of acceptance. The whole epistle rejects that thought. Nor are we to think, as we ponder verse 18, that because 'the condemnation' was 'to all men' in the sense of their being not only condemnable but actually condemned, therefore 'the justification of life' was 'to all men' in the sense that all mankind are actually justified. Here again the whole epistle, and the whole message of St Paul about our acceptance, are on the other side. The provision is for the race, for mankind; but the possession is for those who believe. We should be cautious about drawing parallels in the details. The force of the parallel lies in the broader and deeper factors of the two matters. It lies in the mysterious phenomenon of covenant headship, that affects both our fall and our acceptance; in the power upon the many, in each case, of the deed of the One; and then in the magnificent fullness and positiveness of result in the case of our salvation. In our fall, sin merely worked itself out into doom and death. In our acceptance, the Judge's award is positively crowned and as it were loaded with gifts and treasures. It brings with it, in ways not described here, but amply shown elsewhere, a living union with a Head who is our life, and in whom we already possess the powers of heavenly being in their essence. It brings with it not only the approval of the law, but accession to a throne. The justified sinner is a king already, in his Head, over the power of sin and the fear of death. And he is on his way to a royalty in the eternal future which shall make him great in his Lord.

The main message of this passage is the absolute dependence of our justification upon the atoning act of our Head, and the relation of our Head to us accordingly as our centre and our root of blessing. The mystery of our congenital guilt is there, though it is only incidentally there. And after all what is that mystery? It is undoubtedly a fact. What is the statement of this paragraph, that the many were 'constituted sinners by the disobedience of the one'? It is the Scripture expression, and in some guarded sense the Scripture explanation, of a consciousness deep as the awakened soul of man; that I, a member of this homogeneous race, made in God's image, not only have sinned, but have been a sinful being from my first personal beginning; and that I ought not to be so, and ought never to have been so. It is my calamity, but it is also my accusation. I cannot explain it, but I know it. And to know it, with a knowledge that is not just speculative but moral, is to be put in a self-despair which can go nowhere else than to Christ for acceptance, peace, holiness and power.

Let us translate, as they stand, the closing sentences of this chapter.

Vv 18–19. *Accordingly therefore, as through one transgression* there came a result *to all men, to condemnation*, to sentence of death, *so through one deed of righteousness there came a result to all men* (to 'all' in the sense we have indicated, so that whoever of mankind receives the acceptance owes it always and wholly to the act of Christ) to *justification of life*, to an acceptance which not only bids the guilty 'not die', but opens to the accepted the secret, in him who is their sacrifice, of powers which live in him for them as he is their life. *For as, by the disobedience of the one man, the many*, the many of that case, *were constituted sinners*, constituted guilty of the fall of their nature from God, so that their being sinful is not only their calamity but their sin, *so too by the obedience of the One*, 'not according to their works', that is, to their conduct, past, present, or to come, but 'by the obedience of the One', *the many*, his 'many brethren', his Father's children through faith in him, *shall be*, as each comes to him in all time, and then by the final open proclamation of eternity, *constituted righteous*, qualified for the acceptance of the holy Judge.

Before Paul ends this part of his message, and turns to the next, he adds a word, indicating a theme to be discussed more fully later. It is on the function of the law, in view of this wonderful acceptance of the guilty. He has suggested the question already (3. 31); he will treat some aspects of it more fully later. But here one at least needs to ask if law was just an anomaly, impossible to put into relation with justifying grace? Might it have been as well out of the way, never heard of in the human world? No, God forbid. One deep purpose of acceptance was to glorify the law, making the declared will of God as dear to the justified as it is terrible to the guilty. But now, besides this, it has a function that comes before justification as well as follows it. Applied as positive command to the human will in the fall, what does it do? It does not create sinfulness; God forbid. Not God's will but the creature's will did that. But it occasions sin's declaration of war. It brings out the hidden rebellion of the will. It forces the disease to the surface. It is a merciful force, for it shows the sick man his danger, and it gives point to his doctor's words of warning and hope. It reveals to the criminal his guilt; as it is sometimes found that information of a statutory human penalty awakens a law-breaker's conscience in the midst of a half-unconscious course of crime. And so it brings out to the opening eyes of the soul the wonder of the remedy in Christ. He sees the law; he sees himself; and now at last it becomes a profound reality to him to see the cross. He believes, adores, and loves. The merit of his Lord covers his demerit, as the waters cover the sea. And he passes from the dread but salutary view of the reign of sin over him, in a death he cannot understand, to submit to the reign of grace, in life, in death, for ever.

Vv 20–21. *Now law came sideways in*; law in its widest sense, as it affects the fallen, but with a special reference, no doubt, to its statement at Sinai. It came in 'sideways' as to its relation to our acceptance; as something which should indirectly promote it, by not causing but occasioning the blessing; *that the transgression might abound*, that sin, that sins, in the most inclusive sense, might develop the hidden evil, and as it were expose it to the work of grace. *But where the sin multiplied*, in the place, the region, of fallen humanity, *there did superabound the grace*; with that mighty overflow of the bright ocean of love which we have watched already. *That just as our sin came to reign in our death*, our penal death, *so too might the grace come to reign*, having its glorious way against our foes and over us, *through righteousness*, through the justifying work, *to life eternal*, which we have here and which hereafter will receive us into itself, *through Jesus Christ our Lord*.

The last words of Mr Honest in Bunyan's *Pilgrim's Progress* were ' "Grace reigns." So he left the world'. Let us walk with the same watchword through the world, till we too, crossing that Jordan, lean with a final simplicity of faith upon 'the obedience of the One'.

CHAPTER 14

Justification and Holiness (6.1–13)

In a certain sense, St Paul has completed his exposition of justification. He has brought us on, from his denunciation of human sin, and his detection of the futility of mere privilege, to propitiation, faith, acceptance, love, joy, and hope, and finally to our mysterious but real connection in all this blessing with the One who won our peace. From this point onwards we shall find many mentions of our acceptance and of its cause, underlying the argument everywhere. But we shall now think less directly of the foundations than of the superstructure, for which the foundation was laid. We shall be less occupied with the fortifications of our holy city than with the resources they contain, and with the life which is to be lived, on those resources.

Everything will fit together. But the transition will be marked, and will call for our deepest, most reverent and prayerful thought.

'We need not, then, be holy, if such is your programme of acceptance.' Such was the objection, bewildered or deliberate, which St Paul heard in his mind at this pause in his dictation; he had doubtless often heard it with his ears. Here was a wonderful provision for the free and full acceptance of the ungodly by the eternal Judge. It was explained and stated so as to leave no room for human virtue. Faith itself was no commendatory virtue. It was not 'a work', but the antithesis to 'works'. Its power was not in itself but in its Object. It was itself only the emptiness which received 'the obedience of the One' as the sole meriting cause of peace with God. Then – may we not live on in sin, and yet be in his favour now, and in his heaven hereafter?

Let us recollect, as we pass on, one important lesson of these recorded objections to St Paul's message. They tell us, incidentally, how explicit and unreserved his delivery of the message had been, and how justification by faith, by faith only, meant what was said, when it was said by him. Christian thinkers, of more schools than one, and at many periods, have hesitated not a little over that point. The medieval theologian mingled his thoughts of justification with those of renewal, and accordingly taught our acceptance on lines impossible to lay along those of St Paul. In later days, the meaning of faith has sometimes become hazy, till it has seemed to be only an indistinct summary-word for Christian consistency, exemplary conduct, or good works. But if this, or anything like it, had been St Paul's message, we should not have had Romans 6.1 worded as it is. Whatever objections were encountered by a gospel of acceptance expounded on such lines (and no doubt it would have encountered many, if it called sinful men to holiness), it would not have encountered the objection that it seemed to allow men to be unholy. What such a gospel would seem to do would be to emphasize the urgency of obedience in order to gain acceptance; the vital importance on the one hand of an internal change in our nature (through the operation of the sacraments, according to many); and then on the other hand the practice of Christian virtues, with the hope, in consequence, of acceptance, more or less complete, in heaven. Whether the objector or enquirer was dull or subtle, it could not have occurred to him to say, 'You are preaching a gospel of licence; I may, if you are right, live as I please, only drawing a little deeper on the fund of free acceptance as I go on.' But just this was the feeling, and such were very nearly the words, of those who either hated St Paul's message as unorthodox, or wanted an excuse for the sin they loved, and found it in quotations from St Paul. Then St Paul must have meant by faith what faith ought to mean, simple trust. And he must have meant by justification without works, what those words ought to mean, acceptance irrespective of any conduct that could recommend us. Such a gospel was no doubt liable to be mistaken and misrepresented, and in just the way we mention. But it was also, and it is so still, the only gospel which is the power of God unto salvation – to the fully awakened conscience, to the soul that sees itself, and truly asks for God.

This accidental witness to the meaning of the Pauline doctrine of justification by faith only will appear still more strongly when we come to the apostle's answer to his questioners. He does not meet them by modifying his assertions. He has not a word to say about additional and corrective conditions that precede our peace with God. He makes no impossible hint that 'justification' means the making of us good, or that 'faith' is a summary word for Christian practice. No; there is no reason for such assertions either in the nature of words, or in the whole form of his argument. What does he do? He takes this great truth of our acceptance in Christ our Merit, and puts it unreserved, unrelieved, unspoiled, in contact with other truth, of similar, no, of superior greatness, for it is the truth to which justification leads us. He places our acceptance through Christ Atoning in organic connection with our life in Christ Arisen. He indicates, as a truth evident to the conscience, that as the thought of our share in the Lord's merit is inseparable from union with the meriting person, so the thought of this union is inseparable from that of a spiritual harmony, a common life, in which the accepted sinner finds both a direction and a power in his Head. Justification has indeed set him free from the condemning claim of sin, from guilt. He is as if he had died Christ's death of sacrifice, oblation, and satisfaction; as if he had passed through the desolation in Gethsemane, and had poured out his soul for sin. So he is 'dead to sin', in the sense in which his Lord and Representative died to it; the atoning death has killed sin's claim on him for judgment. As having so died, in Christ, he is 'justified from sin'. But then, because he died in Christ, he is in Christ still, in respect also of resurrection. He is justified, not that he may go away, but that in his Justifier he may live, with the powers of that holy and eternal life with which the Justifier rose again.

The two truths are concentrated as it were into one, by their equal relation to the same person, the Lord. The previous argument has made us intensely conscious that justification, while a definite transaction in law, is not a mere transaction; it lives and glows with the truth of connection with a person. That person is the bearer for us of all merit. But he is also, and equally, the bearer for us of new life; in which the sharers of his merit share, for they are in him. So that, while the way of justification can be isolated for study, as it has been in this epistle, the justified man cannot be isolated from Christ, who is his life. And thus he can never ultimately be considered apart from his possession, in Christ, of a new possibility and power, a new and glorious call to living holiness.

In the simplest and most practical terms the apostle tells us that our justification is not an end in itself, but a means to an end. We are accepted that we may be possessed, and possessed not like a thing, but like an organic limb. We have received the reconciliation that we may now walk, not away from God, as if released from a prison, but with God, as his children in his Son. Because we are justified, we are to be holy, separated from sin, separated to God; not as a mere indication that our faith is real, and that therefore we are legally safe, but because we were justified for this very purpose, that we might be holy. To return to a simile we have used already, the grapes on a vine are not merely a living sign that the tree is a vine, and is alive; they are the product for which the vine exists. No-one should think that the sinner should accept justification – and live to himself. It is a moral contradiction of the very deepest kind, and cannot be entertained without betraying an initial error in the man's whole spiritual creed.

And further, there is not only this profound connection of purpose between acceptance and holiness. There is a connection of endowment and capacity. Justification has done for the justified a twofold work, both aspects of which are all important for the man who asks, 'How can I walk and please God?' First, it has decisively broken the claim to sin upon him as guilt. He stands clear of that exhausting and enfeebling load. The pilgrim's burden has fallen from his back, at the foot of the Lord's cross, into the Lord's grave. He has peace with God, not in emotion, but in covenant, through our Lord Jesus Christ. He has a permanent and unreserved introduction into a Father's loving and welcoming presence, in the merit of his Head. But, as we have already noted, justification has also been to him as it were the sign of his union with Christ in new life. Not only therefore does it give him, as indeed it does, an eternal occasion for gratitude.

It gives him a new power with which to live the grateful life; a power that is not in justification itself, but in what it opens up. It is the gate through which he passes to the fountain; it is the wall which protects the fountain, the roof which shields him as he drinks. The fountain is his justifying Lord's exalted life, his risen life, poured into the man's being by the Spirit who makes Head and member one. And it is as justified that he has access to the fountain, and drinks as deep as he will of its life, power, and purity. In the contemporary passage, 1 Corinthians 6.17, St Paul had already written (in a most practical context), 'He that is joined unto the Lord is one spirit.' It is a sentence which might stand as a heading to the passage we now come to translate.

Vv 1–2. *What shall we say then? Shall we cling to the sin that the grace may multiply*, the grace of the acceptance of the guilty? *Away with the thought! We, the very men who died to that sin*, – when our Representative, in whom we have believed, died for us to it, died to meet and break its claim – *how shall we any longer live*, have congenial being and action, *in it*, as in an air we like to breathe? It is a moral impossibility that the man freed from this thing's tyrannic claim to slay him in this way should wish for anything else than to be separated from it in all respects.

V 3. Or *do you not know that we all, when baptized into Jesus Christ*, when the sacred water sealed to us our faith-received contact with him and interest in him *were baptized into his death*, baptized as coming into union with him as, above all, the Crucified, the Atoning? Do you forget that your covenant-Head, of whose covenant of peace your baptism was the divine physical sign, is nothing to you if not your Saviour who died, and who died because of this very sin with which your thought now plays; died because only in this way could he break its legal bond upon you, in order to break its moral bond?

V 4. *We were entombed therefore with him by means of our baptism*, as it symbolized and sealed the work of faith, *into his death*; it certified our interest in that vicarious death, even to its climax in the grave which, as it were, swallowed up the Victim; *that just as Christ rose from the dead by means of the glory of the Father*, as that death resulted for him in a new and endless life, not by accident, but because the character of God, the splendour of his love, truth, and power, secured the result, *so we too should begin to walk in newness of life*, should step forth in a power altogether new, in our continuing union with him. All possible emphasis lies upon those words, 'newness of life'. They bring out what has been indicated already (vv 17, 18), the truth that the Lord has won us not only remission of a death-penalty, not only even an extension of existence under happier circumstances, and in a more grateful and hopeful spirit – but a new and wonderful life-power. The sinner has fled to the Crucified, that he may not die. He is now not only amnestied but accepted. He is not only accepted but incorporated into his Lord. He is not only incorporated but, because his Lord, being crucified, is also risen, he is incorporated into him as Life. The Last Adam, like the First, transmits not only legal but life-giving effects to his member. In Christ the man has, in a sense as perfectly practical as it is inexplicable, new life and power, as the Holy Spirit applies to his inmost being the presence and virtues of his Head. 'In him he lives, by him he moves.'

To countless people the discovery of this ancient truth, or the fuller grasp of it, has been just like a beginning of new life. They have been long and painfully aware, perhaps, that their strife with evil was a serious failure on the whole, and their deliverance from its power sadly partial. And they could not always command as they would the emotional energies of gratitude, the warm consciousness of affection. Then it was seen, or seen more fully, that the Scriptures set forth this great mystery, this powerful fact of our union with our Head, by the Spirit, for life, for victory and deliverance, for dominion over sin, for willing service. And the hands are lifted up, and the knees strengthened, as the man uses the now open secret – Christ in him, and he in Christ – for the real walk of life. But let us listen to St Paul again.

Vv 5–6. *For if we became vitally connected*, he with us and we with him, *by the likeness of his death*, by the baptismal plunge, symbol and seal of our faith-union with the Buried Sacrifice, *why we shall be* vitally connected with him by the likeness *also of his resurrection*, by the baptismal emergence, symbol and seal of our faith-union with the risen Lord, and so with his risen power. *This knowing, that our old man*, our old state, as out of Christ and under Adam's headship, under guilt and in moral bondage, *was crucified with Christ*, was as it were nailed to his atoning cross, where he represented us. In other words, he on the cross, our Head and Sacrifice, so dealt with our fallen state for us, *that the body of sin*, this our body viewed as sin's stronghold, or instrument, *might be cancelled*, might be put down or deposed, so as to be no more the fatal door to admit temptation to a powerless soul within.

'Cancelled' is a strong word. Let us lay hold upon its strength, and remember that it gives us not a dream, but a fact, to be found true in Christ. Let us not turn its fact into fallacy, by forgetting that, whatever 'cancel' means it does not mean that grace lifts us out of the body; that we are no longer to 'keep under the body, and bring it into subjection', in the name of Jesus. Alas for us, if any promise, any truth, is allowed to 'cancel' the call to watch and pray, and to think that in no sense is there still a foe within us. But all the rather let us always grasp, and use, the glorious positive. Let us recollect, let us confess our faith, that this is the way it is with us, through him who loved us. He died for us for this very end, that our 'body of sin' might be wonderfully 'in abeyance', regarding the power of temptation upon the soul. Yes, as St Paul proceeds, *that henceforth we should not do bondservice to sin*; that from now onwards, from our acceptance in him, from our realization of our union with him, we should say to temptation a 'no' that carries with it the power of the inward presence of the risen Lord. Yes, for he has won that power for us in our justification through his death. He died for us, and we in him, as to sin's claim, as to our guilt; and he died in this way, as we have seen, so that we might be not only legally accepted, but vitally united to him.

V 7. Such is the connection of the following clause, strangely translated in the Authorized Version, and often therefore misapplied, but whose literal wording is, *For he who died*, he who has died, *has been justified from his sin*; stands justified from it, stands free from its guilt. The thought is of the atoning death of Christ, in which the believer is interested as if it were his own. And the implied thought is that, as that death is an accomplished fact, as 'our old man' *was* 'crucified with Christ', therefore we may, we must, claim the spiritual freedom and power in the Risen One which the Slain One secured for us when he bore our guilt. Vv 8–11. This possession is also a glorious prospect, for it is permanent with the eternity of his life. It not only is, but shall be. *Now if we died with Christ, we believe,* we rest upon his word and work for it, *that we shall also live with him,* that we shall share not only now but for all the future the powers of his risen life. For he lives for ever – and we are in him! *Knowing that Christ, risen from the dead, no longer dies,* no death is in his future now; *death over him has no more dominion,* its claim on him is gone for ever. *For as to his dying, it was as to our sin he died;* it was to deal with our sin's claim; and he has dealt with it so that his death is 'once', once for ever; *but as to his living, it is as to God he lives;* it is in relation to his Father's acceptance, it is as welcomed to his Father's throne for us, as the Slain One Risen. *Even so must you too reckon yourselves,* with the sure 'calculation' that his work for you, his life for you, is infinitely valid, *to be dead indeed to your sin,* dead in his atoning death, dead to the guilt exhausted by that death, *but living to your God, in Christ Jesus;* welcomed by your eternal Father, in your union with his Son, and in that union filled with a new and blessed life from your Head, to be spent in the Father's smile, on the Father's service.

Let us too, like the apostle and the Roman Christians, 'reckon' this wonderful reckoning; counting upon these bright mysteries as upon imperishable facts. All is bound up not with the tides or waves of our emotions, but with the living rock of our union with our Lord. 'In Christ Jesus': – that great phrase, here first explicitly used in the connection, includes everything else. Union with the slain and risen Christ, in faith, by the Spirit – here is our inexhaustible secret, for peace with God, for life to God, now and for ever.

V 12. *Therefore do not let sin reign in your mortal body,* mortal, because not yet fully emancipated, though your Lord has 'cancelled' for you its character as 'the body of sin', the seat and instrument of conquering temptation. Do not let sin reign there, *so that you should obey the lusts of it,* of the body. Note the implied instruction. The body 'cancelled' as 'the body of sin', still has its 'lusts' or desires; or rather desires are still occasioned by it to the man, desires which potentially, if not actually, are desires away from God. And the man, justified through the Lord's death and united to the Lord's life, is not therefore to mistake *laissez-faire* for faith. He is to use his divine possessions, with a real energy of will. It is for him, in a most practical sense, to see that his wealth is put to use, that his wonderful freedom is realized in act and habit. 'Cancelled' does not mean annihilated. The body exists, and sin exists, and 'desires' exist. It is for you, O man in Christ, to say to the enemy, defeated yet present, 'You shall not reign; I forbid thee in the name of my King.'

V 13. *And do not present your limbs*, your bodies in the detail of their faculties, *as implements of unrighteousness, to sin*, to sin regarded as the holder and employer of the implements. *But present yourselves*, your whole being, centre and circle, *to God, as men living after death*, in his Son's risen life, *and your limbs*, hand, foot, and head, with all their faculties, *as implements of righteousness for God*.

The idea of self-surrender, sometimes cloudy, sometimes radiant, has been present in every age of history. The spiritual fact that the creature, as such, can never find its true centre in itself, but only in the Creator, has expressed itself in many ways. The gospel view of self-surrender is that it is done in the fullness of personal consciousness and choice. It is done with revealed reasons of infinite truth and beauty to guarantee its rightness. And it is a placing of the surrendered self into hands which will both foster its true development as only its Maker can, as he fills it with his presence, and will use it, in the bliss of an eternal usefulness, for his beloved will.

CHAPTER 15

*Justification and Holiness: Illustrations from Human Life
(6.14–7.6)*

At this point the apostle's thought pauses for a moment. He has
brought us to self-surrender. We have seen the sacred obligations
of our divine and wonderful freedom. We have had the miserable
question, 'Shall we cling to sin?' answered by an explanation of
the rightness and the bliss of giving over our accepted persons,
in the fullest freedom of will, to God, in Christ. Now he pauses,
to illustrate and enforce his argument with two examples from
human experience: slavery (which shows the absolute nature of
surrender) and marriage (which shows its results).

V 14. *For sin shall not have dominion over you;* sin shall not put in
its claim upon you, the claim which the Lord has met in your
justification; *for you are not brought under law, but under grace.* The
whole previous argument explains this sentence. He refers to our
acceptance. He goes back to the justification of the guilty by the
act of free grace; and briefly restates it, so that he may take up
once more the position that this glorious liberation means not
license but divine order. Sin shall be no more your tyrant-creditor,
holding up the broken law in evidence that it has the right to
lead you off to prison and death. Your dying Saviour has met
your creditor in full for you, and in him you have entire discharge
in that eternal court where the terrible plea once stood against
you. Your dealings as debtors are now not with the enemy who
cried for your death, but with the Friend who has bought you
out of his power.

V 15. *What then? are we to sin, because we are not brought under law,
but under grace?* Shall our life be a life of license, because we are
thus wonderfully free? The question clearly is one which, like
that of verse 1, and like those suggested in 3.8,31, had often been

asked of St Paul, by the bitter opponent or false follower. And again it illustrates and defines, by the direction of its error, the line of truth from which it strayed. It helps to do what we noted above (p. 109), to assure us that when St Paul taught 'justification by faith, without deeds of law,' he meant what he said, without reserve or compromise. He called the sinner, just as he was, to receive at once, and without fee, the acceptance of God for Another's blessed sake. It must have been a bitter experience to see, from the first, this holy freedom distorted into an unholy permission to sin. But Paul will not meet it by an impatient compromise, or untimely confusion. It shall be answered by a new argument; the liberty shall be seen in its relation to the Liberator; and behold, the perfect freedom is a perfect service, willing but absolute, a slavery joyfully accepted, with open eyes and open heart, and then lived out as the most real of obligations by a being who has entirely seen that he is not his own.

V 16. *Away with the thought. Do you not know that the party to whom you present*, surrender, *yourselves* bondservants, slaves, *so as to obey* him, – *bondservants you are*, not the less for the freewill of the surrender, *of the party whom you obey*; no longer merely contractors with him, who may bargain, or withdraw, but his bondservants through and through; *whether of sin, to death, or of obedience, to righteousness?* (As if their assent to Christ, their 'Amen' to his terms of peace, acceptance, and righteousness were personified; they were now the bondsmen of this their own act and deed, which had put them, as it were, into Christ's hands for all things.)

V 17. *Now thanks be to our God, that you were bondsmen of sin*, in legal claim, and under moral sway; yes, every one of you was this, whatever forms the bondage took upon its surface; *but you obeyed from the heart the mould of teaching to which you were handed over.* They had been sin's slaves. Verbally, not really, he 'thanks God' for that fact of the past. Really, not verbally, he 'thanks God' for the pastness of the fact, and for the bright contrast to it in the renewed present. They had now been 'handed over', by their Lord's transaction about them, to another ownership, and they had accepted the transfer, 'from the heart'. It was done by

Another for them, but they had said their humble, thankful 'yes'
as he did it. And what was this new ownership? We shall find
soon (v 22), as we might expect, that it is the mastery of God.
But the bold, vivid introductory imagery has already called it (v
16) the slavery of 'obedience'. Just below (vv 19, 20) it is the
slavery of 'righteousness', that is, if we read the word correctly
in context, of 'the righteousness of God', his acceptance of the
sinner as his own in Christ. And here, in a phrase most unlikely
of all, whose personification strikes life into the most abstract
aspects of the message of the grace of God, the believer is one
who has been transferred to the possession of 'a mould of teaching'. The apostolic doctrine, the mighty message, the living creed
of life, the teaching of the acceptance of the guilty for the sake
of him who was their sacrifice, and is now their peace and life –
this truth has, as it were, grasped them as its slaves, to form and
mould them, for its purposes. It holds them; a thought far different from what is too often meant when we say of a doctrine that
'we hold it'. Justification by their Lord's merit, union with their
Lord's life; this was a doctrine, reasoned, ordered, verified. But
it was a doctrine warm and full of the love of the Father and of
the Son. And it had laid hold of them with a mastery which
swayed thought, affection, and will; ruling their whole view of
self and of God.

V 18. *Now, liberated from your sin, you were enslaved to the righteousness
of God*. Here is the point of the argument. It is a point of steel,
for all is fact; but the steel is steeped in love, and carries life and
joy into the heart it penetrates. They are not for one moment
their own. Their acceptance has magnificently emancipated them
from their tyrant-enemy. But it has absolutely bound them to
their Friend and King. Their glad consent to be accepted has
carried with it a consent to belong. And if that consent was at
the moment rather implied than explicit or conscious, they have
now only to understand their blessed slavery better to give the
more joyful thanksgivings to him who has thus claimed them
altogether as his own.

The apostle's aim in this whole passage is to awaken them,
with the strong, tender touch of his holy reasoning, to clarify
their position to themselves. They have trusted Christ, and are

in him. Then, they have entrusted themselves altogether to him. Then, they have, in effect, surrendered. They have consented to be his property. They are the bondservants, they are the slaves, of his truth, that is, of him robed and revealed in his truth, and shining through it on them in the glory both of his grace and of his claim. Nothing less than such an obligation is the fact for them. Let them feel, let them weigh, and then let them embrace, the chain which after all will only prove their pledge of rest and freedom.

What St Paul did for our ancestors, let him do for us today.

Now he follows up the thought. Conscious of the superficial repulsiveness of the metaphor – quite as repulsive in itself to the Pharisee as to people today – he as it were apologizes for it; not least because so many of his first readers were actually slaves. He does not lightly go for his picture of our Master's hold of us to the market of Corinth, or of Rome, where men and women were bought and sold to belong absolutely to their buyers like cattle or furniture. Yet he does go there, to shake slow perceptions into consciousness, and bring the will face to face with the claim of God.

V 19. So he proceeds: *I speak humanly*, I use the terms of this utterly undivine bond of man to man, to illustrate man's glorious bond to God, *because of the weakness of your flesh*, because your still imperfect state enfeebles your spiritual perception, and demands a harsh paradox to direct and fix it. *For* – here is what he means by 'humanly' – *just as you surrendered your limbs*, your functions and faculties in human life, *slaves to your impurity and to your lawlessness, unto that lawlessness*, so that the bad principle came out in bad practice, *so now*, with as little reserve of liberty, *surrender your limbs slaves to righteousness*, to God's righteousness, to your justifying God, unto *sanctification* – so that the surrender shall come out in your Master's sovereign separation of his purchased property from sin.

Paul has appealed to the moral reason of the renewed soul. Now he speaks straight to the will. You are, with infinite rightfulness, the bondmen of your God. You see your deed of purchase; it is the other side of your warrant of emancipation. Take it, and write your own unworthy names with joy upon it, consenting and assenting to your Owner's perfect rights. And then live out your life, keeping the signature of your own surrender before your eyes. Live, suffer, conquer, labour, serve, as men who have themselves walked to their Master's door, and presented the ear to the awl which pins it to the doorway, each in his turn saying, 'I will not go out free' (see Ex. 21. 5, 6; Dt. 15. 16, 17).

To such an act of the soul the apostle calls these saints, whether they had done something similar before or not. They were to sum up the perpetual fact, then and there, into a definite act of thankful will. And he calls us to do the same today. By the grace of God, it shall be done. With eyes open, and fixed upon the face of the Master who claims us and with hands placed helpless and willing within his hands, we will, and do, present ourselves bondservants to him; for discipline, for service, for all his will.

V 20. *For when you were slaves of your sin, you were freemen as to righteousness*, God's righteousness. It had nothing to do with you, whether to give you peace or to receive your tribute of love and loyalty in return. In practice, Christ was not your atonement, and so not your Master; you stood, in a dismal independence, outside his claims. To you, your lips were your own; your time was your own; your will was your own. You belonged to self; that is to say, you were the slaves of your sin. Will you go back? Will the word 'freedom' (he plays with it, as it were, to prove them) make you wish yourselves back where you were before you had endorsed by faith your purchase by the blood of Christ? No, for what was that 'freedom', seen in its results on yourselves?

Vv 21–23. *What fruit*, therefore (the 'therefore' of the logic of facts), *used you to have then*, in those old days, *from things over which you are ashamed now?* Ashamed indeed; *for the end*, the result, as the fruit is the tree's 'end', *the end of those things is – death;* loss of all true life, here and hereafter too. *But now*, in the blessed actual state of your case, as by faith you have entered into Christ, into his work and into his life, *now liberated from sin and enslaved to God, you have your fruit*, you possess indeed, at last, the true results of being for which you were made, all contributing *to sanctification*, to that separation to God's will in practice which is the development of your separation to that will in fact, when you met your Redeemer in self-renouncing faith. Yes, this fruit you have indeed; *and as its end*, the purpose for which it is produced, to which it always and for ever tends, you have *life eternal. For the pay of sin*, sin's military stipend punctually given to the being which has joined its war against the will of God, *is death; but the free gift of God is life eternal, in Jesus Christ our Lord.*

Is life worth living? Yes, infinitely well worth, for the living man who has surrendered to the Lord that bought him. Outside that ennobling captivity, that invigorating while most genuine bondservice, the life of man is at best complicated and tired with a bewildered quest, and gives results at best abortive, matched with the ideal purposes of such a being. We present ourselves to God, for his ends, as instruments, slaves, willing bondmen; and lo, our own end is attained. Our life has settled, after its long friction, into gear. The heart, once dissipated between itself and the world, is now united to the will and love of God; and understands itself, and the world, as never before; and is able to deny self and to serve others in a new and surprising freedom. The man, made willing to be nothing but the tool and bondman of God, 'has his fruit' at last; bears the true product of his now re-created being, pleasant to the Master's eye, and fostered by his air and sun. And this fruit issues, as acts produce habits, in the glad experience of a life that is really sanctified, really separated in ever deeper inward reality, to a holy will. And the end or purpose of the whole glad possession, is eternal life.

These words point, surely, to the blessings of heaven, about which Paul will say more in Romans 8. Here he takes the Lord's slave by the hand, amidst his present tasks and burdens, and he points upward – not to a coming setting free in glory; the man would be dismayed to foresee that; he wants to serve for ever – but to a scene of service in which the last remainders of hindrance to its action will be gone, and a perfected being will for ever, perfectly, be not its own, and so will perfectly live in God. And this, so he says to his fellow-servant, to you and to me, is the free and generous 'gift of God'. And it is to be enjoyed as such, by a being which, living wholly for him, will freely and purely exult to live wholly on him, in heaven.

Yet surely the bearing of the sentences is not wholly upon

heaven. Eternal life, to be developed hereafter to such a degree that Scripture speaks of it often as if it began hereafter, really begins here, and develops here, and is already 'more abundant' (Jn. 10. 10) here. It is, as to its secret and also its experience, to know and to enjoy God, to be possessed by him, and used for all his will. In this respect it is 'the end', the result and the goal, now and perpetually, of the surrender of the soul. The Master meets that attitude with more and yet more of himself, known, enjoyed, possessed, possessing. And so he gives, evermore gives, out of his sovereign bounty, eternal life to the bondservant who has embraced the fact that he is nothing, and has nothing, outside his Master. Eternal life is still the free gift of God, not just at the outset of the renewed life, nor only in heaven, but all along the way. Let us now, today, tomorrow, and always, open the lips of surrendering and obedient faith, and drink it in, abundantly, and yet more abundantly. And let us use it for the Giver.

We are already, here on earth, at its very springs; so the apostle reminds us. For it is 'in Jesus Christ our Lord'; and we, believing, are in him, 'saved in his life'. It is in him; no, it is he. 'I am the Life'; 'He that hath the Son, hath the life'. Abiding in Christ, we live because he lives. It is not to be attained; it is given, it is our own. In Christ, it is given, in its divine fullness, as to covenant provision, here, now, from the first, to every Christian. In Christ, it is supplied, as to its fullness and fitness for each arising need, as the Christian asks, receives, and uses for his Lord.

So from, or rather in, our holy bondservice the apostle has brought us to our inexhaustible life, and its resources for willing holiness. But he has more to say in explaining the theme. He turns from slave to wife, from surrender to marriage, from the purchase to the vow, from the results of a holy bondage to the offspring of a heavenly union.

7. 1–4. *Or do you not know, brethren (for I am talking to those acquainted with law*, whether Mosaic or Gentile), *that the law has claim on the man*, the party in any given case, *for his whole lifetime? For the woman with a husband is to her living husband bound by law*, stands all along bound to him. His life, under normal conditions, is his adequate claim. Prove him living, and you prove her his. *But if*

the husband should have died, she stands ipso facto cancelled from the husband's law, the marriage law as he could bring it to bear against her. *So, therefore, while the husband lives, she will earn adulteress for her name, if she weds another* (a second) *husband. But if the husband should have died, she is free from the law* in question, *so as to be no adulteress, if wedded to another,* a second, *husband. Accordingly, my brethren, you too,* as a mystic bride, collectively and individually (see 1 Cor. 6.17) *were done to death as to the law,* so slain that its capital claim upon you is met and done, *by means of the body of the Christ* by 'the doing to death' of his sacred body for you, on his atoning cross, to satisfy for you the aggrieved law; *in order to your wedding Another,* a second party, *him who rose from the dead; that we might bear fruit for God;* 'we', Paul and his converts, in one happy fellowship, which he delights thus to remember and indicate in passing.

The parable is stated and explained with a clearness which leaves us at first more surprised that in the application the illustration is reversed. In the illustration, the husband dies, the woman lives, and marries again. In the application, the law does not die, but we, its unfaithful bride, are 'done to death to it', and then, strange sequel, are wedded to the risen Christ. We are taken by him to be 'one spirit' with him (1 Cor. 6. 17). We are made one in all his interests and wealth, and fruitful with holy deeds. Shall we call all this a confused simile? Not if we recognize the deliberate and explicit carefulness of the whole passage. St Paul, we may be sure, was quite as quick as we are to see the inverted imagery. But he is dealing with a subject which would be distorted by a mechanical correspondence in the treatment. The law cannot die, for it is the declared will of God. Its claim is, like that of the injured Roman husband, to sentence its own unfaithful wife to death. And so it does; so it has done. But behold, its Maker and Master steps upon the scene. He surrounds the guilty one with himself, takes her whole burden on himself, and meets and exhausts her doom. He dies. He lives again, after death, because of death; and the law acclaims his resurrection as infinitely just. He rises, clasping in his arms her for whom he died, and who thus died in him, and now rises in him. Out of his sovereign love, while the law witnesses to the sure contract, and rejoices as 'the Bridegroom's Friend', he claims her – herself, yet in him another – for his blessed bride. All is love, and all is law. The Church, the soul, is married to her Lord, who has died for her, and in whom now she lives. The transaction is infinitely happy. And it is absolutely right. All the old terrifying claims are met fully and for ever. And now the mighty, tender claims which take their place instantly, and of course, begin to bind the bride. The law has 'given her away' – not to herself, but to the risen Lord.

For this, let us remember, is the point and bearing of the passage. It puts before us, not only the mystic marriage, but its relation to holiness. The apostle's object is this. From various angles he reminds us that we belong. He has shown us our redeemed selves in their blessed bondservice; 'free from sin, enslaved to God'. He now shows us to ourselves in our divine wedlock; 'married to Another', 'bound to the law of' the heavenly Husband; clasped to his heart, but also to his rights, without which the very joy of marriage would be only sin. From either parable the inference is direct, powerful, and compelling. You are set free, into a liberty as supreme and as happy as possible. You are appropriated, into a possession, and into a union, more close and absolute than language can show. You are wedded to One who 'has and holds from this time forward'. And the sacred bond is to produce many results. A life of willing and loving obedience, in the power of the risen Bridegroom's life, is to have as it were for its offspring the graces of love, joy, peace, longsuffering, gentleness, goodness, fidelity, meekness, and self-control.

Vv 5–6. Alas, in the time of the first marriage there was offspring. But that was the fruit not of the union but of its violation. *For when we were in the flesh*, in our unrenewed days, when our rebel self (the best word for 'flesh' in this context), the antithesis of 'the Spirit', ruled and denoted us (a state, he implies, in which we all were once, whatever our outward differences were), *the passions*, the strong but reasonless impulses, *of our sins, which* passions *were by means of the law*, occasioned by the fact of its just but unloved claim, fretting the self-life into action, *worked actively in our limbs*, in our bodily life in its varied faculties and senses, *so as to bear fruit for death.* We wandered, restive, from our bride-groom, the law, to sin, our lover. And behold, the result was numerous evil deeds and habits, born as it were into bondage in the house of death. *But now*, now as the wonderful case stands in the grace of God, *we are abrogated from the law*, divorced from our first injured partner, no, slain (in our crucified Head) in satisfaction of its righteous claim, *as having died with regard to that in which we were held captive*, even the law and its violated bond, *so that we do bondservice in* the *Spirit's newness, and not in* the *letter's oldness.*

Thus he comes back, through the imagery of wedlock, to that other parable of slavery which has become so precious to his heart. 'So that we do bondservice', 'so that we live a slave-life'. It is as if he must break in on the heavenly marriage itself, not to disturb the joy of the Bridegroom and the bride, but to engrave on the bride's heart the vital fact that she is not her own; that fact so blissful, but so powerful also and so practical that it is worth anything to bring it home.

It is to be no dragging and dishonouring bondage, in which the poor worker can't wait for evening. It is to be 'not in the letter's oldness'; no longer on the old principle of the dread and unrelieved 'Thou shalt', cut with a pen of legal iron upon the stones of Sinai; bearing no provision of enabling power, but all possible provision of doom for the disloyal. It is to be 'in the Spirit's newness'; on the new, wonderful principle, new in its full manifestation and application in Christ, of the Holy Spirit's empowering presence. In that light and strength the new relations are discovered, accepted, and fulfilled. Joined by the Spirit to the Lord Christ, so as to have full benefit of his justifying merit; filled by the Spirit with the Lord Christ, so as to derive freely and always the blessed virtues of his life; the willing bond-servant finds in his absolute obligations an ever-new inward liberty. And the worshipping bride finds in the holy call to 'keep her only unto him' who has died for her life, nothing but a perpetual surprise of love and gladness, 'new every morning,' as the Spirit shows her the heart and the riches of her Lord.

Thus closes, in effect, the apostle's exposition of the self-surrender of the justified. Happy the person who can respond to it all with the 'Amen' of a life which, resting on the righteousness of God, always answers to his will with the loyal gladness found in the newness of the Spirit. It is 'perfect freedom' to understand, in experience, the bondage and marriage of the saints.

CHAPTER 16

The Function of the Law in the Spiritual Life (7. 7–25)

The apostle has led us a long way in his great argument; through sin, propitiation, faith, union, surrender, to the wonderful and excellent mystery, the bridal oneness of Christ and the Church, of Christ and the believer. He has yet to unfold the secrets and glories of the experience of a life lived in the power of the Spirit of whose newness he has just spoken. But his last parable has brought him straight to a question which has repeatedly been indicated and deferred. He has told us that the law of God was at first, ideally, our mystic husband, and that we were unfaithful in our wedded life, and that the injured lord sentenced to death his guilty spouse, and that the sentence was carried out – but carried out in Christ. Thus a death-divorce took place between us, the justified, and the law, regarded as the violated party in the covenant.

Is this former husband then a party whom we are now to suspect, and to defy? Our wedlock with him brought us little joy. Alas, its main experience was that we sinned. At best, if we did right (in any deep sense of right), we did it against the grain; while we did wrong (in the deep sense of wrong, difference from the will of God) naturally. Was not our old lord to blame? Was there not something wrong about the law? Did not the law misrepresent God's will? Was it not, after all, sin itself in disguise, though it charged us with adultery with sin?

We cannot doubt that the statement and the treatment of this question here are in effect a record of personal experience, as we can see by the use of 'I', 'me' and 'mine'. We overhear the discussions and arguments of will with conscience, of will with will, almost of self with self, carried on in a region which only self-consciousness can penetrate, and which only the subject of it all can thus describe. Yes, the person Paul is here, analysing and reporting upon himself; drawing the veil from his own inmost life, according to the will of God, who bids him, for the Church's sake, expose himself to view. Nothing in literature, no *Confessions* of an Augustine, no *Grace Abounding* of a Bunyan, is more intensely individual. Yet on the other hand nothing is more universal in its searching application.

This profound paragraph has been interpreted in various ways. Firstly, it has been held by some to be only St Paul's intense way of presenting the great phenomenon, wide as fallen humanity of human will colliding with human conscience. But this is an extremely inadequate explanation on two counts. On the one hand the long groaning confession is no artificial embodiment of a universal fact; it is the cry of a human soul, if ever there was a personal cry. On the other hand the passage betrays a kind of conflict far deeper and more mysterious than merely that of 'I ought' with 'I will not'. It is a conflict of 'I will' with 'I will not', of 'I hate' with 'I do'. And in the later stages of the confession we find the subject of the conflict claiming a wonderful sympathy with the law of God; recording not merely a claim that right is right, but a consciousness that God's command is a delight.

Secondly, it has been held that the passage records the experiences of a half-renewed soul; struggling on its way from darkness to light, stumbling across a border-zone between the power of Satan and the kingdom of God; deeply convinced of sin, but battling with it in the old impossible way after all. But this explanation does not fit the passage as a whole. It is no experience of a half-renewed life to 'take delight with the law of God after the inner man'. A half-renewed soul cannot describe itself as so beset by sin that 'it is not I, but sin that dwelleth in me'. No more dangerous form of thought about itself could be adopted by a soul not fully acquainted with God.

Thirdly, it has been held that our passage lays it down that a stern but on the whole disappointing conflict with internal evil is the permanent lot of the true Christian, that the renewed and believing man is, if indeed awake to spiritual realities, to feel at every step, 'O wretched man that I am'; 'What I hate, that I do'; and to expect deliverance from such a consciousness only when he attains his final heavenly rest with Christ. Here the difficulty is with the context of surrounding passages about freedom, power, joy, and life in the Holy Spirit.

What is the right interpretation? Is there yet another line of exegesis which will better satisfy the facts of both the passage and its context? We think there is one, which is both distinctive in itself, and combines elements of truth indicated by the others. For the passage does have a reference to the universal conflict of conscience and will; it does say some things quite appropriate to the man who is awake to his bondage but has not yet found his Redeemer; and there is, we dare to say, a sense in which it may be held that the picture is true for the whole course of Christian life here on earth. For there is never an hour of that life when the person who 'says he has no sin' does not 'deceive himself' (1 Jn. 1. 8). And if that sin be just a simple defect, a falling short of the glory of God; if it be only that mysterious tendency which, felt or not, hourly needs a divine counteraction; still, the individual 'has sin', and must long for a final emancipation, with a longing which carries in it at least a latent 'groan'.

So we begin by recognizing that Paul takes us first to his earliest deep convictions of right and wrong, when, apparently after a previous complacency with himself, he woke to see – but not to welcome – the absoluteness of God's will. He glided along a smooth stream of moral and mental culture and reputation till he struck the rock of 'Thou shalt not covet', 'Thou shalt not desire', 'Thou must not have self-will'. Then, as from a grave, which was however only an ambush, 'sin' sprang up; a conscious force of opposition to the claim of God's will as against the will of Paul; and his dream of religious satisfaction died. We are certainly in the unrenewed state until the end of verse 11. The tenses are past; the narrative is explicit. He made a discovery of law which was like death after life to his then religious experience. He has nothing to say of counter-facts in his soul. It was conviction of sin, with rebellion as its only result.

Then we find ourselves in a range of confessions of a different order. There is a continuity. The law is there, and sin is there, and a profound moral conflict. But there are now counter-facts. The man, the ego, now 'wills not', indeed, 'hates', what he practises. He wills what God commands, though he does it not. His sinful deeds are, in a certain sense, in this respect, not his own. He actually 'delights, rejoices, with the law of God'. Yet there is a sense in which he is 'sold', 'enslaved', 'captured', in the wrong direction.

Here, as we have admitted, there is much which is appropriate to the not yet renewed state, where however the man is awakening morally, to good purpose, under the hand of God. But the passage as a whole refuses to be satisfied thus, as we have seen. He who can truly speak in this way of an inmost sympathy with the most holy law of God, is no half-Christian; certainly not in St Paul's view of things.

But now note one great negative phenomenon of the passage. We read words about this renewed sinner's moral being and faculties; about his 'inner man', his 'mind', 'the law of his mind'; about 'himself', as distinguished from the 'sin' which haunts him. But we read not one clear word about the eternal Spirit, whose glorious presence we have seen (7. 6) characterizing the gospel, and of whom we are soon to hear so much. Once only is he even distantly indicated; 'the law is spiritual' (7. 14). But that is no comfort, no deliverance. The Spirit is indeed in the law; but he must be also in the individual, if there is to be effectual response, and harmony, and joy.

But he was renewed, you say. And if so, he was an instance of the Spirit's work, a receiver of the Spirit's presence. True. He could not 'delight in the law of God', and 'with his true self serve the law of God' without the Spirit working in him. But does this necessarily mean that he, as a conscious agent, was fully using his eternal Guest as his power and victory?

We are not merely discussing a literary passage. We are pondering an oracle of God about man. So we ask the reader, and ourselves, whether our heart can help explain this difficult paragraph. Christian man, by grace – that is to say, by the Holy Spirit of God – you have believed, and live. You are a limb of Christ, who is your life. But you are a sinner still; always, actually and potentially. For whatever the presence of the Spirit in you has done, it has not so altered you that, if he should go, you would not instantly revert to unholiness. Do you, if I may put it so, use your renewed self in an unrenewed way, meeting temptation and the tendency to sin by yourself alone, with only high resolves, moral scorn of wrong, and discipline on body or mind? God forbid we should call these things evil. They are good. But they are aspects, not the essence, of the secret. It is the Lord himself dwelling in you who is your victory; and that victory is to be realized by a conscious and decisive appeal to him. And is this not proved true in your experience? When, in your renewed state, you use the true renewed way, is there not a better record to be given? When, realizing that the true principle is indeed a Person, you resolve and struggle less, and appeal and confide more – is not sin's reign broken?

We are aware of the objection that the indwelling Spirit works always through the being in whom he dwells; so we are not to think of him as a separable ally, but just to act ourselves, leaving it to him to act through us. Well, we are willing to state the matter almost exactly in those last words, as a theory. But the subject is too deep – and too practical – for neat logical consistency. He does indeed work in us, and through us. But then – it is he. And to the hard pressed soul there is an indescribable reality and power in thinking of him as a separable, let us say simply a personal ally, who is also Commander, Lord, Life-Giver; and in calling him definitely in.

So we read this passage again, and note this absolute and eloquent silence in it about the Holy Spirit. And we dare, in that view, to interpret it as St Paul's confession, not of a long past experience, not of an imagined experience, but of his own normal experience always – when he acts out of character as a renewed man. He fails, or reverts, when, still being a sinner by nature and still in the body, he meets the law, and meets temptation, in any strength short of the definitely sought power of the Holy Spirit, making Christ all to him for peace and victory. And he implies, surely, that this failure is not a bare hypothesis, but that he knows what it is. It is not that God is not sufficient. He is so, always, now, for ever. But the man does not always adequately use God. And when he does not, the resultant failure, however slight, is a sorrow, burden and shame. It tells him that the 'flesh' is still present, present at least in its elements, though God can keep them out of combination. It tells him that, though immensely blessed, and knowing now exactly where to seek, and to find, a constant practical deliverance, he is still 'in the body', and that its conditions are still of 'death'. And so he looks with great desire for its redemption. The present of grace is good, beyond all his previous hopes. But the future of glory is far better.

Thus the man both serves the law of God, as its willing bondman (7.25), in the life of grace, and submits himself, with reverence and shame, to its convictions, when, if just for an hour or a moment, he reverts to the life of the flesh.

Let us take the passage up now for a nearly continuous translation.

Vv 7–13. *What shall we say then*, in face of the thought of our death-divorce, in Christ, from the law's condemning power. *Is the law sin?* Are they only two phases of one evil? *Away with the thought! But* – here is the connection of the two – *I should not have known*, recognized, understood, *sin but by means of law.* For coveting, for example, *I should not have known*, should not have recognized as sin, *if the law had not been saying, 'Thou shalt not covet'. But sin, making a fulcrum of the commandment, produced*, effected, *in me all coveting*, every variety of application of the principle. *For, law apart, sin is dead* – in the sense of lack of conscious action. It needs a holy will, more or less revealed, to occasion its collision. Given no holy will, known or surmised, and it is 'dead' as rebellion, though not as pollution. *But I*, the person in whom it lay buried, *was all alive* conscious and content, *law apart, once on a time. But when the commandment came* to my conscience and my will, *sin rose to life again* ('again' so it was no new creation after all), *and I – died*; I found myself legally doomed to death, morally without life-power, and without the self-satisfaction that seemed my vital breath. *And the commandment that was life-wards*, prescribing nothing but perfect right, the straight line to life eternal, *proved for me deathwards. For sin, making a fulcrum of the commandment, deceived me*, into thinking fatally wrong of God and of myself, *and through it killed me*, revealed me to myself as legally and morally a dead man. *So that the law, indeed, is holy, and the commandment*, the special instruction which was my actual death-blow, *holy, and just, and good*. (He says, 'the law, indeed', with the implied antithesis that 'sin, on the other hand', is the opposite; the whole fault of his misery beneath the law lies with sin.) *The good thing then*, this good law, *has it to me become death? Away with the thought! No, but sin did so become that it might come out* as *sin, working out death for me by means of the good law – that sin might prove overwhelmingly sinful, through the commandment*, which at once called it up, and, by awful contrast, exposed its nature. Note, he does not say merely that sin 'appeared' unutterably evil. More boldly, in this sentence of mighty paradoxes, he says that it 'became' such. As it were, it developed its character into its fullest action, when it thus used the eternal Will to set creature against Creator. Yet even this was overruled; all happened in this way so that the very virulence of the plague might effectually demand the glorious Remedy.

Vv 14–17. *For we know*, we men with our conscience, we Christians with our Lord's light, *that the law*, this law which sin so foully abused, *is spiritual*, the expression of the eternal Holiness, framed by the sure guidance of the Holy Spirit; *but then I*, I Paul, taken as a sinner, viewed apart from Christ, *am fleshly*, a child of self, *sold to be under sin*; yes, not only when, in Adam, my nature sold itself at first, but still and always, just so far as I am considered apart from Christ, and just so far as, in practice, I live apart from Christ, reverting, if only for a minute, to my self-life. *For the work I work out, I do not know*, I do not recognize; I am lost amidst its distorted conditions; *for* it is *not what I will that I practise, but* it is *what I hate that I do. But if what I do is what I do not will, I assent to the law that it*, the law, *is good*; I show my moral sympathy with the commandment by the endorsement given it by my will, in the sense of my earnest moral preference. *But now*, in this situation, *it is no longer I who work out the work, but the indweller in me – sin.*

He implies by 'no longer' that once it was different; once the central choice was for self, now, in the renewed life, even in its conflicts and failures, it is for God. A mysterious 'other self' is still hidden, and asserts itself in awful reality when the true man, the renewed man, ceases to watch and to pray. And in this sense he dares to say 'it is no more I'. It is a sense the very opposite to the dream of self-excuse; for though the renewed ego does not do the deed, it has, by its sleep, or by its confidence, betrayed the soul to the true doer. And thus he passes naturally into the following confessions, in which we read at once the consciousness of a state which ought not to be, though it is, and also the conviction that it is a state out of character with himself, with his redeemed and re-created personality. There is no false thought in this confession that he cannot help doing evil, or that evil is only an aspect of good. It is a groan of shame and pain, from a man who could not be tortured in this way if he were not born again. Yet it is also a claim – as if to assure himself that deliverance is intended, and is at hand – that the treacherous tyrant he has let into the place of power is an alien to him as he is a renewed man. He says this to himself, and to us, not to make an excuse, but to clear his thought, and direct his hope.

Vv 18–20. *For I know that there dwells not in me, that is, in my flesh, good*; in my personal life, so long, and so far, as it reverts to self as its working centre, all is evil, for nothing is as God would have it be. And that flesh or self-life, is ever there, hidden if not obvious; present in that it is ready for instant reappearance, from within, if any moral power less than that of the Lord himself is in command. *For the willing lies at my hand; but the working out what is right, does not.* 'The willing', as throughout this passage, means not the ultimate will of the man's soul, deciding his action, but his earnest moral approval or sympathy, the convictions of the enlightened being. *For not what I will, even good, do I; but what I do not will, even evil, that I practise. Now if what I do is what I do not will, no longer*, as once, *do I work it out, but the indweller in me, sin.* Again his purpose is not excuse, but deliverance. There is no deadly antinomianism here, of the kind that has withered count-less lives, where the thought has been admitted that sin may be in the man, and yet the man may not sin. Paul's thought is, as all along, that it is his own shame that this is the situation; yet that the evil is, ultimately, a thing alien to his true character, and that therefore he is right to call the lawful King and Victor in upon it.

And now comes up again the solemn problem of the law. The man hears its voice, and in his newly-created character he loves it. But he has reverted, ever so little, to his old attitude, to the self-life, and so there is also rebellion in him when that voice says 'Thou shalt'.

Vv 21–25. *So I find the law* – he would have said, 'I find it my monitor, honoured and loved, but not my helper'; but he breaks the sentence up in the stress of this intense confession; *so I find the law – for me*, me *with a will to do the right – that for me the evil lies at hand. For I have glad sympathy with the law of God*; what he commands I endorse with delight as good, *as regards the inner man*, that is, my world of conscious insight and affection in the new life; *but I see* (as if I were a watcher from outside) *a rival law*, another and contradictory command, 'serve thyself', *in my limbs*, in the world of my senses and faculties, *at war with the law of my mind*, the law of God, adopted by my now enlightened thinking-power as its sacred code, *and seeking to make me captive in that war to the law of sin*, the law *which is in my limbs. Unhappy man am I. Who will rescue me out of the body of this death*, out of a life conditioned by this mortal body, which in the fall became sin's special vehicle, directly or indirectly, and which is not yet (7. 23) actually redeemed? *Thanks be to God*, who gives that deliverance, in promise and in part now, fully and in eternal reality hereafter, *through Jesus Christ our Lord*.

So then, to sum up the whole phenomenon of the conflict, leaving aside for the moment this glorious hope of the result, *I, myself, with the mind indeed do bondservice to the law of God, but with the flesh*, with the life of self, wherever and whenever I revert that way, I do bondservice *to the law of sin*.

Do we leave the passage with a sigh, and almost with a groan? Do we sigh over the difficulty and complexity of the thought, or groan over the consciousness that no analysis of our spiritual failures can console us for the fact of them, and that the apostle seems in his last sentences to relegate our consolations to the future, while it is in the present that we fail, and in the present that we long with all our souls to do, as well as to approve, the will of God?

Let us be patient, and also let us think again. Let us find a solemn and sanctifying peace in the patience which meekly accepts the mystery that we must still wait for the redemption of our body; that the conditions of this present existence must still for a while give ambushes and advantages to temptation, which will be all annihilated hereafter. But let us also think again. If we were correct in our remarks previous to this passage, there are glorious possibilities for the present readable between the lines of St Paul's confession. We have seen in conflict the Christian man, renewed, yet taken, in a practical sense, apart from his renewer. We have seen him really fight, though he really fails. We have seen him unwittingly, but guiltily, betray his position to the foe, by occupying it as it were alone. We have seen also, nevertheless, that he is not his foe's ally but his antagonist. Listen; he is calling for his King.

That cry will not be in vain. The King will take a double line of action in response. While his soldier-bondservant is still in the body, Christ will transfigure it, into the counterpart – even as it were into the part – of his own body of glory; and the man shall rest, and serve, and reign for ever, with a being completely like the Lord.

CHAPTER 17

The Justified: Their Life by
The Holy Spirit (8.1–11)

To study the way Romans 8 follows Romans 7 is both interesting and fruitful. No-one can read the two chapters without feeling the contrasting and complementary connection between them. The stern analysis of the one, unrelieved except by the fragment of thanksgiving at its close, is to the revelations and triumphs of the other like an almost starless night compared with the splendour of a midsummer morning. The day is related to the night, which has prepared us for it, as hunger prepares for food. Precisely what was absent from the former passage is supplied richly in the latter. There the name of the Holy Spirit, 'the Lord, the Life-Giver', was unheard. Here the fact and power of the Holy Spirit are present everywhere, so present that there is no other part of the whole of Scripture (except Jesus' words in John 14–17) which presents us with so much revelation on this precious theme. And here we find the secret that is to still the strife which we have just witnessed, and which in our own souls we know so well. Here is the way 'how to walk and to please God' (I Thess. 4.1) in our justified life. Here is the way how, not to be victims of the 'body', and slaves of the 'flesh', but to 'do to death the body's practices' in a continuous exercise of inward power, and to 'walk after the Spirit'. Here is the resource on which we may be for ever joyfully paying 'the debt' of such a walk; giving our redeeming Lord his due, the value of his purchase, even our willing, loving surrender, in the all-sufficient strength of the Holy Spirit 'given unto us'.

The way this glorious truth is introduced is worth noting. It does not appear without preparation and intimation; we have heard already of the Holy Spirit in the Christian's life (5.5, 7.6.).

The heavenly water has been seen and heard in its flow; as in limestone country the traveller may see and hear, through cracks in the fields, the buried but living floods. But here the truth of the Spirit, like those floods, finding at last their exit at the base of a cliff, pours itself into the light, and animates all the scene. There is both a spiritual and practical lesson, in this way of treating the matter. We are surely reminded, as to the experiences of the Christian life, that in a certain sense we possess the Holy Spirit, yes, in his fullness, from the first hour of our possession of Christ. We are reminded also that it is at least possible on the other hand that we may need so to realize and to use our covenant possession, after sad experiments in other directions, so that life shall be from then onwards a new experience of liberty and holy joy. We are reminded meanwhile that such a new departure, when it occurs, is new rather from our side than from the Lord's. The water was running all the while beneath the rocks. Insight and faith, given by his grace, have not called it from above, but as it were from within, liberating what was there.

The practical lesson of this is important for the Christian teacher and pastor. On the one hand, let him make very much in his public and private teaching of the revelation of the Spirit. Let him leave no room, so far as he can do it, for doubt or forgetfulness in his friends' minds about the absolute necessity of the fullness of the presence and power of the Holy One, if life is to be truly Christian. Let him describe as boldly and fully as the Word describes it what life may and must be where that sacred fullness dwells; how assured, how happy, how ready for service, how pure, free, strong, heavenly, practical and humble. Let him urge any who have yet to learn it to learn all this in their own experience, claiming on their knees the mighty gift of God. On the other hand, let him be careful not to over-elaborate his theory, and to prescribe too rigidly the methods of experience. Not all believers fail in the first hours of their faith to realize, and to use, the fullness of what the covenant gives them. And where that realization comes later than our first sight of Christ, as with so many of us it does come, the experience and action are not always the same. To one it is a crisis of memorable consciousness, a private Pentecost. Another wakes up as from sleep to find the unsuspected treasure at hand—hid from him till then by nothing thicker than shadows. And another is aware that somehow, he knows not how, he has come to use the Presence and Power as a while ago he did not; he has passed a frontier—but he knows not when.

In all these cases, meanwhile, the believer had, in one great respect, possessed the great gift all along. In covenant, in Christ, it was his. As he stepped by penitent faith into the Lord, he trod on ground which, wonderful to say, was all his own. And beneath it ran, that moment, the river of the water of life, but he had to discover it, to draw from it, and to apply it.

Again the relation we have just indicated between our possession of Christ and our possession of the Holy Spirit is a matter of the utmost spiritual and practical importance, presented prominently in this passage. All along, as we read the passage, we find linked inextricably together the truths of the Spirit and of the Son. 'The law of the Spirit of life' is bound up with 'Christ Jesus'. The Son of God was sent, to take our flesh, to die as our sin-offering, that we might 'walk according to the Spirit'. 'The Spirit of God' is 'the Spirit of Christ'. The presence of the Spirit of Christ is such that, where he dwells, 'Christ is in you'. Here we read both a caution, and a truth of the richest positive blessing. We are warned to remember that there is no separable 'Gospel of the Spirit'. Not for a moment are we to advance, as it were, from the Lord Jesus Christ to a higher or deeper region, ruled by the Holy Spirit. All the reasons, methods, and results of the work of the Holy Spirit are eternally and organically connected with the Son of God. We have him at all because Christ died. We have life because he has joined us to the living Christ. Our experimental proof of his fullness is that Christ to us is all. And we are to be on the guard against any exposition of his work and glory which shall for one moment leave out those facts. But not only are we to be on our guard; we are to rejoice in the thought that the mighty and endless work of the Spirit is all done always in Christ Jesus. And we are to draw every day on the indwelling Giver of Life to do for us his own, his characteristic, work; to show us 'our King in his beauty', and to 'fill our springs of thought and will with him'.

To return to the connection of the two great chapters. We have seen how close are the contrast and the complement. But it is also true, surely, that the eighth chapter is not just the counterpart to the seventh. Rather the eighth, though the seventh applies to it a special motive, is also a review of the whole previous argument of the epistle, or rather the crown on the whole previous structure. It begins with a deep re-assertion of our justification; a point not mentioned in 7.7–25. It does this using the word 'therefore', to which, surely, nothing in the immediately preceding verses is related. And then it unfolds not only the present acceptance and present freedom of the saints, but also their amazing future of glory, already indicated, especially in 5.2. And its closing strains are full of the great first wonder, our Acceptance: 'Them he justified'; 'It is God that justifieth'. So we avoid taking chapter eight as simply the successor and counterpart of chapter seven. It is this, in some great respects. But it is more; it is the meeting point of all the great truths of grace which we have studied.

As we approach the first paragraph of the chapter, we ask ourselves what is its message. It is our possession of the Holy Spirit of God, for purposes of holy loyalty and holy liberty. The foundation of that fact is indicated once more, in the brief assertion of our full justification in Christ, and of his propriatory sacrifice (v. 3). Then from those words 'in Christ', he opens this ample revelation of our possession, in our union with Christ, of the Spirit who, having joined us to him, now liberates us in him, not just from condemnation but from sin's dominion. If we are indeed in Christ, the Spirit is in us, dwelling in us, and we are in the Spirit. And so, possessed and filled by the blessed Power, we indeed have power to walk and to obey. Nothing is mechanical or automatic; we are still fully persons; he who annexes and possesses our personality does not for a moment violate it. But he does possess it; and the Christian, so possessing and so possessed, is not only bound but enabled, in humble but practical reality, in an otherwise unknown freedom, to 'fulfil the just demand of the law', 'to please God', in a life lived not to self but to Christ.

Thus, as we shall see in detail as we proceed, the apostle, while he still firmly keeps his hand, so to speak, on justification, is occupied fully now with its result, holiness. And this he explains as not merely a matter of grateful feeling, the outcome of the loyalty supposed to be natural to the pardoned, but as a matter of divine power.

If we approach these words, remembering that they are written for us, as well as for the original readers, we shall be humbled as well as gladdened; and so our gladness will be sounder. We shall find that whatever be our 'walk according to the Spirit', and our dominion over sin, we shall still have 'the practices of the body' with which to deal — of the body which still is 'dead because of sin', 'mortal', not yet 'redeemed'. We shall be practically reminded, even by the most joyful exhortations, that possession and personal condition are one thing in covenant, and another in realization; that we must watch, pray, examine self, and deny it, if we would 'be' what we 'are'. Yet all this is only the salutary addition to the main thrust of every line. We are accepted in the Lord. In the Lord we have the Eternal Spirit for our inward Possessor. Let us arise, and walk humbly, but also in gladness, with our God.

St Paul speaks again, perhaps after a silence, and Tertius writes down for the first time the now immortal and beloved words.

Vv 1–2. *So no adverse sentence is there now*, in view of this great fact of our redemption, *for those in Christ Jesus*. 'In Christ Jesus' — mysterious union, blessed fact, worked by the Spirit who linked us sinners to the Lord. *For the law of the Spirit of the life which is in Christ Jesus freed me*, the man of the conflict just described, *from the law of sin and of death*. The law, which legislates the covenant of blessing for all who are in Christ, has set him free. By what appears to us a strange paradox, the gospel — the message which carries with it acceptance, and also holiness, by faith — is here called a 'law'. For while it is free grace to us it is also immovable decree with God. The amnesty is his edict. It is by heavenly statute that sinners, believing, possess the Holy Spirit in possessing Christ. And here, with a sublime abruptness and directness, the great gift of the covenant, the Spirit, for which the covenant gift of justification was given, is put forward as the covenant's characteristic and crown. It is for the moment as if this were all—that 'in Christ Jesus' we, I, are under the command which assures to us the fullness of the Spirit. And this 'law', unlike the stern 'letter' of Sinai, has actually 'freed me'. It has endowed me not only with place but with power, in which to live emancipated from a rival law, the law of sin and of death. And what is that rival law? We dare to say that it is the command of Sinai; 'Do this, and thou shalt live'. This is a hard saying; for in itself that very law has been recently vindicated as holy, just, good, and spiritual. And only a few lines above in the epistle we have heard of a law of sin which is served by the flesh. And we should unhesitatingly explain this 'law' to be identical with that one, were it not for the next verse here, a still nearer context, in which 'the law' is unmistakably the divine moral code, considered how-ever as powerless. Must they not both be the same? And to call that sacred code 'the law of sin and of death' is not to say that it is sinful and deathful. It need only mean, and we think it does mean, that it is the occasion of sin and the warrant for death, through the collision of its holiness with fallen man's will. It must command; he, being what he is, must rebel. He rebels; it must condemn. Then comes his Lord to die for him, and to rise again; and the Spirit comes, to unite him to his Lord. And now, the man is 'freed' from the law provoking the helpless, guilty will, and claiming the sinner's penal death.

V 3. *For*—(the process is now explained more fully) *the impossible of the law*—what it could not do, for this was not its function, even to enable us sinners to keep its demands inwardly—*God, when he sent his own Son in likeness of flesh of sin*, incarnate, in our identical nature, under all those conditions of earthly life which for us are sin's vehicles and occasions, *and as sin-offering*, expiatory and reconciling, *sentenced sin in the flesh*; not pardoned it, note, but sentenced it. He ordered it to execution; he killed its claim and its power for all who are in Christ. And this, 'in the flesh', making man's earthly conditions the scene of sin's defeat, for our everlasting encouragement in our 'life in the flesh'.

V 4. And what was the aim and result? *That the righteous demand of the law might be fulfilled in us, us who walk not flesh-wise, but Spirit-wise*; that we, accepted in Christ, and using the Spirit's power in the daily 'walk' of circumstance and experience, might be freed from the life of self-will, and meet the will of God with simplicity and joy.

Such, and nothing less or else, was the law's 'righteous demand'; an obedience both universal and from the heart. For its first requirement, 'Thou shalt have no other God', meant, in essence, the dethronement of self from its central place, and its place taken by the Lord. But this could never be while there was a still unsettled reckoning between the man and God. There must be friction while God's law remained not only violated but unsatisfied and unatoned. And so it necessarily remained, till the sole adequate Person, one with God, one with man, stepped into the gap; our peace, our righteousness, and also, by the Holy Spirit, our life. At rest because of his sacrifice, at work by the power of his Spirit, we are now free to love, and divinely enabled to walk in love. Meanwhile the dream of an unsinning perfectness, which could be the basis of a claim to merit, is not so much rejected as put far out of the question. For the central truth of the new position is that the Lord has fully dealt, for us, with the law's claim that man shall deserve acceptance. 'Boasting' is totally and permanently 'excluded' from this new kind of law-fulfilling life. For the 'fulfilment' which means legal satisfaction is taken out of our hands for ever by Christ. The only humble 'fulfilment' that is ours is the one which means a restful, unanxious, reverent, unreserved loyalty in practice. To this our 'mind', the tendency of our soul, is now brought, in the life of acceptance, and in the power of the Spirit.

Vv 5–8. *For they who are flesh-wise*, the unchanged children of the self-life, *think*, 'mind', have moral affinity and converse with, *the things of the flesh; but they who are Spirit-wise, think the things of the Spirit*, his love, joy, peace, and all that holy 'fruit'. Their liberated and Spirit-bearing life now goes that way, in its true bias. *For the mind*, the moral affinity, *of the flesh*, of the self-life, *is death*; it involves the ruin of the soul, in condemnation, and in separation from God; *but the mind of the Spirit*, the affinity given to the believer

by the indwelling Holy One, *is life and peace*; it implies union
with Christ, our life and our acceptance; it is the state of soul in
which he is realized. *Because*—this absolute opposition of the two
'minds' is such because—*the 'mind' of the flesh is personal hostility
towards God; for to God's law it is not subject. For indeed it cannot be*
subject to it;—*those who are in flesh*, surrendered to the life of self
as their law, *cannot please God*, 'cannot meet the wish' of him
whose loving but absolute claim is to be Lord of the whole man.

'They cannot': it is a moral impossibility. The law of God is,
'Thou shalt love me with all thy heart, and thy neighbour as
thyself'; the mind of the flesh is, 'I will love my self and its will
first and most.' However well this is hidden, even from the man
himself, it is always the same thing in essence. It may mean a
defiant choice of open evil. It may mean a subtle and almost
imperceptible preference of literature, or art, or work, or home,
to God's will as such. In either case, it is 'the mind of the flesh',
a thing which cannot be refined and educated into holiness, but
must be surrendered when discovered, as its eternal enemy.

Vv. 9–10. *But you* (there is a glad emphasis on you) *are not in
flesh, but in Spirit*, surrendered to the indwelling Presence as your
law and secret, *on the assumption that* (he suggests not weary
misgivings but a true examination) *God's Spirit dwells in you*; has
his home in your hearts, humbly welcomed into a continuous
residence. *But if any one has not Christ's Spirit* (who is the Spirit as
of the Father so of the Son, sent by the Son, to reveal and to
impart him), *that man is not his.* He may bear his Lord's name,
he may be a Christian externally, he may enjoy the divine sacraments of union; but he has not the reality. The Spirit, shown by
his holy fruit, is no Indweller there; and the Spirit is our vital
bond with Christ. *But if Christ is*, thus by the Spirit, *in you*,
dwelling by faith in the hearts which the Spirit has strengthened
to receive Christ (Eph. 3. 16, 17)—*true, the body is dead, because of
sin*, the primeval sentence still holds its sway there; the body is
deathful still, it is the body of the fall; *but the Spirit is life*, he is
in that body, your secret of power and peace eternal, *because of
righteousness*, because of the merit of your Lord, in which you are
accepted, and which has won for you this wonderful Spirit-life.

Then even for the body a glorious future is assured, organically one with this living present. Let us listen as he goes on.

V 11. *But if the Spirit of him who raised Jesus*, the slain Man, *from the dead, dwells in you, he who raised from the dead Christ Jesus*, the Man so revealed and glorified as the Anointed Saviour, *shall also bring to life your mortal bodies, because of His Spirit, dwelling in you.* That 'frail temple', which was once so much defiled, and so defiling, is now precious to the Father because it is the place where the Spirit of his Son lives. Nor only so; that same Spirit, who, by uniting us to Christ, made our redemption actual, shall surely, in ways unknown to us, carry the process to its glorious completion, and be somehow the cause of the redemption of our body.

This gospel for the body is a wonderful theme of Scripture. In Christ, the body is seen to be something very different from the mere prison, or chrysalis, of the soul. It is its destined instrument, may we not say its mighty wings in prospect, for the life of glory. As invaded by sin, it has to pass through either death or, at the Lord's return, an equivalent transfiguration. But as created in God's plan of human nature it is permanently congenial to the soul, no, it is necessary to the soul's full action. And whatever be the mysterious mode (it is absolutely hidden from us as yet) of the event of resurrection, we do know, if only from this statement, that the glory of the immortal body will have profound relations with the work of God in the sanctified soul. It will be brought about, not through material, physical events, but 'because of the Spirit'; and 'because of the Spirit dwelling in you', as your power for holiness in Christ.

So the Christian reads the account of his present spiritual wealth, and of his coming completed life. Let him take it to heart, with most humble but quite decisive assurance, as he looks again, and believes again, on his redeeming Lord. For him, in his inexpressible need, God has gone about to provide 'so great salvation'. He has accepted his person in his Son who died for him. He has not only forgiven him through that great sacrifice, but in it he has condemned his sin, which is now a doomed thing, beneath his feet, in Christ. And he has given to him, as a personal and perpetual Indweller, to be claimed, hailed, and used by humble faith, His own eternal Spirit, the Spirit of his Son, the Blessed One who, dwelling infinitely in the Head, comes to dwell fully in the members, and make Head and members wonderfully one. Now then let him give himself up with joy, thanksgiving, and expectation, to the 'fulfilling of the righteous demand of God's law', 'walking Spirit-wise', with steps always moving away from self and towards the will of God. Let him meet the world, the devil, and that mysterious 'flesh' (all ever in potential presence) with no less a name than that of the Father, and the Son, and the Holy Spirit. Let him stand up not like a defeated and disappointed combatant, maimed, half-blinded, half-persuaded to give up, but as one who treads upon 'all the power of the enemy', in Christ, by the indwelling Spirit. And let him reverence his mortal body, even while he 'keeps it in subjection', and while he willingly tires it, or gives it to suffer, for his Lord. For it is the temple of the Spirit.

CHAPTER 18

Holiness by the Spirit, and the Glories That Shall Follow
(8.12–25)

Now the apostle goes on to develop his argument. How true to himself, and to his Inspirer, is the line he follows! First come the most practical possible of reminders of duty; then, and closely, the inmost experiences of the renewed soul in both its joy and its sorrow, and the most radiant and far-reaching prospects of glory to come. We listen still, always remembering that this letter from Corinth to Rome is to reach us too.

St Paul begins with holiness viewed as duty and debt. He has led us through our vast treasury of privilege and possession. What are we to do with it? Shall we treat it as a museum, in which we may occasionally observe the mysteries of new nature, and with more or less learning talk about them? Shall we just boast about them? No, we are to live upon our Lord's magnificent bounty—to his glory, and in his will. We are rich; but it is for him. We have his talents; and those talents, in respect of his grace, as distinct from his 'gifts', are not one, five, or ten, but ten thousand—for they are Jesus Christ. But we have them all for him. We are free from the law of sin and of death; but we are in perpetual and delightful debt to him who has freed us. And our debt is, to walk with him.

The paragraph begins, 'So, brethren, we are debtors'. For a moment Paul turns to say what we owe no debt to; 'the flesh', the self-life. But it is plain that his main purpose is positive, not negative. He implies in the whole rich context that we are debtors to the Spirit, to the Lord, 'to walk Spirit-wise'.

What a salutary thought it is! Too often in the Christian Church the great word 'holiness' has been practically banished to a supposed almost inaccessible background, to the heights of a spiritual ambition, to a region where a few might with difficulty climb in the quest, men and women who had enough spare time to be good, or who perhaps had exceptional instincts for piety. God be thanked, he has always kept many consciences alive to the illusion of such a notion; and in our own day, more and more, his mercy brings it home to his children that 'this is his will, even the sanctification'—not of some of them, but of all. Far and wide we are coming to see, as the fathers of our faith saw before us, that whatever else holiness is, it is a sacred and binding debt. It is not an ambition; it is a duty. We are bound, every one of us who names the name of Christ, to be holy, to be separate from evil, to walk by the Spirit.

Alas for the misery of indebtedness, when funds fall short! Whether the unhappy debtor examines his affairs, or guiltily ignores their condition, he is—if his conscience is not dead—a haunted man. But when an honourable indebtedness coincides with ample means, then one of the moral pleasures of life is paying it off promptly.

Christian, partaker of Christ, and of the Spirit, we also owe, to him who owns. But it is an indebtedness of the happy type. Once we owed, and there was worse than nothing in the purse. Now we owe, and we have Christ in us, by the Holy Spirit, with which to pay. The eternal neighbour comes to us and shows us his holy demand; to live today a life of truth, of purity, of confession of his name, of unselfish readiness to serve, of glad forgiveness, of unbroken patience, of practical sympathy, of the love which seeks not her own. What shall we say? That it is a beautiful ideal, which we should like to realize, and may yet some day seriously attempt? That it is admirable, but impossible? No, 'we are debtors'. And he who claims has first immeasurably given. We have his Son for our acceptance and our life. His very Spirit is in us. Holiness is beauty. But it is first duty, practical and present, in Jesus Christ our Lord.

Vv 12–13. *So then, brethren, debtors are we—not to the flesh, with a view to living flesh-wise*; but to the Spirit—who is now both our law and our power—with a view to living Spirit-wise. *For if you are living flesh-wise, you are on the way to die. But if by the Spirit you are doing to death the practices*, the strategems, the machinations, *of*

the body, you will live. Ah, the body is still there, and is still a seat
and vehicle of temptation. 'It is for the Lord, and the Lord is
for it' (1 Cor. 6.13). It is the temple of the Spirit. Our call is (1
Cor. 6.20) to glorify God in it. But all this, from our point of
view, passes from realization into mere theory, woefully contradicted by experience, when we let our acceptance in Christ, and
our possession in him of the almighty Spirit, pass out of use into
mere phrase. Say what some will, we are never for an hour here
on earth exempt from elements and conditions of evil residing
not merely around us but within us. There is no stage of life
when we can dispense with the power of the Holy Spirit as our
victory and deliverance from 'the evil schemes of the body'. And
the body is no separate and as it were minor personality. If the
man's body 'schemes', it is the man who is the sinner.

But then, thanks be to God, this fact is not the real concern
of the words here. What St Paul has to say is that the man who
has the indwelling Spirit has with him, in him, a divine and all-
effectual counter-agent to the subtlest of his foes. Let him do
what we saw him above (7.7–25) neglecting to do. Let him with
conscious purpose, and firm recollection of his wonderful position
and possession (so easily forgotten!), call up the eternal Power
which is indeed not himself, though in himself. Let him do this
with habitual recollection and simplicity. And he shall be 'more
than conqueror' where he was so miserably defeated. His path
shall be like that of a person who walks over foes who threatened,
but who fell, and who die at his feet. It shall be less a struggle
than a march, over a battlefield, certainly, yet a field of victory
so continuous that it shall be like peace.

'If by the Spirit you are doing them to death'. Note the words
well. He says nothing here of things often thought to be of
the essence of spiritual remedies; nothing of 'will-worship, and
humility, and unsparing treatment of the body' (Col. 2.23);
nothing even of fasting and prayer. Self-discipline is sacred and
precious, the watchful care that act and habit are true to the
'temperance' which is a vital ingredient in the Spirit's 'fruit'
(Gal. 5.22, 23). It is the Lord's own voice (Matt. 26.41) which
bids us always 'watch and pray'; 'praying in the Holy Spirit'
(Jude 20). Yes, but these true exercises of the believing soul are

after all only as the covering fence around that central secret—
our use by faith of the presence and power of the Holy Spirit
given to us. The Christian who neglects to watch and pray will
most surely find that he knows not how to use this his great
strength, for he will be losing realization of his oneness with his
Lord. But then the man who actually, and in the depth of his
being, is 'doing to death the practices of the body', is doing so,
in the first instance, not by discipline, nor by direct effort, but
by the believing use of the Spirit. Filled with him, he treads
upon the power of the enemy. And that fullness is according to
surrendering faith.

Vv 14–15. *For as many as are led by God's Spirit, these are God's sons;
for you did not receive a spirit of slavery*, to take you *back again to fear;
no, you received a Spirit of adoption* to sonship, in which Spirit,
surrendered to his holy power, *we cry*, with confidence, not hesitation, '*Abba, our Father*'. This is Paul's argument: If you would
truly live indeed, you must do sin to death by the Spirit. And
this means, from another aspect, that you must yield yourselves
to be led along by the Spirit, with the leading which is sure to
conduct you always away from self and into the will of God. You
must welcome the Indweller to have his holy way with your
springs of thought and will. So, and only so, will you truly answer
the idea, the description, 'sons of God'—a glorious term, never
to be satisfied by the relation of mere creaturehood, or by that
of merely exterior holiness, mere membership of an organization,
even the church itself. But if you meet sin by the Spirit in this
way, if you are so led by the Spirit, you show yourselves nothing
less than God's own sons. He has called you to nothing lower
than sonship; to living connection with a divine Father's life, and
to the eternal embraces of his love. For when he gave and you
received the Spirit, the Holy Spirit of promise, who reveals Christ
and joins you to him, what did that Spirit do? Did he lead you
back to the old position, in which you shrunk from God, as from
a master who bound you against your will? No, he showed you
that in the Only Son you are nothing less than sons, welcomed
into the inmost home of eternal life and love. You found yourselves indescribably near the Father's heart, because accepted,
and new-created, in his own Beloved. And so you learnt the

happy, confident call of the child, 'Father, O Father; Our Father, Abba.'

So it was, and so it is. The living member of Christ is nothing less than the dear child of God. He is other things as well; he is disciple, follower, bondservant. He never ceases to be a bond-servant, though here he is expressly told that he has received no 'spirit of slavery'. So far as 'slavery' means service forced against the will, he has done with this, in Christ. But so far as it means service rendered by one who is his master's absolute property, he has entered into its depths, for ever. Yet all this is exterior as it were to the inmost fact, that he is—in an ultimate sense, which alone really fulfils the word—the child, the son, of God. He is dearer than he can know to his Father. He is more welcome than he can ever realize to take his Father at his word, and lean upon his heart, and tell him all.

V 16. *The Spirit itself bears witness with our spirit, that we are God's children*, born children. The Holy One, on his part, makes the once cold, reluctant, apprehensive heart 'know and believe the love of God'. He 'sheds abroad God's love in it'. He brings home to consciousness and insight the sober certainty of the promises of the Word; that Word through which, above all other means, he speaks. He shows to the man 'the things of Christ', the Beloved, in whom he has adoption and renewal; making him see, as souls see, what a paternal welcome there must be for those who are in Christ. And then, on the other part, the believer meets Spirit with spirit. He responds to the revealed paternal smile with not just a subject's loyalty but a son's deep love; a deep, reverent, tender, genuine love. 'Doubtless you are his own child', says the Spirit. 'Doubtless he is my Father', says our wondering, believing, seeing spirit in response.

V 17. *But if children*, then *also heirs; God's heirs, Christ's co-heirs*, prospective possessors of our Father's heaven (towards which the whole argument now moves), in union of interest and life with our First-born Brother, in whom lies our right. That unseen bliss, which from one point of view is an infinitely merciful and surprising gift, from another point of view will be the lawful portion of the lawful child, one with the Beloved of the Father. We are such heirs *if indeed we share his sufferings*, those deep but hallowed pains which will surely come to us as we live in and for him in a fallen world, *that we may also share his glory*, for which that path of sorrow is, not indeed the meriting, but the qualifying, preparation.

Amidst the truths of life and love, of the Son, of the Spirit, of the Father, he thus throws in the truth of pain. Let us not forget it. In one form or another, it is for all 'the children'. Not all are martyrs, not all are exiles or captives, not all are called to meet open insults in a defiant world of paganism or unbelief. Many are still so called, as many were at first, and as many will be to the end; for 'the world' is no more now than it ever was in love with God, and with his children as such. But even for those whose path is—not by themselves but the Lord—most protected, there must be 'suffering', somehow, sooner, later, in this present life, if they are really living the life of the Spirit, the life of the child of God, 'paying the debt' of daily holiness, even in its humblest and gentlest forms. We must note, by the way, that it is to such sufferings, and not to sorrows in general, that the reference lies here. The Lord's heart is open to all the griefs of his people, and he can use them all for their blessing and for his ends. But the 'suffering with him' must imply a pain due to our union with him. It must be involved in our being his members, used by the Head for his work. It must be the hurt of his 'hand' or 'foot' in serving his sovereign thought. What will the bliss be of the corresponding sequel! 'That we may share his glory', not merely, 'be glorified', but share his glory; a splendour of life, joy, and power whose eternal law and soul will be union with him who died for us and rose again.

Now St Paul's whole thought turns towards that prospect, and the mention of that glory, after suffering, draws him to a sight of the mighty 'plurity' of the glory.

V 18. *For I reckon*, 'I calculate'—word of sublimest prose, more moving here than any poetry, because it asks us to treat the hope of glory as a fact—*that not worthy* of mention *are the sufferings of the present season, in view of the glory about to be unveiled upon us*, unveiled, and then heaped upon us, in its golden fullness.

For (V 19) he is going to give us a deep reason for his 'calculation'; wonderfully characteristic of the gospel. It is that the final glory of the saints will be a crisis of mysterious blessing for the whole created universe. In ways absolutely unknown, certainly as regards anything said in this passage, but none the less divinely fit and sure, the ultimate and eternal manifestation of the mystical Christ, the Perfect Head with his perfected members, will be the occasion, and in some sense too the cause, of the freeing of Nature, in its heights and depths, from the cancer of decay, and its entrance on an endless age of indissoluble life and splendour. No doubt that goal shall be reached through long processes and intense crises of strife and death. Nature, like the saint, may need to pass to glory through a tomb. But the result will indeed be glory, when he who is the Head of 'Nature', of the heavenly nations, and of redeemed man, shall bid the vast periods of conflict and dissolution cease, in the hour of eternal purpose, and shall clearly 'be what he is' to them all.

Science, by its nature, has nothing to say about what the universe shall be, or shall not be, under new and unknown conditions. Revelation announces that there are to be profoundly new conditions, and that they bear a mysterious but necessary relation to the coming glorification of Christ and his Church. And what we now see and feel as the imperfections and shocks and seeming failures of the universe are only as it were the throes of birth, in which Nature, impersonal, but so to speak animated by the thinking of the intelligent orders who are a part of her universal being, prepares for her wonderful future.

Vv 19–23. *For the longing outlook of the creation is expecting—the unveiling of the sons of God. For to vanity*, to evil, to failure and decay, *the creation was subjected not willingly, but because of him who made it subject*; its Lord and sustainer, who in his inscrutable but holy will commanded physical evil to correspond to the moral evil of his conscious fallen creatures, whether angels or men. So that there is a deeper connection than we can yet analyse between sin, the primal and central evil, and everything that is really wreck or pain. But this subjection was *in hope, because the creation itself shall be liberated from the slavery of corruption into the freedom of the glory of the children of God*, the freedom brought in for it by their eternal liberation from the last relics of the fall. *For we know*, by observation of natural evil, in the light of the promises, *that the whole creation is uttering a common groan* of burden and yearning, *and suffering a common birth-pang, even till now*, when the gospel has heralded the coming glory. *Nor only so, but even the actual possessors of the first-fruits of the Spirit*, possessors of the presence of the Holy One in them now, which is the sure pledge of his eternal fullness yet to come, *even we ourselves*, richly blest as we are in our wonderful Spirit-life, *yet in ourselves are groaning* still burdened with mortal conditions full of temptation, lying not only around us but deep within, *expecting adoption*, full instatement into the fruition of the sonship which already is ours, *even the redemption of our body*.

From the coming glories of the universe Paul returns, in the consciousness of an inspired but human heart, to the present discipline and burden of the Christian. Let us observe the noble honesty of the words; this 'groan' inserted in the middle of such a song of the Spirit and of glory. He has no ambition to pose as the possessor of an impossible experience. He is more than conqueror; but he is conscious of his enemies. The Holy Spirit is in him; he does the body's practices victoriously to death by the Holy Spirit. But the body is there, as the seat and vehicle of many temptations. And though there is a joy in victory which can sometimes make even the presence of temptation seem 'all joy' (Jas 1.2), he knows that something 'far better' is yet to come. His longing is not merely for a personal victory, but for an eternally unhindered service. That will not fully be his till his whole being is actually, as well as in God's covenant, redeemed. That will not be till both the spirit and the body are delivered from the last dark traces of the fall, at the resurrection.

Vv 24–25. *For it is as to our hope that we were saved*. When the Lord laid hold of us we were indeed saved, but with a salvation which was only in part actual. Its total was not to be realized till the whole being was in actual salvation. Such salvation (see below, 13.11) coincided with 'the Hope', the Lord's return and the resurrection glory. So, to paraphrase this clause, 'It was in the sense of the hope that we were saved'. *But a hope in sight is not a hope; for, what a man sees, why does he hope for?* Hope, in that case, has, in its nature, expired in possession. And our full 'salvation' is a hope; it is bound up with a promise not yet fulfilled; therefore, in its nature, it is still unseen, still unattained. But then, it is certain; it is infinitely valid; it is worth any waiting for. *But if, for what we do not see, we do hope*, looking on good grounds for the sunrise in the dark east, *with patience we expect it*. 'With patience', literally 'through patience'. The 'patience' is as it were the means, the secret, of the waiting. In New Testament use, 'patience' means the saint's active submission, submissive action, beneath the will of God. It is no nerveless, motionless prostration; it is the going on and upward, step by step, as the believer 'waits upon the Lord, and walks, and does not faint'.

CHAPTER 19

The Spirit of Prayer in the Saints: Their Present and Eternal Welfare in the Love of God (8.26–39)

In the last paragraph the music of this glorious prophecy passed, in some solemn phrases, into the minor mood. 'If we share his sufferings'; 'The sufferings of this present season'; 'We groan within ourselves'; 'In the sense of our hope we were saved.' All is well. The deep harmony of the Christian's full experience, if it is full downwards as well as upwards, sometimes demands such tones; and they are all music, for they all express a life in Christ, lived by the power of the Holy Spirit. But now the strain is to ascend again. We are now to hear how our salvation, though its ultimate issues are still things of hope, is itself a thing of eternity, from everlasting to everlasting. We are to be made sure that all things are working now, together, for the believer's good; and that his justification is sure; and that his glory is so certain that its future is, from his Lord's viewpoint, present; and that nothing, absolutely nothing, shall separate him from the eternal Love.

But first comes a very deep and tender word, the last of its kind in the long argument, about the presence and power of the Holy Spirit. The apostle has the Christian's 'groan' still in his ear, in his heart; in fact, it is his own. And he has just pointed himself and his fellow believers to the coming glory, as to a wonderful antidote; a prospect which is both great in itself and indescribably suggestive of the greatness given to the most suffering and tempted saint by his union with his Lord. As if to say to the pilgrim, in his moment of distress, 'Remember, you are more to God than you can possibly know; he has made you such, in Christ, that Nature as a whole is concerned in your future glory.' But now, as if nothing must suffice except what is directly

divine, he commands him to remember also the presence in him
of the eternal Spirit, as his mighty but tenderest indwelling
friend. Even as 'that blessed Hope', so, 'likewise also', this
blessed present Person, is the weak person's power. He takes the
man in his bewilderment, when troubles from without press him,
and fears from within make him groan, and he is in great need,
yet at a loss for the right cry. And he moves in the tired soul,
and breathes himself into its thought, and his mysterious 'groan'
of divine yearning mingles with our groan about our troubles,
and the man's longings go out above all things not towards rest
but towards God and his will. So the Christian's innermost and
ruling desire is both fixed and animated by the blessed Indweller,
and he seeks what the Lord will love to grant, God himself and
whatever shall please him. The man prays correctly because
(what a divine miracle is put before us in the words!) the Holy
Spirit, within him, prays through him.

Thus we attempt, in advance, to explain the sentences which
now follow. It is true that St Paul does not explicitly say that
the Spirit makes intercession in us, as well as for us. But must
it not be so? For where is he, from the point of view of Christian
life, but in us?

Vv 26–27. *Then, in the same way, the Spirit also*—as well as 'the
hope'—*helps*, as with a clasping, supporting hand, *our weakness*,
our shortness and bewilderment of insight, our feebleness of faith.
*For what we should pray for as we ought, we do not know; but the
Spirit itself interposes to intercede for us, with groanings unutterable; but*
(whatever be the utterance or no utterance) *the Searcher of our
hearts knows what is the mind*, the purpose, *of the Spirit; because God-
wise*, with divine insight and sympathy, the Spirit with the
Father, *he intercedes for saints*.

Did he not intercede in this way for Paul, and in him, fourteen
years before these words were written, when (2 Cor. 12.7–10)
the man asked three times that the 'thorn' might be removed,
and the Master gave him a better blessing, the victorious overshadowing power? Did he not intercede in this way for Monica,
and in her, when she sought with prayers and tears to keep her
rebellious Augustine by her, and the Lord let him fly from her
side—to Italy, to Ambrose, and so to conversion?

But the strain rises now, finally and fully, into the rest and triumph of faith. 'We not know what we should pray for as we ought'; and the blessed Spirit meets this deep need in his own way. And this, with all else that we have in Christ, reminds us of something that 'we know' indeed; namely, that all things, favourable or not in themselves, combine in blessing for the saints. And then Paul looks backward (or rather, upward) into eternity, and sees the throne, and the King with his sovereign will, and the lines of perfect and infallible plan and provision which stretch from that centre to infinity. Who are these 'saints'? From one viewpoint, they are simply sinners who have seen themselves, and fled for safety to the one possible hope; a hope set before every soul that cares to win it. From another viewpoint, that of the eternal Mind and Order, they are those whom, for reasons infinitely wise and just, but wholly hidden in himself, the Lord has chosen to be his own for ever, so that his choice takes effect in their conversion, acceptance, spiritual transformation, and glory.

There, as regards this great passage, the thought ends in the glorification of the saints. What their Glorifier will do with them, and through them, glorified in this way, is another matter. Assuredly he will make use of them in his eternal kingdom. The Church, made most blessed for ever, is blessed ultimately, not for itself but for its Head, and for his Father. It is to be, in its final perfection, 'an habitation of God, in the Spirit' (Eph. 2.22). Is he not so to possess it that the universe shall see him in it, in a manner and degree now unknown and unimaginable? Is not the endless 'service' of the chosen to be such that all orders of being shall through them behold and adore the glory of the Christ of God? They will be for ever what they become here, the bondservants of their redeeming Lord, his bride, his vehicle of power and blessing; having nothing of their own in him all, and all for him. No selfish exaltations await them in heaven; or the whole history of sin would begin all over again. They will have no spirit of heavenly Pharisaism; a look downward upon less blessed regions of existence, as from a sanctuary of their own. Who can tell what ministries of boundless love will be the expression of their life of inexpressible and inexhaustible joy?

Always, like Gabriel, in the presence of God, will they not always also, like him, be sent (Luke 1.19) on the messages of their glorious Head, in whom at length, 'all things shall be gathered together'?

But this is not the thought of the present passage. Here, as we have said, the thought ends in the final glorification of the saints of God, as the immediate goal of the process of their redemption. V 28. *But we know that for those who love God all things work together for good, even for those who, purpose-wise, are his called ones.* 'We know it', with the knowledge of faith; that is to say, because he, absolutely trustworthy, guarantees it by his character and word. The mystery, is deep, no insoluble, from every other point of view. The lovers of the Lord cannot explain, to themselves or others, how this coincidence of 'all things' works out its infallible results in them. And the observer from outside cannot understand their certainty that it is so. But the fact is there, given and assured, not by speculation about events, but by personal knowledge of an eternal Person. Love God, and you will know.

They love God, with the genuine affection of human hearts, hearts not the less human because divinely new-created, renewed from above. Their immediate consciousness is just this; we love him. Not, we have read the book of life; we have had a glimpse of the eternal purpose in itself; we have heard our names recited in the roll of the chosen; but, we love him. We have found in him the eternal Love. In him we have peace, purity, and that deep, final satisfaction, that view of 'the King in his beauty', which is the supreme good of the creature. It was our fault that we did not see it sooner, that we did not love him sooner. It is the duty of every soul that he has made to reflect upon its need of him, and upon the fact that it owes it to him to love him in his holy beauty of eternal Love. If we could not it was because we would not. If you cannot it is because, somehow and somewhere, you will not; will not put yourselves without reserve in the way of the sight. 'Oh taste and see that the Lord is good'; oh love the eternal Love.

But those who simply and genuinely love God in this way are also, on the other side, 'purpose-wise, his called ones'; 'called', in the sense which we have found above (p. 22) to be consistently traceable in the epistles; not merely invited, but brought in; not just evangelized, but converted. In each case the man or the woman, came to Christ, came to love God with the freest possible coming of the will and heart. Yet each, having come, had the Lord to thank for the coming. The human personality had traced its orbit of will and deed, as truly as when it willed to sin and to rebel. But, in ways past our finding out, its free track lay along a previous track of the purpose of the Eternal; its free 'I will' was the precise and fore-ordered correspondence to His 'Thou shall'. It was the act of man; it was the grace of God.

Can we get beyond such a statement? If we are right in our reading of the whole teaching of Scripture on the sovereignty of God, our thoughts on it must rest just here. The doctrine of the choice of God refuses, it seems to us, to be explained away so as to mean in effect little but the choice of man. But then the doctrine is 'a lamp, not a sun'. It is presented to us everywhere, and not least in this epistle, as a truth not meant to explain everything, but to enforce this thing—that the man who as a fact loves the eternal Love has to thank not himself but that Love that his eyes, guiltily shut, were effectually opened. Not one link in the chain of actual redemption is forged by us, or the whole would indeed be fragile. It is of God that we, in this great matter, will as we ought to will. I ought to have loved God always. It is of his mere mercy that I love him now.

With this humbling lesson the truth of the heavenly choice, and its effectual call, brings us one of divine encouragement. Such a 'purpose' is no fluctuating thing, shifting with the currents of time. Such a call to such an embrace means a tenacity, as well as a welcome, worthy of God. 'Who shall separate us?' 'Neither shall any pluck them out of my Father's hand.' And this is the motive of the words in this wonderful context, where everything is made to bear on the safety of the children of God, in the midst of all imaginable dangers.

V 29. *For whom he knew beforehand*, with a foreknowledge which, in this argument, can mean nothing short of foredecision (see Rom. 11.2; Acts 2.23; 1 Pet. 1.2, 20) no mere foreknowledge of what they would do, but rather of what he would do for them— *those he also set apart beforehand, for confirmation*, a deep and genuine

resemblance due to like being, *to the image*, the revealed counten-
ance, *of his Son, that he might be firstborn amongst many brethren*,
surrounded by his Father's children by their union with himself.
So, as ever in the Scriptures, mystery bears full on character.
The man is saved that he may be holy. His 'predestination' is
not merely not to perish, but to be made like Christ, in a spiritual
transformation, coming out in the moral features of the family
of heaven. And all bears ultimately on the glory of Christ. The
gathered saints are an organism, a family, before the Father; and
their living centre is the Beloved Son, who sees in their true
sonship the fruit of 'the travail of his soul'.

V 30. *But those whom he thus set apart beforehand, he also called*,
effectually drew so as truly and freely to choose Christ; *and those
whom he* thus *called* to Christ, *he also justified* in Christ, in the great
way of propitiation and faith of which the epistle has so fully
spoken; *but those whom he* thus *justified, he also glorified*. 'Glorified'
is a marvellous past tense. It reminds us that in this passage we
are placed, as it were, upon the mountain of the throne of God;
our finite thought is allowed to speak for once (however little it
understands it) the language of eternity, to utter the facts as the
Eternal sees them. To God, the pilgrim is already in heaven; the
bondservant is already at the end of his day's work receiving his
Master's 'Well done, good and faithful'. He to whom time is not
as it is to us thus sees his purposes complete, always and for
ever. We see through his sight, in hearing his word about it. So
for us, in wonderful paradox, our glorification is presented, as
truly as our call, in terms of accomplished fact.

Here, in one sense, the teaching of the epistle ends; what remains
is its application. But what an application! The apostle brings
his converts out into the open field of trial, and commands them
to use his doctrine there. Are they dear to the Father in the Son?
Is their every need met? Is their guilt cancelled in Christ's mighty
merit? Is their existence filled with Christ's eternal Spirit? Is sin
cast beneath their feet, and is such a heaven opened above their
heads? Then what have they to fear, before man, or before God?
What power in the universe, of whatever order of being, can
really hurt them? For what can separate them from their share

in their glorified Lord, and in his Father's love in him? Again
we listen, with Tertius, as the voice goes on:

Vv 31–39. *What therefore shall we say in view of these things? If God
is for us, who is against us?* He *who did not spare his own true Son, but
for us all handed him over* to that awful expiatory, propitiatory,
darkness and death, so that he was 'pleased to bruise him, to
put him to grief' (Is. 53.10), all for his own great glory, but, no
whit the less, all for our pure blessing; *how* (wonderful 'how'!)
shall he not also with him, because all is included and involved in
him who is the Father's All, *give us also freely all things* ('the all
things that are')? And do we want to be sure that he will not,
after all, find a flaw in our claim, and find us guilty in his court?
*Who will lodge a charge against God's chosen ones? Will God—who
justifies them? Who will condemn them,* if the charge is lodged? *Will
Christ—who died, no rather who rose, who is on the right hand of God,
who is actually interceding for us?* (Note this one mention in the
whole epistle of Christ's ascension, and his action for us above,
as he is, by the fact of his being seated on the throne, our sure
channel of eternal blessing, unworthy that we are.) Do we need
assurance, amid 'the sufferings of this present time', that through
them the invincible hands of Christ always clasp us, with untired
love? We 'look upon the covenant' of our acceptance and life in
him who died for us, and who lives both for and in us, and we
meet the fiercest buffet of these waves in peace. *Who shall sunder
us from the love of Christ?* There rise before him, as he asks,
like so many angry personalities, the outward troubles of the
pilgrimage. *Tribulation? or Perplexity? or Persecution? or Famine? or
Nakedness? or Peril? or Sword? As it stands written,* in that deep song
of anguish and faith (Ps. 44) in which Israel the elder Church,
one with us in deep continuity, tells her story of suffering, *For
thy sake we are done to death all the day long; we have been reckoned,*
estimated, *as sheep of slaughter.'* Even so. *But in these things, all of
them, we more than conquer;* not only do we tread upon our foes; we
spoil them, we find them occasions of glorious gain, *through him
who loved us. For I am sure that neither death, nor life,* life with
its natural attractions or its bewildering tasks, *nor angels, nor
principalities, nor powers,* whatever orders of being unfriendly to
Christ and his saints the vast unseen contains, *nor present things,*

nor things to come, in all the boundless field of circumstance and possibility, *nor height, nor depth*, in the limitless sphere of space, *nor any other creature*, no thing, no being, under the Uncreated One, *shall be able to sunder us*, 'us' with an emphasis upon the word and thought, *from the love of God, which is in Christ Jesus our Lord*—from the eternal embrace in which the Father embraces the Son, and, in the Son, all who are one with him.

So we return to the subject of 'Jesus Christ our Lord' (see 4.25, 5.21, 6.23, 7.25). Our 'righteousness, and sanctification, and redemption' (I Cor. 1.33), the themes of Romans 3, 6, and 8, are all, in their living ultimate essence, 'Jesus Christ our Lord'. He makes every truth, every doctrine of peace and holiness, every certain presupposition and conclusion, to be life as well as light. He is pardon, and sanctity, and heaven. Here, finally, the eternal Love is seen not as it were diffused into infinity, but gathered up wholly and for ever in Christ. Therefore to be in him is to be in it.

CHAPTER 20

The Sorrowful Problem:
Jewish Unbelief: Divine Sovereignty (9.1–33)

We may well think that again there was silence for a while in that room in Corinth, when Tertius had written down the last words we have studied. A 'silence in heaven' follows, in the Apocalypse (8.1), the vision of the white hosts of the redeemed, gathered at last before the throne and the Lamb. A silence in the soul is the fittest immediate sequel to the revelation of grace and glory that has passed before us here. And did not the man whose work it was to utter it, and whose personal experience was as it were the informing soul of the whole argument of the epistle from the first, and not least in this last declaration of faith, keep silence when he had done, hushed and tired by this 'exceeding weight' of grace and glory?

But Paul has a great deal more to say to the Romans, and in due time the dictation continues. What will the next theme be? It will be in significant contrast to the last; a lament, a discussion, an instruction, and then a prophecy, not about himself and his happy fellow-saints, but poor self-blinded unbelieving Israel.

The occurrence of that subject just here is true to the inmost nature of the gospel. The apostle has just been counting up the wealth of salvation, and claiming it all, as present and eternal property, for himself and his brothers in the Lord. Justifying righteousness, liberty from sin in Christ, the Indwelling Spirit, electing love, coming and certain glory, all have been recounted, and asserted, and embraced. Is this great present and future joy selfish? Let those who see these things only from outside say so. Make proof of what they are in their inner nature, enter into them, learn yourself what it is to have peace with God, to receive the Spirit, to expect the eternal glory; and you will find that nothing is so sure to expand the heart towards others as the personal reception into it of the truth and life of God in Christ. It is possible to hold a true creed — and to be spiritually hard and selfish. But is it possible to be like this when not only the creed is held, but the Lord of it, its heart and life, is received with wonder and great joy? The person whose certainties, riches, and freedom, are all consciously in Christ, cannot but love his neighbour, and long that he too should come into 'the secret of the Lord'.

So St Paul, just at this point of the epistle, turns with a unique intensity of grief and yearning towards the Israel which he had once led, and now had left, because they would not come with him to Christ. Both his natural and spiritual sympathies go out to this self-afflicting people, so privileged, so divinely loved, and now so blind. Oh that he could offer any sacrifice that would bring them reconciled, humbled, happy, to the feet of the true Christ! Oh that they might see the fallacy of their own way of salvation, and submit to the way of Christ, taking his yoke, and finding rest to their souls! Why do they not do it? Why does not the light which convinced him shine on them? Why do not the voices of the prophets prove to them, as they do now to Paul, absolutely convincing of the historical as well as the spiritual claims of the Man of Calvary? Has the promise failed? Has God finished with the race to which he guaranteed such a perpetual blessing? No, that cannot be. Paul looks again, and he sees in the whole past a long warning that, while an outer circle of benefits might affect the nation, the inner circle, the true light and life of God, embraced only a remnant; even from the day when Isaac and not Ishmael was made heir of Abraham. And then he meditates on the impenetrable mystery of the relation of the Infinite Will to human wills; he remembers how, in a way whose full reasons are unknowable (but they are good, for they are in God), the Infinite Will has to do with our willing; genuine and responsible though our willing is. And before that opaque veil he rests. He knows that only righteousness and love is behind it; but he know that it is a veil, and that in front of it man's thought must cease and be silent. Sin is completely man's fault. But when man turns from sin it is all God's mercy, free, special, distinguishing. Be silent, and trust him, O man whom God has made. Remember, he has made you. It is not only that he is greater or stronger than you, but he has made you. Be reasonably willing to trust, without seeing them, the reasons of your Maker.

Then Paul turns again with new regrets and yearnings to the thought of the wonderful gospel which was meant for Israel and for the world, but which Israel rejected, and now would like to hinder on its way to the world. Lastly, he recalls the future, still full of eternal promises for the chosen race, and through them full of blessing for the world; till he rises at length from perplexity and anguish, and the wreck of once eager expectations, into the great hymn of praise in which he blesses the Eternal Sovereign for the very mystery of his ways, and adores him because he is his own eternal end.

Vv 1–5. *Truth I speak in Christ*, speaking as the member of the All-Truthful; *I do not lie, my conscience, in the Holy Spirit*, informed and governed by him, *bearing me concurrent witness* — the soul within affirming to itself the word spoken without to others — *that I have great grief, and my heart has incessant pain*, yes, the heart in which (v 5) the Spirit has 'poured out' God's love and joy; there is room for both experiences in its human depths. *For I was wishing, I myself, to be anathema from Christ*, to be devoted to eternal separation from him, an awful dream of the greatest sacrifice, made impossible only because it would mean self-robbery from the Lord who had bought him; a spiritual suicide by sin — *for the sake of my brethren, my kinsmen flesh-wise. For they are Israelites*, bearers of the glorious divine name, sons of the 'Prince with God, (Gen. 32.28); *theirs is the adoption*, the call to be God's own race, 'his son, his first-born' (Exod. 4.22) of the peoples; *and the glory*, the glory of the eternal presence of God, sacramentally seen in tabernacle and temple, spiritually spread over the race; *and the covenants*, with Abraham, Isaac, Levi, Moses, Aaron, Phinehas, and David; *and the legislation*, the holy moral code, *and the ritual*, with its divinely ordered symbolism, the vast parable of Christ, *and the promises*, of 'the pleasant land', and the perpetual favour, and the coming Lord; *theirs are the fathers*, the patriarchs, priests, and kings; *and out of them, as to what is flesh-wise, is the Christ* — he who is over all things, God, blessed to all eternity. Amen.

It is indeed a splendid roll of honours, recited over this race 'separate among the nations', a race which to-day as much as ever remains the enigma of history, to be solved only by revelation. It is indeed a riddle, made of indissoluble facts, this people scattered everywhere yet everywhere individual; scribes of a Book which has profoundly influenced mankind, and which is recognized by many races as an impressive and lawful claimant to be divine, yet themselves, in so many aspects, provincial to the heart; historians of their own glories, but at least equally of their own unworthiness and disgrace; transmitters of predictions which may be disregarded, but can never, as a whole, be explained away, yet obstinate deniers of the majestic fulfilment in the Lord of Christendom; human in every fault and imperfection, yet so concerned in bringing to man the message of the Divine that Jesus himself said of them, 'Salvation comes from the Jews' (John 4.22). On this wonderful race this its most illustrious member (after his Lord) here fixes his eyes, full of tears. He sees their glories pass before him—and then realizes the spiritual squalor and misery of their rejection of the Christ of God. He groans, and in real agony asks how it can be. Only one thing cannot be. The promises have not failed; there has been no failure in the Promiser. What may seem such is rather man's misreading of the promise.

Vv 6–13. *But it is not as though the word of God has been thrown out*, the 'word' whose divine honour was dearer to him than even that of his people. *For not all who come from Israel constitute Israel; nor, because they are seed of Abraham, are they all his children*, in the sense of family life and rights; *but 'In Isaac shall a seed be called thee'* (Gen. 21.12); Isaac, and not any son of thy body begotten, is father of those whom thou shalt claim as thy covenant-race. *That is to say, not the children of his flesh are the children of his God; no, the children of the promise*, indicated and limited by its developed terms, *are reckoned as seed. For of the promise this was the word* (Gen. 18.10, 14), 'According to this time I will come, and Sarah, she and not any spouse of yours; no Hagar, no Keturah, but Sarah, *shall have a son.' Nor only so, but Rebecca too—being with child*, with twin children, *of one husband*—no problem of complex parentage, as with Abraham, occurring here—*even of Isaac our father*, just named as the selected heir—*(for it was while they were not yet born, while they had not yet shown any conduct good or bad, that the choice-wise purpose of God might remain,* sole and sovereign, *not based on works, but* wholly *on the Caller)—it was said to her* (Gen. 25.23), '*The greater shall be bondman to the less.' As it stands written,* in the prophet's message a millennium later, '*Jacob I loved, but Esau I hated.*' I repudiated him as heir.

So the limit has run always along with the promise. Ishmael is Abraham's son, yet not his son. Esau is Isaac's son, yet not his son. And though we trace in Ishmael and in Esau, as they grow, characteristics which may seem to explain the limitation, this will not really do. For the chosen one in each case has his conspicuous unfavourable characteristics too. And the whole tone of the record (not to speak of its apostolic interpretation here) looks towards mystery, not explanation. Esau's 'profanity' was the occasion, not the cause, of the choice of Jacob. The reason of the choice lay hidden in God.

So we are led up to the shut door of the sanctuary of God's choice. It is locked, but not by fate or an indifferent tyrant. If you listen you will hear words within, like the soft deep voice of many waters, yet of an eternal Heart; 'I am that I am; I will that I will; trust me.' But the door is locked; and the voice is mysterious.

God knows, with infinite kindness and sympathy, the indescribable pain that can be felt by people trying to understand his eternal nature and choice. We do not find in Scripture, surely, anything like a condemnation for that awful sense of the unknown which can gather on the soul drawn—irresistibly as it sometimes seems to be—into the problems of the choice of God, and oppressed by the very questions stated here by the apostle. The Lord knows, not only his will, but our heart, in these matters. And where he entirely declines to explain (surely because we are not yet of age to understand him if he did) he shows us Jesus, and commands us meet the silence of the mystery with the silence of a personal trust in the personal character revealed in him.

Shall we approach the following paragraph in some such stillness? Shall we listen, not too explain away, not even over much to explain, but to submit, with a submission which is not a

suppressed resentment but a complete reliance? We shall find
that the whole matter, in practice, has a voice clear enough for
the soul which sees Christ, and believes in him. It says to that
soul, 'Who makes you different? Why are you not now, as once,
guiltily rejecting Christ, or, what is the same, postponing him?
Thank him who has "compelled you", yet without violating your
integrity "to come in". See in your choice of him his mercy on
you. And now, fall at his feet, to bless, serve, and trust him.
Think ill of yourself. Think reverently of others. And remember
(the Infinite, who has chosen you, says it), he does not will the
death of a sinner, he loved the world, he commands you to tell
it that he loves it, to tell it that he is Love.'

Now we listen. With a look which speaks of awe, but not
misgiving, disclosing past storms of doubt, but now a rest of
faith, the apostle dictates again:

V 14. *What therefore shall we say? Is there injustice at God's bar? Away
with the thought.* The thing is, in the deepest sense, unthinkable.
God, the God of Revelation, the God of Christ, is a Being who,
if unjust—ceases to be, 'denies himself'. But the thought that his
reasons for some given action should be, at least to us now,
absolute mystery, he being the Infinite Personality, is not
unthinkable at all. And in such a case it is not unreasonable, but
the deepest reason, to ask for no more than his clear guarantee, so
to speak, that the mystery is fact; that he is conscious of it, alive
to it (speaking humanly); and that he claims it as his will. For
when God, the God of Christ, commands us 'take his will for it',
it is different from an attempt, however powerful, to frighten us
into silence. It is a reminder who it is who speaks; the Being
who is related to us, who loved us, but who also has absolutely
made us, and cannot (because we are sheer products of his will)
make us his equals so as to tell us all.

Vv 15–17. So the apostle proceeds with a 'for' whose bearing we
have already indicated: *For to Moses he says* (Exod. 34.19), in the
dark sanctuary of Sinai, '*I shall pity whomsoever I do pity, and
compassionate whomsoever I do compassionate*'; my account of my
saving action shall stop there. *It appears therefore that it,* the ultimate account of salvation, *is not of* (as the effect is 'of' the first
cause) *the willer, nor of the runner,* the carrier of willing into work,

but of the Pitier — God. For the Scripture says (Exod. 10.16) *to Pharaoh,* that great example of defiant human sin, real and guilty, but also, concurrently, of the sovereign choice which sentenced him to go his own way, and used him as a beacon at its end, '*For this very purpose I raised thee up,* made thee stand, even beneath the plagues, *that I might display in thee my power, and that my name,* as of the just God who strikes down the proud, *might be told far and wide in all the earth.*'

Pharaoh's was a case of phenomena that coincided. On the one hand there was a man willingly, deliberately, and most guiltily, battling with right, and rightly bringing ruin on his own head, wholly of himself. On the other hand, there was God, making that man a monument not of grace but of judgment. And that aspect is isolated here, and treated as if it were all.

V 18. *It appears then that whom he pleases, he pities, and whom he pleases, he hardens,* in that sense in which he 'hardened Pharaoh's heart', made it 'stiff', 'heavy', 'harsh' — by sentencing it to have its own way. Yes, this is how it appears (see Ps. 81.12; Rom. 1.24, 26). And beyond that inference we can take no step of thought except that the subject of that mysterious 'will', he who thus 'pleases', 'pities', and 'hardens', is no other than the God of Jesus Christ. He may be, not only submitted to, but trusted, in that unknowable sovereignty of his will.

Vv 19–22a. Yet listen to the question which speaks out the problem of all hearts: *You will say to me therefore, Why does he still,* after such a statement of his sovereignty, softening this heart, hardening that, why does he still *find fault?* Ah why? *For his act of will who has withstood?* (No, you have withstood his will, and so have I. Not one word of the argument has contradicted the primary fact of our will, nor therefore our responsibility. But this he does not bring in here.) No rather, rather than take such an attitude of narrow and helpless logic, think deeper; *No rather, O man,* O mere human being, *you — who are you, who are answering back to your God? Shall the thing formed say to its Former, Why did you make me like this? Has not the potter authority over his clay, out of the same kneaded mass to make this vessel for honour but that for dishonour? But if God, being pleased to demonstrate his wrath, and to evidence what he can do* — what will St Paul go on to say? That God created

responsible beings on purpose to destroy them, gave them personality, and then compelled them to sin? No, he does not say
so. The stern and simple illustration of the potter and his clay,
gives way, in its application, to a statement of the work of God
on man full of significance in its variation. Here indeed are the
'vessels' still; and the vessels 'for honour' are such because of
'mercy', and his own hand has 'prepared them for glory'. And
there are the vessels 'for dishonour', and in a sense of awful
mystery they are such because of 'wrath'. But the 'wrath' of the
Holy One can fall only on those who deserve it; so these 'vessels'
have merited his displeasure of themselves. And they are 'prepared for ruin'; but where is any mention of his hand preparing
them? And meanwhile he 'bears them in much longsuffering'.
The mystery is there, impenetrable as ever, when we try to pierce
behind God's will. But on every side it is limited and qualified
by facts which witness to the compassions of the Infinite Sovereign even in his judgments, and remind us that sin is altogether
'of' the creature.

Vv 22b–24. So we take up the words where we dropped them
above: *What if he bore* (the tense throws us forward into eternity,
to look back from these on his ways in time) *in much longsuffering,
vessels of wrath, adjusted for ruin?* And acted otherwise with others,
that he might evidence the wealth of his glory, the resources of his
inmost character, poured *upon vessels of pity, which he prepared in
advance for glory*, by the processes of justifying and hallowing
grace—*whom in fact he called*, effectually, in their conversion, *even
us, not only from the Jews, but also from the Gentiles?* For while the
historical Israel, with its privilege and its apparent failure, is
here first in view, there lies behind it the phenomenon of 'the
Israel of God', the heaven-born heirs of the fathers, a race not
of blood but of the Spirit. The great promise, all the while, had
pointed towards that Israel as its final scope; and now he gives
proof from the prophets that this intention was at least half
revealed all along the line of revelation.

Vv 25–26. *As actually in our Hosea* (2.23, Heb., 25) in the book we
know as such, *he says, 'I will call* what was not my people, my
people; *and the not-beloved one, beloved. And* (another Hosean oracle,
in line with the first) *it shall be, in the place where it was said to them,*

Not my people are ye, there they shall be called sons of the living God.'
In both places the first reference of the words is to the restoration
of the Ten Tribes to covenant blessings. But the apostle, in
the Spirit, sees an ultimate and satisfying reference to a vaster
application of the same principle; the bringing of the rebelling
and banished ones of all mankind into covenant and blessing.

Meanwhile the prophets who foretell that great in-gathering
indicate with equal seriousness the spiritual failure of all but a
fraction of the direct heirs of promise.

Vv 27–29. *But Isaiah cries over Israel, 'If the number of the sons of*
Israel should be as the sand of the sea, the remnant only *shall be saved;*
for as one who completes and cuts short will the Lord do his work upon
the earth.' Here again is a first and second reference of the prophecy. In every stage of the history of sin and redemption the
apostle, in the Spirit, sees an embryo of the great development.
So, in the sadly limited numbers of the exiles who returned from
the old captivity he sees an embodied prophecy of the fewness
of the sons of Israel who shall return from the exile of incredulity
to their true Messiah. *And as Isaiah* (1.9) *has foretold*, so it is;
'*Unless the Lord of Hosts had left us a seed, like Sodom we had become,*
and to Gomorrah we had been resembled.'

Such was the mystery of the facts, both in the earlier and in
the later story of Israel. A remnant, still a remnant, not the
masses, entered upon an inheritance of such generous provision,
and so sincerely offered. And behind this lay the insoluble
shadow within which is concealed the relation of the Infinite
Will to the wills of men. But also, in front of the phenomenon,
concealed by no shadow except that which is cast by human sin,
the apostle sees and records the reasons, as they reside in the
human will, of this 'salvation of a remnant'. The promises of God,
all along, and supremely now in Christ, had been conditioned (it
was in the nature of spiritual things that it should be so) by
submission to his way of fulfilment. The golden gift was there,
in the most generous of hands, stretched out to give. But it could
be put only into a hand that was open and empty. It could be
taken only by submissive and self-forgetting faith. And man, in
his fall, had twisted his will out of gear for such an action. Was
it strange that, by his own fault, he failed to receive?

Vv 30–33. *What therefore shall we say? Why, that the Gentiles, though they did not pursue righteousness*, though no oracle had set them on the track of a true divine acceptance and salvation, *achieved righteousness*, grasped it when once revealed, *but the righteousness that results on faith; but Israel, pursuing a law of righteousness*, aiming at what is, for fallen man, the impossible goal, a perfect meeting of the law's one principle of acceptance, 'This do and thou shalt live', *did not attain that law*; that is to say, did not attain the acceptance to which that law was to be the avenue. The Pharisee as such, the Pharisee Saul of Tarsus for example, neither had peace with God, nor really dared to think he had. He knew enough of the divine ideal to be hopelessly uneasy about his realization of it. He could say, stiffly enough, 'God, I thank thee' (Luke 18. 11, 14); but he 'went down to his house' unhappy, unsatisfied, unjustified. *On what account? Because* it was *not of faith, but as of works*; in the unquiet dream that man must, and could, acquire a valid claim. *They stumbled on the Stone of their stumbling; as it stands written* (Isa. 8.14, 28.16), in a passage where the great perpetual Promise is in view, and where the blind people are seen rejecting it in favour of policy or formalism, *Behold, I place in Sion*, in the very centre of light and privilege, *a stone of stumbling, and a rock of upsetting*; and *he who confides in him* (or, perhaps, *in it*), he who rests on it, on him, *shall not be put to shame*.

Was ever prophecy more profoundly proved by events? Not just for Israel, but for mankind, the King Messiah is, as ever, the Stone of either stumbling or foundation. He is, as ever, 'a sign spoken against'. He is, as ever, the Rock of Ages, where the believing sinner hides, and rests, and builds.

Have we known what it is to stumble over him? 'We will not have this man to reign over us'; 'We were never in bondage to any man; who is he that he should set us free?' And are we now lifted by a Hand of all-powerful kindness to a place where we 'know nothing' for peace of conscience, satisfaction of thought, liberation of the will, and the abolition of death, 'but Jesus Christ, and him crucified'? Then let us think with always humbled sympathy of those who, for whatever reason, still 'forsake their own mercy' (Jon. 2.8). And let us inform them where we are, and how we got here. And for ourselves, that we may do

this the better, let us often read again the simple, strong assurance which closes this chapter of mysteries; 'He who confides in
him shall not be put to shame'; 'shall not be disappointed'; 'shall
not make haste'. No, we shall not make haste. No hurried retreat
shall ever need to be beaten from that safe Place. That Fortress
cannot be stormed. It cannot be surprised. It cannot crumble.
For 'It is he'; the Son, the Lamb, of God; the sinner's everlasting
righteousness, the believer's unfailing source of peace, purity,
and power.

CHAPTER 21

*Jewish Unbelief and Gentile Faith:
Prophecy (10.1–21)*

The problem of Israel is still upon the apostle's mind. He has explored the fact that his brethren, as a mass, have rejected Jesus. He has expressed his grief over it. He has reminded himself, and then his readers, that the fact however involves no failure of the purpose and promise of God; for God from the first had indicated limitations within the apparent scope of the promise to Abraham. He has looked in the face, once for all, the mystery of the relation between God's efficient will and the will of the creature, finding a shelter, under the moral strain of that mystery, not away from it but as it were behind it, in remembering the infinite trustworthiness, as well as eternal rights, of man's Maker. Then he has returned to the underlying main theme of the whole epistle, the acceptance of the sinner in God's own one way; and we have seen how, from Israel's own point of view, Israel has stumbled and fallen just by his own fault. Israel would not rest upon 'the Stone of stumbling'; he would collide with it. Divine sovereignty here or there—the heart of Jewish man, in its responsible personality, and wholly of itself, rebelled against a man-humbling salvation. And so all its religiousness, earnestness, and intensity, went for nothing in the quest for peace and purity. They really stumbled at the Stumbling Stone; which all the while lay ready to be their foundation and rest.

Paul cannot leave the subject, with its sadness, its lessons, and its hope. He must say more of his love and longing for Israel; and also more about this aspect of Israel's fall—this collision of man's will with the Lord's way of peace. And he will unfold the deep witness of the prophecies to the nature of that way, and to the reluctance of the Jewish heart to accept it. Moses shall come in with the law, and Isaiah with the Scriptures of the prophets; and we shall see how their Inspirer, all along from the first, indicated what should surely happen when a divine salvation should be presented to hearts filled with themselves.

V 1. *Brethren*, he begins, *the deliberate desire of my heart*, whatever discouragements may oppose it, *and my petition unto God for them, is salvationwards*. He is inevitably moved to this by the pathetic sight of their earnestness, misguided indeed, guiltily misguided, and utterly inadequate to earn the slightest merit; yet, to the eyes that watch it, something different from indifference or hypocrisy. He cannot see their real struggles and not long that they may reach the shore.

V 2. *For I bear them witness*, the witness of one who once was the example of the class, *that they have zeal of God*, an honest jealousy for his name, Word, and worship, *only not in the line of spiritual knowledge*. They have not seen all he is, all his Word means, all his worship implies. They are sure, and rightly sure, of many things about him; but they have not seen him. And so they have not despised themselves (Job 42.5, 6). And thus they are not in their own conviction, restricted to a salvation which must be altogether of him; which is not a contract with him, but an eternal gift from him.

What a solemn and heart-moving scene! There are now, and were then, those who would have surveyed it, and come away with the comfortable reflection that so much earnestness would surely somehow work out right in the end; no, that it was already sufficiently good in itself to secure these honest zealots a place in some comprehensive heaven. If there was ever an excuse for such thoughts, surely it was here. The 'zeal' was quite sincere. It was ready to suffer, as well as to strike. The zealot was not afraid of a world in arms. And he felt himself on fire not for evil, but for God, for the God of Abraham, of Moses, of the prophets, of the promise. Would not this do? Would not the lamentable rejection of Jesus which accompanied it be condoned as a tremendous but mere accident, while the 'zeal of God' remained as the substance and essence, of the spiritual state of the zealot? Surely a very large allowance would be made; to put it at the lowest terms.

Yet such was not the view of St Paul, himself once the most
honest and unbiased Jewish zealot in the world. He had seen
the Lord. And so he had seen himself. The deadly mixture of
motive which may underlie what nevertheless we may have to
call an honest hatred of the gospel had been shown to him in
the white light of Christ. In that light he had seen—what it
alone can fully show—the condemnableness of all sin, and the
hopelessness of self-salvation. From himself he reasons, and
rightly, to his fellow Jews. He knows, with a solemn sympathy,
how much they are in earnest. But his sympathy conceals no
false liberalism; it is not cheaply generous about the claims of
God. He does not think that because they are in earnest they
are saved. Their earnestness drives his heart to a deeper prayer
for their salvation.

V 3. *For knowing not the righteousness of our God,* his way of being
just, yet the Justifier, *and seeking to set up their own righteousness,* to
construct for themselves a claim which should 'stand in judgment', *they did not submit to the righteousness of our God,* when it
appeared before them, embodied in 'the Lord our Righteousness'.
They aspired to acceptance. God commanded them submit to it.
In their view, it was a matter of attainment; an ascent to a
difficult height, where the climber might glory in his success. As
God presented it, it was a matter of surrender, as when a patient
places himself helpless in a master-healer's hands, for a recovery
which will be due to those hands alone.

Alas for such ignorance in these earnest souls; for such a failure
in Israel to strike the true line of 'knowledge'! For it was a guilty
failure. The law had been indicating all the while that God's
revelation to them was not its own end, but one vast complex
means to guide man to a Redeemer who was both to satisfy every
example, and every oracle, and to supply 'the impossible of the
law' (8.3), by giving himself to be the believer's merit.

V 4. *For the law's end,* its goal, its final cause in the plan of
redemption, *is—Christ, unto righteousness,* to effect and secure this
wonderful acceptance, *for every one who believes.* Yes, he is no
arbitrary sequel to the law; he stands organically related to it.
And to this the law itself is witness, both by presenting a relentless and condemning standard as its only possible code of accept-

ance, and by mysteriously pointing the soul away from that code, in its quest for mercy, to something altogether different, both accessible and divine.

Vv 5–11. *For Moses writes down* thus *the righteousness* got *from the law, 'The man who does them, shall live in it'* (Lev. 18.5); it is a matter of personal action and personal meriting alone. So the code, feasible and good on the plane of national and social life, which is its lower field of action, is necessarily fatal to fallen man when the question lies between his conscience and the eternal Judge. *But the righteousness* got *from faith,* the acceptance received by surrendering trust, *thus speaks* (Deut. 30. 12–14)—in Moses's words indeed (and this is one main point in the reasoning, that he is witness), yet as it were with a deep and tender personal voice of its own; *'Say not in thy heart, Who shall ascend to the heaven?' that is, to bring down Christ,* by human efforts, by a climbing merit; *'or, Who shall descend into the abyss? that is, to bring up Christ from the dead'* as if his victorious sacrifice needed your supplement in order to gain its resurrection triumph. *But what does it say? 'Near thee is the utterance,* the explicit account of the Lord's willingness to bless the soul which casts itself on him, *in thy mouth,* to recite it, *and in thy heart',* to welcome it. And *this* message *is the utterance of faith,* the creed of acceptance by faith alone, *which we proclaim; that if you shall confess in your mouth Jesus as Lord,* as divine King and Master, *and shall believe in your heart* that God *raised him from the dead,* owning in the soul the glory of the resurrection, as revealing and sealing the triumph of the atonement, *you shall be saved. For with the heart faith is exercised, unto righteousness,* with acceptance for its result; *while with the mouth confession is made, unto salvation,* with present deliverance and final glory for its result, the moral sequel of a life which owns its Lord as all in all. *For the Scripture says* (Isa. 28.16), *'Everyone who believes on him shall not be ashamed',* shall never be disappointed; shall be 'kept, through faith, unto the salvation ready to be revealed in the last time' (1 Pet. 1 5).

Here we have crossed an area full of questions and mystery. We have to remember here also, as in previous places, that the Scripture is 'not a sun, but a lamp'. Much, very much, which this passage suggests as problem finds no answer here. We do not, and cannot, know what the words of Moses quoted from Deuteronomy meant to him. If Christ's words are to be taken as final, it is quite certain that 'Moses wrote of him' (John 5.46). But it is not certain that he always knew he was so writing when he so wrote; nor is it certain how far his consciousness went when it was most awake that way. In the passage here cited by St Paul, Moses may have been aware only of a reference of his words to the seen, the temporal, the national, to the blessings of loyalty to Israel's God-given political organization, and of a return to it after times of revolt and decline. But then, St Paul neither affirms this nor denies it. As if on purpose, he almost drops the personality of Moses out of sight, and personifies justification as the speaker. His concern is less with the prophet than with his Inspirer, the ultimate Author behind the immediate author. And his own prophet-insight is guided to see that in the thought of that Author, as he moved Moses's mind and diction at his will, Christ was the inmost reference of the words.

We may ask again what are the laws by which Paul modifies Moses' phrases here. 'Who shall descend into the abyss?' The Hebrew reads, 'Who shall go over (or on) the sea?' The Greek Old Testament reads, 'Who shall go to the other side of the sea?' Here too 'we know in part'. Undoubtedly the change of terms was neither unconsciously nor arbitrarily made; and it was made for readers who could challenge it, if it seemed to them to be done in either way. But we should need to know the whole relation of the One inspiring Master to the minds of both his prophet and his apostle to answer the question completely. However, we can see that prophet and apostle both have in their thought here the contrast of depth to height; that the sea is, to Moses here, the antithesis to the sky, not to the land; and that St Paul intensifies the imagery in its true direction accordingly when he writes, 'into the abyss'.

Again, he finds justification by faith in Moses' words about the subjective 'nearness' of 'the utterance' of mercy. Once more we admit our ignorance of the conscious intention of the words, as Moses' words. We shall quite decline, if we are reverently cautious, to say that for certain Moses was not aware of such an inmost reference in what he said; it is very much easier to assert than to know what the limitations of the consciousness of the prophets were. But here also we rest in the fact that behind both Moses and Paul, in their free and mighty personalities, stood their one Lord, building his Scripture slowly into its varied oneness through them both. He was in the thought and word of Moses; and meantime the thought and word of Paul was already present to him, and was in his plan. And the earlier utterance had this at least to do with the later, that it drew the mind of the meditating and worshipping Israel to the idea of a contact with God in his promises which was not external and mechanical but deep within the individual himself, and manifested in the individual's free and living acknowledgment of it.

As we leave the passage, let us mark and cherish its insistence upon 'confession', 'confession with the mouth that Jesus is Lord'. This Paul particularly connects with 'salvation', with the believer's preservation to eternal glory. 'Faith' is 'unto righteousness'; 'confession' is 'unto salvation'. Why is this? Is faith after all not enough for our union with the Lord, and for our safety in him? Must we bring in something else? If this is what he means, he is contradicting the whole argument of the epistle. No; it is eternally true that we are justified, accepted, incorporated, and kept, through faith only; that is, that Christ is all for all things in our salvation, and our part and work in the matter is to receive and hold him in an empty hand. But then this empty hand, holding him, receives life and power from him. The believer is rescued so that he may live and serve. He cannot truly serve without loyalty to his Lord. He cannot be truly loyal while he hides his relation to him. In some clear way he must 'confess him'; or he is not treading the path where the Shepherd walks before the sheep.

The 'confession with the mouth' here in view is, surely, nothing less than the believer's open loyalty to Christ. It is not a recitation of the Creed. It is the witness of the whole man to Christ, as his own discovered life and Lord. And thus it means in effect the path of faithfulness along which the Saviour actually leads to glory those who are justified by faith.

That no slackened emphasis on faith is to be felt here is clear from verse 11. There, in the summary and close of the passage, nothing but faith is named, 'whosoever believeth on him'. It is as if he would correct even the slightest uneasy thought that our repose upon the Lord has to be secured by something other than himself, through some means more complex than taking him at his word. Here, as much as anywhere in the epistle, this is the message; 'from faith to faith'. The 'confession with the mouth' is not a different something added to this faith; it is its result, its manifestation, its embodiment. 'I believed; therefore have I spoken' (Ps. 116.10).

This return to his great theme gives the apostle's thought a direction once again towards the truth of the world-wide scope of the gospel of acceptance. In the middle of this section of the epistle, on his way to say glorious things about abiding mercy and coming blessings for the Jews, he must pause again to assert the equal welcome of 'the Greeks' to the righteousness of God, and the foreshadowing of this welcome in the prophets.

Vv 12–13. *For there is no distinction between Jew and Greek* (a wonderful contrast to the 'no distinction' of 3.23!). *For the same Lord is Lord of all, wealthy to all who call upon him,* who invoke him, who appeal to him, in the name of his own mercies in his redeeming Son. *For* we have the prophecies with us here again. Joel, in a passage (2.32) full of Messiah, the passage with which the Spirit of Pentecost filled Peter's lips, speaks thus without a limit; '*Every one, whoever shall call upon the Lord's name, shall be saved.*' As Paul cites the words, and the thought of this immense welcome to the sinful world comes to him, he feels once more all the need of the heathen, and all the cruel narrowness of the Pharisaism which would shut them out from such blessing.

Vv 14–15. *How then can they call on him on whom they never believed? But how can they believe on him whom they never heard? But how can they hear him apart from a proclaimer? But how can they proclaim unless they are sent,* unless the Church which holds the sacred light sends her messengers out into the darkness? And in this again the prophets are with the Christian apostle, and against the loveless Judaist: *As it stands written* (Isa. 52.7), '*How fair the feet of the gospellers of peace, of the gospellers of good!*'

Here, as an incident in this deep discussion, is given for ever to the Church of Christ one of the most distinct and compelling

of her missionary 'marching-orders'. Let us think on this, forgetting for a while the problem of Israel and the exclusiveness of
ancient Pharisaism. What is there here for us? What motive facts
are here, ready to energize and direct the will of the Christian,
and of the Church, in the matter of the 'gospelling' of the world?

We take note first of what is written last, the moral beauty and
glory of the enterprise: 'How fair the feet!' From the viewpoint of
heaven there is nothing on the earth more lovely than the bearing
of the name of Jesus Christ into the needy world, when the bearer
is one 'who loves and knows'. The work may have, and probably
will have, very little of the rainbow of romance about it. It
will often lead the worker into the most difficult and trying
circumstances. He will often be tempted to think 'the journey
too great for him', and long to let his tired and heavy feet rest
for ever. But his Lord is saying of him, all the while, 'How fair
the feet!' He is doing a work whose inmost conditions even now
are full of moral glory, and whose eternal results, perhaps where
he thinks there has been most failure, shall be, by grace, worthy
of 'the King in his beauty'. It is the continuation of what the
King himself 'began to do' (Acts 1.1), when he was his own first
missionary to a world which needed him immeasurably, yet did
not know him when he came.

Secondly, this paragraph asserts the necessity of the missionary's work still more urgently than its beauty. True, it suggests
many questions (what great Scripture does not do so?) which we
cannot answer yet at all:—'Why has God left the Gentiles in this
situation? Why is so much, for their salvation, suspended (in our
view) upon the too precarious and too lingering diligence of the
Church? What will the King say at last to those who never could,
through the Church's fault, even hear the blessed name, that
they might believe in it, and call upon it?' He knows the whole
answer to such questions; not we. But it has been revealed to us
that in the Lord's normal order, which is for certain the order
of eternal spiritual right and love, however little we can see all
the conditions of the case, man is to be saved through a personal
'calling upon his name'. And for that 'calling' there is need of
personal believing. And for that believing there is need of personal hearing. And for that hearing, God does not speak from

the sky, nor send visible angels up and down the earth, but commands his Church, his children, to go and tell.

Nothing can be stronger and surer than the practical logic of this passage. The need of the world, it says to us, is not only improvement or evolution. It is salvation. It is pardon, acceptance, holiness, and heaven. It is God; it is Christ. The work is to be done now, in the name of Jesus Christ, and by his name. And his name, in order to be known, has to be announced and explained. And that work is to be done by those who already know it, or it will not be done at all. 'There is none other name.' There is no other method of evangelization.

Why is not the name of Christ already at least externally known and reverenced in every place of human dwelling? It would have been so, for a long time now, if the Church of Christ had followed better the teaching and the example of St Paul. Had the apostolic missions been sustained more adequately throughout Christian history, and had the apostolic gospel been better maintained in the Church in all the energy of its divine simplicity and fullness, the globe would have been covered — not indeed in a hurry, yet ages ago now — with the knowledge of Jesus Christ as Fact, Truth and Life.

But Paul anticipates an objection from facts to his burning plea for the rightness of an unrestrained evangelism. The proclamation might be universal; but were not the results partial, even when a Paul, a Barnabas, a Peter, was the missionary? Everywhere some faith; but everywhere more hostility, and still more indifference! Could this, after all, be the main track of the divine purposes — these often ineffectual excursions of the 'fair feet' of the messengers of an eternal peace? Ah, that objection must have offered no mere logical difficulty to St Paul; it must have pierced his heart. For while his Master was his first motive, his fellow-men themselves were his second. He loved their souls; he longed to see them blessed and saved in Christ. The man who shed tears over his converts as he warned them (Acts 20.31) had tears also, we may be sure, for those who would not be converted (see Phil. 3.18). But here too he leans back on the solemn comfort, that prophecy had taken account of this beforehand. Moses, and Isaiah, and David, had foretold on the one hand a universal message of good, but on the other hand a sorrowfully limited response from man, and notably from Israel. So he proceeds:

Vv 16–17. *But not all obeyed the good tidings*, when the word reached them; *for*—we were prepared for such a mystery, such a grief—*for Isaiah says* (53.1), in his great oracle of the Crucified, *'Lord, who believed our hearing'*, the message they heard of us, about One 'on whom were laid the iniquities of us all'? And as he dictates that word 'hearing', it emphasizes to him the fact that it is not mystic intuitions born out of the depths of man that are the means of revelation, but clear messages given from the depths of God, and spoken by men to men. And he throws the thought into a brief sentence, like a footnote in a modern book: *So we gather that faith* comes *from hearing; but the hearing* comes *through Christ's utterance*; the messenger has it because it was first given to him by the Master who proclaimed himself to be the Way, Truth, Life, Light, Bread, Shepherd, Ransom and Lord. All is revelation, not reverie; utterance, not insight.

Vv 18–21. Then the swift thought turns, and returns again. The prophecies *have* foretold an evangelical utterance to the whole human world. They not only do so in explicit prediction but also in their more remote allusions. *But I say, Did they not hear?* Was this failure of belief due to a limitation of the messenger's range in the plan of God? *No, rather, 'Unto all the earth went out their tone, and to the ends of man's world their utterances'* (Ps. 19.4). The words are the voice of the Psalm where the glories of the visible heavens are put with the glories of the Word of God. The apostle hears more than nature in the Psalm; he hears grace and the gospel in the deep harmony which carries the immortal melody along. The God who meant the skies, with their 'silent voices', to preach a Creator not to one race but to all, also meant his Word to preach a Redeemer for all. Yes, and there were clear predictions that it should be so, as well as starry parables; predictions too that showed the prospect not only of a world that had been evangelized, but of an Israel put to shame by the faith of pagans. *But I say* (his rapid phrase meets with an anticipating answer the objection so far unspoken) *did not Israel know?* Had they no distinct forewarning of what we see today? *First comes Moses,*

saying, in his prophetic song, sung at the foot of Mount Pisgah
(Deut. 32.21), *I*—the 'I' is emphatic; the Person is the Lord, and
the action shall be nothing less than his—*I will take a no-nation to
move your jealousy; to move your anger I will take a nation non-intelligent*;
a race not only not informed by a previous revelation, but not
trained by thinking about it to an insight into new truth. And
what Moses indicates, Isaiah, standing later in the history, indig-
nantly explains: *But Isaiah dares anything and says (65.1), 'I was
found by those who sought not me; manifest I became to those who consulted
not me'. But as to Israel he says* in the words that follow (65.2), *'All
the day long I spread my hands open,* to beckon and to embrace,
towards a people disobeying and contradicting.'

So the servant brings his sorrows for consolation to—may we
write the words in reverence?—the sorrows of his Master. He
mourns over an Athens, an Ephesus, and above all over a Jerusalem, that 'will not come to the Son of God, that they might
have life' (John 5.40). And his grief is not only inevitable; it is
profoundly right, wise, holy. But he need not bear it unrelieved.
He grasps the Scripture which tells him that his Lord has called
those who would not come, and opened the eternal arms for an
embrace—to be met only with a contradiction. He weeps, but it
is as on the breast of Jesus as he wept over Jerusalem. And in
the double certainty that the Lord has felt such grief, and that
he is the Lord, he yields, he rests, he is still. 'The King of the
Ages' (1 Tim. 1.17) and 'the Man of Sorrows' are one. To know
him is to be at peace even under the griefs of the mystery of sin.

CHAPTER 22

Israel However not Forsaken (11.1–10)

'A people disobeying and contradicting.' So the Lord of Israel, through the prophet, had described the nation. Let us remember as we pass on what a major feature in the prophecies, and indeed in the whole Old Testament, such accusations and exposures are. From Moses to Malachi, in histories, and songs, and instructions, we find everywhere this tone of stern truth-telling, this unsparing detection and description of Israelite sin. And we reflect that every one of these utterances, humanly speaking, was the voice of an Israelite; and that whatever reception it met with at the time—it was sometimes a scornful or angry reception, more often a reverent one—it was ultimately treasured, venerated, almost worshipped, by the religious establishment of this same rebuked and humiliated Israel. We ask ourselves what this has to say about the true origin of these statements, and the true nature of the environment into which they fell. Do they not bear witness to the supernatural in both? It was not 'human nature' which, in a race quite as prone, at least, as any other, to assert itself, produced these intense and persistent rebukes from within, and secured for them a profound and lasting veneration. The Hebrew Scriptures, in this as in other things, are a literature which mere man, mere Israelite man, could not have written if he would, and would not have written if he could. Somehow, the prophets not only spoke with an authority more than human, but they were known to speak with it. There was a national consciousness of divine privilege; and it was inextricably bound up with a national conviction that the Lord of the privileges had an eternal right to reprove his privileged ones, and that he had, as a fact, his accredited messengers of reproof, whose voice was not theirs but his. It was not just the outcry of patriotic zealots, but the Oracle of God. Yes, an awful privilege was involved in the reception of such reproofs: 'You only have I known; therefore will I punish you' (Amos 3.2).

But this is a recollection by the way. St Paul, as we saw in our last study, has quoted Isaiah's stern message, only now to comfort his troubled heart with the fact that the unbelief of Israel in his day was, if we may dare to put it so, no surprise to the Lord, and therefore no shock to the servant's faith. But is he to stop there, and sit down, and say, 'This must be so'? No; there is more to follow, in this discourse on Israel and God. He has 'good words, and comfortable words' (Zech. 1.13), after the woes of the last two chapters, and after those earlier passages of the epistle where the Jew is seen only in his hypocrisy, rebellion, and pride. Paul has to speak of a faithful remnant, now as always present, who make as it were the golden unbroken link between the nation and the promises. And then he has to lift at least a corner of the curtain from the future, and to indicate how there is there a might blessing for Israel, and through Israel for the world. Even now they were serving a spiritual purpose in their very unbelief; they were occasioning a vast transfer of blessing to the Gentiles, by their own refusal of blessing. And hereafter they were to serve a still greater purpose. They were yet, in their crowds, to return to their rejected Christ. And their return was to be used as the means of a crisis of blessing for the world.

We seem to see the look and hear the voice of the apostle, once a mighty Rabbi and the persecuting patriot, as he starts to dictate again. His eyes brighten, and his brow clears, and a happier emphasis comes into his words, as he sets himself to speak of his people's good, and to remind his Gentile colleagues how, in God's plan of redemption, all their blessing, all they know of salvation, all they possess of life eternal, has come to them through Israel. Israel is the stem, drawing truth and life from the unfathomable soil of the covenant of promise. They are the grafted branches, rich in every blessing—because they are the mystical seed of Abraham, in Christ.

Vv 1–6. *I say therefore, Did God ever thrust away his people? Away with the thought! For I am an Israelite, of Abraham's seed, Benjamin's tribe;* a full member of the race ruled by God, and of its first royal and always loyal tribe; in my own person, therefore, I am an instance of Israel still in covenant. *God never thrust away his people, whom he foreknew* with the foreknowledge of eternal choice and purpose. That foreknowledge was not according to their works or power; and so it holds its sovereign way across and above their long unworthiness. *Or do you not know, in Elijah,* in his story, *what the Scripture says? How he intercedes before God,* on God's own behalf, *against Israel, saying* (1 Kgs 19.10), *'Lord, thy prophets they killed, and thy altars they dug up; and I was left solitary, and they seek my life'? But what says the oracular answer to him? 'I have left for myself seven thousand men, men who never bowed a knee to Baal'* (1 Kgs 19.18). *So therefore at the present season also there proves to be a remnant,* 'a leaving' left by the Lord for himself, *on the principle of election of grace;* their persons and their number following a choice and gift whose reasons lie in God alone. And then follows one of those character- istic footnotes of which we saw an instance above (10.17): *But if by grace, no longer of works;* 'no longer', in the sense of a logical succession and exclusion; *since the grace proves,* on the other prin- ciple, *no longer grace. But if of works, it is no longer grace; since the work is no longer work.* That is to say, when once the principle of grace is admitted, as it is here assumed to be, 'the work' of the man who is its subject is 'no longer work' in the sense which makes a contrast with grace; it is no longer so much work done for so much pay. In other words, the two supposed principles of the divine choice are in their nature mutually exclusive. Admit the one as the condition of the 'election', and the other ceases; you cannot combine them. If the election is of grace, no previous merit to it is possible in the subject of it. If it is according to previous merit, no sovereign freedom is possible in the divine action. No freedom to bring the saved man, the saved remnant, to an adoring confession of inexpressible and mysterious mercy.

This is the point, here in this passing footnote, as in the longer similar statements above (ch. 9), of the emphasized allusion to 'choice' and 'grace'. He writes in this way so as to bring the believer, Gentile or Jew, to his knees in humility, wonder, grati- tude, and trust. 'Why did I, the self-ruined wanderer, the self- hardened rebel, come to the Shepherd who sought me, surrender my sword to the King who reclaimed me? Did I reason myself into harmony with him? Did I lift myself, hopelessly maimed, into his arms? No; it was the gift of God; from first to last. And if so, it was the choice of God.' That point of light is surrounded by a cloud-world of mystery, though within those surrounding clouds there lurks, as far as God is concerned, only rightness and love. But the point of light is there, despite the clouds; where fallen man chooses God, it is thanks to God who has chosen fallen man. Where a race is not 'thrust away', it is because 'God foreknew'. Where some thousands of members of that race, while others fall away, are found faithful to God, it is because he has 'left them for himself, on the principle of choice of grace'. Where, in the middle of a widespread rejection of God's Son Incarnate, a Saul of Tarsus, an Aquila, a Barnabas, behold in him their Redeemer, King, Life, and All, it is on that same principle. Let the man who sees and believes in this way give the whole thanks for his salvation in the quarter where it is all due. Let him not confuse one truth by another. Let not this truth disturb for a moment his certainty of personal moral freedom, and of its responsibility. Let it not for a moment turn him into a fatalist. But let him abase himself, and give thanks, and humbly trust the One who has laid hold of him for blessing in this way. As he does so, in simplicity, not speculating but worshipping, he will need no subtle logic to assure him that he is to pray, and to work, without reserve, for the salvation of all men. It will be more than enough for him that his Sovereign commands him to do it, and tells him that it is according to his will.

To retrace our steps a little, in the matter of the apostle's doctrine of the divine choice: the reference in this paragraph to the seven thousand faithful in Elijah's day suggests a special reflection. To us, it seems to say distinctly that the choice or 'election' intended all along by St Paul cannot possibly be explained adequately by making it either an election (to whatever benefits) of mere masses of men, as for instance of a nation, considered apart from its individuals; or an election merely to privilege, or opportunity, which may or may not be used by the receiver. As regards national election, it is undoubtedly present and even prominent in the passage, and in this whole section of the epistle. For ourselves, we tend to see it quite simply in verse 2 above; 'His people, whom he foreknew'. We read there, what we find so often in the Old Testament, a sovereign choice of a nation to stand in special relation to God; of a nation taken, so to speak, in the abstract, viewed not as the mere total of so many individuals, but as a kind of personality. But we maintain that the idea of election takes another line when we come to the 'seven thousand'. Here we are thrown at once on the thought of individual experiences, and the ultimate secret of them, found only in the divine Will affecting the individual. The 'seven thousand' formed no organism or quasi-personality. They were 'left' not as a mass, but as units; so isolated, so little grouped together, that even Elijah did not know of their existence. They were just so many individual men, each one of whom found power, by faith, to stand personally firm against the Baalism of that dark time, with the same individual faith which in later days, against other terrors, and other temptations, upheld Christians. And the apostle quotes them as an instance and illustration of the Lord's way and will with the believing of all time. In their case, then, he both passes as it were through national election to individual election, as a permanent spiritual mystery; and he shows that he means by this an election not only to opportunity but to holiness. The Lord's 'leaving them for himself' lay behind their not bowing their knees to Baal. Each resolute confessor was individually enabled, by a sovereign and special grace. He was a true human personality, freely acting, freely choosing not to yield in that terrible storm. But behind his freedom was the higher freedom of the Will of God, saving him from himself that he might be free to confess and suffer. To our mind, no part of the epistle more clearly than this passage affirms this individual aspect of the great mystery. It is truly a mystery; we have admitted this at every step. And it is never for a moment to be treated therefore as if we knew all about it. And it is never therefore to be used to confuse the believer's thought about other sides of truth. But it is there, as a truth among truths; to be received with humility by the creature before the Creator, and with humble hope by the simple believer.

Paul goes on with his argument, taking up the thread broken by the footnote upon grace and works:

Vv 7–10. *What therefore? What Israel*, the nation, the character, *seeks after*, righteousness in the court of God, *this is lighted not upon*, as one who seeks a buried treasure in the wrong field 'lights not upon' it; *but the election*, the chosen ones, the 'seven thousand' of the gospel era, *did light upon it. But the rest were hardened* (not as if God had created their hardness, or injected it; but he gave it to be its own penalty) *as it stands written* (Isa. 29.10, and Deut. 29.4), '*God gave them a spirit of slumber, eyes not to see, and ears not to hear, even to this day*'. A persistent ('unto this day') unbelief was the sin of Israel in the prophets' times, and it was the same in those of the apostles. And the condition was the same; God 'gave' sin to be its own way of retribution. *And David says* (Ps. 69.22), in a Psalm full of Messiah, and of the awful retribution justly ordained to come on his impenitent enemies, '*Let their table turn into a trap, and into toils, and into a stumblingblock, and into a requital to them; darkened be their eyes, not to see, and their back ever bow thou together.*'

The words are awful, in their context here, and in themselves, and as an example of a class. Their purpose here is to enforce the thought that there is such a thing as positive divine action in the self-ruin of the impenitent. Not one word implies the thought that he who acts in this way meets a soul tending upwards and turns it downwards; that he ignores or rejects even the faintest enquiry after himself; that he is author of one scrap of the sin of man. But we do learn that the enemies of God and Christ may be, and, where the Eternal so sees it good, are sentenced to go their own way, even to its results in destruction. The context of every citation here, as it stands in the Old Testament, clearly shows that those so sentenced are no helpless victims of an adverse fate, but sinners of their own will, in a most definite and personal sense.

But then also in themselves, and as an example of a class, the words are a dark shadow over Scripture. It is only by the way that we can note this here, but it must not be quite omitted in our study. Psalm 69 is a leading instance of the several Psalms where the prophet appears calling for the sternest retribution on his enemies. What thoughtful heart has not felt the painful mystery here? Read in private, or chanted in church, they still tend to upset us with the question, Can this possibly be according to the mind of Christ, who when crucified prayed, 'Father, forgive them; for they know not what they do'? Can these curses have his sanction? Can he endorse them as his Word?

This is a pressing and painful question to which no complete answer can be given. Let us note that this same dark Psalm is, by the witness of the apostles, as taught by their Master, a Psalm full of Messiah. It was undoubtedly claimed as his own by the Lamb of the Passion. He who speaks in these dreadful words also says, in the same statement (verse 9), 'The zeal of thine house hath eaten me up'. So the Lord Jesus did endorse this Psalm. He more than endorsed it; he adopted it as his own. Let this remind us further that the speaker of these denunciations, even the first and non-mystical one — David, let us say — appears in the Psalm not merely as a private person crying out about his violated personal rights, but as an ally and servant of God, one whose life and cause is identified with his. In proportion as this is so, the violation of his life and peace, by enemies described as quite consciously and deliberately malicious, is a violation of the whole sanctuary of divine righteousness. If so, is it incredible that even the darkest words of such a Psalm are to be read as a true echo from the depths of man to the Voice which announces 'indignation and wrath, tribulation and anguish, to every soul of man that doeth evil'? Perhaps even the most watchful assertor of the divine character of Scripture is not bound to assert that no human weakness in the least moved the spirit of a David when he, in the sphere of his own personality, thought and said these things. But we have no right to assert, as a known or necessary thing, that it was so. And we have right to say that in themselves these sayings are only a sternly true response to the avenging indignation of the Holy One.

In any case, do not let us talk easily and loosely about their incompatability with the spirit of the New Testament. From one side, the New Testament is an even sterner book than the Old; as it must be of course, when it brings sin and holiness out into the light of the cross of Christ. It is in the New Testament that, 'the souls' of saints at rest are heard saying 'How long, O Lord, holy and true, dost thou not judge and avenge our blood on them that dwell on the earth?' (Rev. 6.10). It is in the New Testament that an apostle writes, 'It is a righteous thing with God to recompense tribulation to them which trouble you' (2 Thess. 1.6). It is the Lord of the New Testament, the offerer of the prayer of the cross, who said 'Fill ye up the measure of your fathers. I send unto you prophets, and wise men, and scribes, and some of them ye shall kill and crucify; that upon you may come all the righteous blood shed upon the earth' (Matt. 23.32–35).

Christ's eyes must have often rested on the denunciations of the Psalms. He saw in them that which struck no real discord, in the ultimate spiritual depth, with his own blessed compassions. Let us not resent what he has countersigned. It is his, not ours, to know all the conditions of those mysterious outbursts from the Psalmists' consciousness. It is ours to recognize in them the intensest expression of what rebellious evil merits, and will find, as its reward.

But we have digressed from the proper matter before us. Here, in the epistle, Psalm 69 is cited only to affirm with the authority of Scripture the mystery of God's action in sentencing the impenitent adversaries of his Christ to more blindness and ruin. Through this dark and narrow door the apostle is about to lead us now into a large room of hope and blessing, and to unveil to us a wonderful future for the now disgraced and seemingly rejected Israel.

CHAPTER 23

Israel's Fall Overruled, for the World's Blessing, and for Israel's Mercy (11.11–24)

The apostle has been led a few steps backwards in the last few verses. His face has been turned once more toward the dark region of the prophetic sky, to see how the sin of Christ-rejecting souls is met and punished by the dreadful 'gift' of sleep, and apathy, and the changing of blessings into snares. But now he points our eyes, with his own, to the morning light of grace and promise. We are to see what Israel's fall has had to do with the world's hope and with life in Christ, and then what blessings await Israel himself, and again the world through him.

V 11. *I say, therefore* (the phrase takes up the point of view to which the same words in verse 1 led us), *did they stumble that they might fall?* Did their national rejection of an unwelcome because unworldly Messiah take place, in the divine permission, with the positive divine purpose that it should bring on a final rejection of the nation, its banishment from its place in the history of redemption? *Away with the thought! But their partial fall is the occasion of God's salvation for the Gentiles, with a view to move them*, the Jews, *to jealousy*, to awake them to a sight of what Christ is, and of what their privilege in him might yet be, by the sight of his work and glory in lives that were once pagan.

Note here the divine blessing which lurks even under the edges of the cloud of judgment. And note too, close to the passage which has put before us the mysterious side of divine action on human wills, the daylight simplicity of this side of that action; the loving skill with which the world's blessing is meant by the God of grace to act upon the will of Israel.

But would that 'the Gentiles' had taken more notice of that last short sentence of St Paul's. It is one of the most marked, as it is one of the saddest, phenomena in the history of the Church that for ages, almost from the days of St John himself, we look in vain either for any appreciable Jewish element in Christendom, or for any extended effort on the part of Christendom to win Jewish hearts to Christ by a wise and loving evangelization. With only relatively insignificant exceptions this was the abiding state of things till well within the eighteenth century, when the German Pietists began to call the attention of believing Christians to the spiritual needs and prophetic hopes of Israel, and to remind them that the Jews were not only a beacon of judgment, or only the most impressive and awful illustration of the fulfilment of prophecy, but the bearers of still unfulfilled predictions of mercy for themselves and for the world. Meanwhile, all through the Middle Age, and through generations before and after, Christendom did little for Israel but retaliate, reproach, and tyrannize.

No doubt there is more than one side to the persistent phenomenon. There is a side of mystery; the permissive sentence of the Eternal has to do with the long affliction, however caused, of the people which once uttered the fatal cry, 'His blood be on us, and on our children' (Matt. 27.25). And the wrong-doings of Jews, beyond a doubt, have often made an opportunity for anti-Semitism on a larger or smaller scale. But all this leaves unaltered, from the point of view of the gospel, the sin of Christendom in its tremendous failure to seek, in love, the good of erring Israel. It leaves as black as ever the guilt of every fierce retaliation upon Jews by so-called Christians, of every slanderous belief about Jewish creed or life, of every unjust anti-Jewish law ever passed by Christian king or senate. It leaves an undiminished responsibility upon the church of Christ, not only for the flagrant wrong of having too often animated and directed the civil power in its oppressions of Israel, and not only for having so awfully neglected to seek the evangelization of Israel by direct appeals for the true Messiah, and by an open setting forth of his glory, but for the deeper and more subtle wrong, persistently inflicted from age to age, in a most guilty unconsciousness—the wrong of having failed to show Christ to Israel through the living holiness of Christendom. Here, surely, is the very point of Paul's thought in the sentence before us: 'Salvation to the Gentiles, to move the Jews to jealousy'. In his inspired idea, Gentile Christendom, in Christ, was to be so pure, generous, and happy, clearly finding in its Messianic Lord such resources for both peace of conscience and a life of noble love, a love above all directed towards opponents and slanderers, that Israel, looking on, with eyes however blinded with prejudice, should soon see a moral glory in the Church's face that was impossible to hide, and be drawn as by a moral magnet to the Church's hope. Is it the fault of God (may he pardon the question, if it is irreverent), or the fault of man, man carrying the Christian name, that facts have been so different in the course of history? It is the fault of us Christians. The narrow prejudice, the unjust law, the rigid application of exaggerated church principle; all these things have been man's perversion of the divine idea, to be confessed, deplored and repented. May the mercy of God awaken Gentile Christendom, in a manner and degree not yet known, to remember our permanent debt to this people everywhere present with us, but everywhere distinct from us; the debt of a life, personal and ecclesiastical, so clearly pure and loving in our Lord the Christ as to 'move them to the jealousy' which shall claim him again for their own. Then we shall truly be hastening the day of full and final blessing, both for themselves and for the world.

Vv 12–14. The apostle points us now, to that bright coming day more directly than ever: *But if their partial fall be the world's wealth, and their lessening* their reduction (a reduction in one aspect to a race of scattered exiles, in another to a mere remnant of true Israelites), *be the Gentiles' wealth*, the occasion by which 'the unsearchable wealth of Messiah' (Eph. 3.8) has been as it were forced into Gentile receptacles, *how much more their fulness*, the filling of the dry channel with its ample ideal stream, the change from a believing remnant, fragments of a fragmentary people, to a believing nation, reanimated and reunited? What blessings for the world, for the Gentiles, may not come through such an Israel? *But to you I speak, the Gentiles*; to you, because if I reach the Jews, in the way I mean, it must be through you. *So far indeed as I, distinctively I, am the Gentiles' apostle, I glorify my ministry* as such; I rejoice, Pharisee that I once was, to be devoted as no other apostle is to a ministry for those whom I once thought of as of outcasts in religion. But I speak as your own apostle, and to you, *if perchance I may move the jealousy of my flesh and blood and may save some from amongst them*, by letting them as it were overhear what are the blessings of you Gentile Christians, and how it is the Lord's purpose to use those blessings as a magnet to wandering Israel. Paul's hope is that, through the Roman congregation, this glorious open secret will come out, as they meet their Jewish neighbours and talk with them. So one here, and another there, would be drawn to the feet of Jesus, 'jealousy' which means little else than the human longing to understand what is evidently the great joy of another's heart; a 'jealousy' on which often grace can fall, and use it to bring divine light and life.

He says only, 'some of them'; as he does in 1 Corinthians 9.22 (see also, 2 Cor. 3.14–16.) He recognizes it as his present task, indicated both by circumstance and revelation, not to be the glad ingatherer of vast crowds to Christ, but the patient winner of scattered sheep. Yet let us note that none the less he spends his whole soul upon that winning, and takes no excuse from a glorious future to slacken a single effort in the difficult present.

V 15. *For if the throwing away of them*, their downfall as the Church of God, was *the world's reconciliation*, the instrumental or occasioning cause of the direct proclamation to the pagan peoples of the atonement of the cross, *what* will *their reception be, but life from the dead?* That is to say, the great event of Israel's return to God in Christ, and his to Israel, will be the signal and the means of a vast rise of spiritual life in the universal Church, and of an unparalleled ingathering of renewed souls from the world. When Israel, as a Church, fell, the fall worked good for the world merely by driving, as it were, the apostolic preachers out from the synagogue, to which they so much longed to cling. The Jews did anything but help the work. Yet even so they were made an occasion for world-wide good. When they are 'received again', as this scripture so definitely affirms that they shall be received, the case will be greatly different. As before, they will be 'occasions'. A national and ecclesiastical return of Israel to Christ will of course give occasion over the whole world for a vastly revitalized attention to Christianity, and for an appeal for the world's faith in the facts and claims of Christianity, as bold and loud as that of Pentecost. But more than this; Israel will now be not only occasion but agent. The Jews, ubiquitous, cosmopolitan, yet invincibly national, coming back in living loyalty to the Son of David, the Son of God, will be a positive power in evangelization such as the Church has never yet felt. Whatever the actual facts shall prove to be in the matter of their return to the Promised Land, no prediction obliges us to think that the Jews will be withdrawn from the wide world by a national resettlement in their land. A nation is not a dispersion merely because it has individual citizens widely dispersed; if it has a true national centre, it is a people at home, a people with a home. Whether as a central mass in Syria, or as also a presence everywhere in the human world, Israel will thus be ready, once restored to God in Christ, to be a more than natural evangelizing power.

Now the argument takes a new direction. This restoration is not only sure to be infinitely beneficial. It is also to be looked for and expected as a thing that is true to the order of God's plan. In his will, when he went about to create and develop his Church, Israel sprung from the dry ground as the sacred olive, rich with the sap of truth and grace, full of branch and leaf. From the tents of Abraham onward, the world's true spiritual light and life was there. There, not elsewhere, was revelation, and God-given ordinance, the covenants, and the glory. There, not elsewhere, the Christ of God, for whom all things waited, towards whom all the lines of man's life and history converged, was to appear. Thus, in a certain profound sense, all true salvation must be not only 'of' Israel (John 4.24) but through him. Union with Christ was union with Abraham. To become a Christian, that is to say, one of Messiah's men, was to become, mystically, an Israelite. From this point of view the Gentile's union with the Saviour, though not in the least less genuine and divine than the Jew's, was, so to speak, less normal. And thus nothing could be more spiritually normal than the Jew's recovery to his old relation to God, from which he had violently dislocated himself. Paul now presses these thoughts on the Romans, as a new motive and guide to their hopes, prayers, and work. (Do we gather from the length and fullness of the argument that already it was difficult to bring Gentiles to think correctly about the chosen people in their fall and rebellion?) He reminds them of the inalienable consecration of Israel to special divine purposes. He points them to the ancient olive, and boldly tells them that they are, themselves, only a graft of a wild stock, inserted into the noble tree. Not that he thinks of the Jew as a superior being. But the Church of Israel was the original of the Christian Church. So the restoration of Israel to Christ, and to the Church, is a recovery of normal life, not a first and abnormal gift of life.

Vv 16–24. *But if the first-fruit was holy, holy is the kneaded lump too.* Abraham was as it were the Lord's first-fruits of mankind, in the field of his Church. 'Abraham's seed' are as it were the mass kneaded from that first-fruits; made of it. Was the first-fruits holy, in the sense of consecration to God's redeeming purpose? Then that which is made of it must somehow still be a consecrated thing, even though put aside for awhile as if 'common'. *And if the root was holy,* holy are *the branches too*; the descendants of Abraham are still, ideally, potentially, consecrated to him who separated Abraham to himself, and moved him to his great self-separation. *But if some of the branches* (how tender is the euphemism of the 'some'!) *were broken off, while you, wild-olive as you were, were grafted in among them,* in their place of life and growth, *and became a sharer of the root and of the Olive's fatness—do not boast over the torn-off branches. But if you do boast over them—not you carry the root, but the root carries you. You will say then, The branches were broken off— that I might be grafted in. Good:* true—and untrue: *because of their unbelief they were broken off, while you because of your faith stand.* They were no better beings than you, in themselves. But neither are you better than they, in yourself. They and you alike are, personally, only subjects of redeeming mercy; owing all to Christ; possessing all only in accepting Christ. 'Where is your boasting, then?' *Do not be high-minded, but fear,* fear yourself, your sin, your enemy. *For if God did not spare the natural branches, take care lest he spare not you either. See therefore God's goodness and sternness. On those who fell,* came his *sternness; but on you,* his *goodness, if you abide by that goodness,* with the grasp and response of faith; *since you too will be cut out* otherwise. *And they too, if they do not abide by their unbelief, shall be grafted in; for God is able to graft them in again. For if you*

*from the naturally wild olive were cut out, and non-naturally were grafted
into the Garden-Olive, how much more shall those, the* branches *naturally,
be grafted into their own Olive!*

There are several topics here that call for reverent notice and
study.

1. The imagery of the olive, with its root, stem, and branches.
The olive, rich and useful, long-lived, and evergreen, stands, as
a nature-parable of spiritual life, beside the vine, palm, and
cedar, in the garden of God. Sometimes it pictures the individual
saint, living and fruitful in union with his Lord (Ps. 52.8). Sometimes it sets before us the fertile organism of the Church, as here,
where the olive is the great universal Church in its long life
before and after the historical coming of Christ; the life which in
a certain sense began with the call of Abraham, and was only
magnificently developed by the incarnation and passion of
Christ. Its root, in this respect, is the great father of faith,
Abraham. Its stem is the Church of the Old Testament, which
coincided, in the matter of external privilege, with the nation of
Israel, and to which at least the immense majority of true
believers of that time belonged. Its branches (by a slight and
easy modification of the image) are its individual members,
whether Jewish or Gentile. The Master of the tree, arriving on
the scene in the gospel age, comes as it were to prune his olive,
and to graft. The Jewish 'branch', if he is what he seems, if he
truly believes, abides in the tree. Otherwise, he is—from the
divine point of view—broken off. The believing Gentile is grafted
in, and becomes a true part of the living organism; as genuinely
and vitally one with Abraham in life and blessing as his Hebrew
brother. But the fact of the Hebrew 'race' in root and stem makes
the re-ingrafting of a repenting Hebrew branch more 'natural'
(not more possible, or more beneficial, but more 'natural') than
the first ingrafting of a Gentile branch. The whole tree is permanently Abrahamic, or Israelite, in stock and growth; though all
mankind has a place now in its forest of branches.

2. The imagery of 'grafting'. Here is an instance of partial,
while truthful, use of a natural process in Scripture parable. In
our gardens and orchards it is the wild stock which receives, in
grafting, the 'good' branch; a fact which lends itself to many

fertile illustrations. Here, on the contrary, the 'wild' branch is inserted into the 'good' stock. But the olive-yard gives Paul all the imagery he really needs. He has before him, ready to hand, the tree of the Church; all that he wants is an illustration of communication and union of life by artificial insertion. And this he finds in the olive-dresser's art, which shows him how a strange graft can by human design be made to grow into the life of the tree, as if it came from the root.

3. The teaching of the passage about the place of Israel in the divine plan of life for the world. We have remarked on this already, but it needs to be noted again. God has dealt with man, and is dealing with him, in the training and development of his life and nature through many races and civilizations. But in the matter of man's spiritual salvation, in the gift to him, in his fall, of eternal life, God has dealt with man, in practice, through one race, Israel. From this point of view, the great Husbandman has planted not a forest but a tree; and the innumerable trees of the forest can get the sap of Eden only as their branches are grafted by his hand into his one tree, by the faith which unites them to him who is the Root below the root, the Root of David and Abraham.

4. The appeal to the newly grafted 'branch' to 'abide by the goodness of God'. We have listened, as St Paul has dictated to his scribe, to many deep words about a divine and sovereign power on man; about man's absolute debt to God for the fact that he believes and lives. Yet here, with equal decision, we have man thrown back on the thought of his responsibility, of the dependence in a certain sense of his safety on his faithfulness. 'If you are true to mercy, mercy will be true to you; otherwise you too will be broken off.' Here, as in our study of earlier passages, let us be willing to go all along with Scripture in the seeming inconsistency of its absolute promises and its conditional cautions. Let us, like it, go to both extremes; then we shall be as near, probably, as our finite thought can be at present to the whole truth as it is in God. Is the Christian worn and wearied with his experience of his own pollution, instability, and helplessness? Let him embrace, without a misgiving, the whole of the promise, 'My sheep shall never perish.' Has he drifted into a

vain confidence, not in Christ, but in privilege, experience, or apparent religious prosperity? Has he caught himself in the act of saying, even in a whisper, 'God, I thank Thee that I am not as other men are'? Then let him listen in time to the warning voice, 'Be not high-minded, but fear'; 'Take heed lest he spare not you.' And let him put no pillow of theory between the sharpness of that warning and his soul. Penitent, self-despairing, resting in Christ alone, let him 'abide by the goodness of God'.

CHAPTER 24

The Restoration of Israel Directly Foretold: All is of and For God (11.25–36)

So far St Paul has rather reasoned than predicted. He has shown his Gentile friends the naturalness, so to speak, of a restoration of Israel to Christ, and the undoubted certainty that such a restoration will bring blessing to the world. Now he advances to the direct assertion, made with a prophet's full authority, that it shall be so. 'How much rather shall they be grafted into their own Olive?' The question implies the assertion; nothing remains but to expand on it.

Vv 25–27. *For I would not have you ignorant, brethren, of this mystery*, this fact in God's purposes, impossible to be known without revelation, but luminous when revealed (*that you may not be wise in your own esteem*, valuing yourselves on an insight which is all the while only a partial glimpse); *that failure of perception, in a measure*, in the case of many, not all, of the nation, *has come upon Israel*, and will continue *until the fulness of the Gentiles shall come in*, until Gentile conversion shall be in some sense a flowing tide. *And so all Israel*, Israel as a mass, no longer as scattered units, *shall be saved*, coming to the feet of him in whom alone is man's salvation from judgment and from sin; *as it stands written* (Ps. 14.7, Isa. 59.20, with Isa. 27.9), '*There shall come from Sion the Deliverer; he shall turn away all impiety from Jacob; and such they shall find the covenant I shall have granted*, such shall prove to be my promise and provision, "ordered and sure", *when I shall take away their sins*', in the day of my pardoning and restoring return to them.

This is a memorable passage. In the first place it is one of the most definitely predictive of all the prophetic utterances of the epistles. Apart from all problems of explanation in detail, it gives us this as its general message: There lies hidden in the future, for the race of Israel, a critical period of overwhelming blessing. If anything is revealed as fixed in the eternal plan, which, never violating the creature's will is yet not subject to it, it is this. We have heard Paul speak fully, and without compromise, of the sin of Israel; the hardened or paralyzed spiritual perception, the refusal to submit to pure grace, the restless quest for a valid self-righteousness, the deep exclusive arrogance. And so the promise of coming mercy, which will surprise the world, sounds all the more sovereign and magnificent. It shall come; so says Christ's prophet Paul. Not because of historical precedents, or in the light of general principles, but because of the revelation of the Spirit, he speaks of that wonderful future as if it were in full view from the present; 'All Israel shall be saved'.

Paul mentions no dates or times. All we gather is that he sees in the future a great advance of Gentile Christianity; a great impression to be made by this on the mind of Israel; a vast and comparatively sudden awakening of Israel, by the grace of God, however brought to bear; the salvation of Israel in Christ on a national scale; 'the receiving of them again'; and 'life from the dead' as the result—life from the dead to the world at large. However late or soon, with whatever accompanying divine or human events, this is how it shall be.

'Believest thou the prophets?' The question, asked of Agrippa by St Paul, comes to us from this prediction of his own. 'Lord, we believe'. Our Master knows that for us, surrounded by materialism and fatalism, it is not easy. And one symptom of their evil influence is the growing tendency in the Church to limit, minimize, or explain if possible away, from the Scriptures, whatever is properly and distinctively superhuman. Some Christians seem to think far otherwise than their Lord thought about this very element of prediction in the Scripture, and would have us believe that it is no great thing to grasp, and to argue for. But as for us, we desire in all things to be of the opinion of him who is the eternal Truth and Light, and who took our nature, expressly, as to one great purpose, in order to clearly reveal his views to us. He lived and died in the light and power of predictive Scripture. He predicted. He rose again to commission his apostles, as the

Spirit should teach them, to see 'things to come' (John 16.13). To us, this prophecy gives faith and hope. We do not understand, but we believe, because it is written here, that after these days of the prevalence of unbelief, after all these questions, loud or half expressed, angry or agonizing, 'Where is the promise?' the world shall see a spiritual miracle on a scale unknown before. 'All Israel shall be saved.' Even so, Lord Jesus Christ, the Deliverer. Fill us with the patience of this hope, for your chosen race, and for the world.

Now for a brief but necessary look at some of the details of the passage.

1. 'Until the fulness of the Gentiles come in'. Does this mean that the stream of Gentile conversions shall have flowed and ceased, before the great blessing comes to Israel? Certainly the Greek may carry this meaning. But this interpretation would give the 'salvation' of Israel no influence of blessing upon the Gentile world, as implied in verses 12 and 15. This leads us to explain the phrase here to refer to a time when that process shall be, so to speak, running high. That time of great and obvious grace shall be the occasion to Israel of the shock, as it were, of blessing; and from Israel's blessing shall date further divine good for the world.

As we pass, let us note the light thrown by these sentences on the duty of the Church in evangelizing the Gentiles for the Jews, as well as the Jews for the Gentiles. Both holy enterprises are destined to have effect outside themselves. The evangelist of Africa, India, or China, is working for the hour of the 'salvation of all Israel'. The evangelist of the Jewish dispersion is preparing Israel for the hour of final blessing when the 'saved' nation shall, in the hand of God, kindle the world with holy life.

2. 'All Israel shall be saved'. It has been held by some interpreters that this points to the Israel of God, the spiritual sons of Abraham. If so, it would be fairly paraphrased as a promise that when the Gentile conversions are complete, and the 'spiritual failure of perception' gone from the Jewish heart, the family of faith shall be complete. But surely it does violence to words, and thought, to explain 'Israel' in this whole passage mystically. Interpretation becomes an arbitrary work if we may

suddenly do so here, where the contrast between Israel and the Gentiles is the very theme of the message. No; we have here the nation, chosen once to a mysterious vocation in the spiritual history of man, chosen with a choice never cancelled, however long suspended. A blessing is in view for the nation; a blessing that is spiritual, divine, all of grace, quite individual in its action on each member of the nation, but national in the scale of its results. We are not obliged to press the word 'all' to its literal sense. Nor are we obliged to limit the crisis of blessing to anything like a moment of time. But we may surely gather that the numbers blessed will be at least the vast majority, and that the work will not be chronic but critical. A relatively swift and wonderful transition shall show the world a nation penitent, faithful, holy, given to God.

3. The quotations from the Psalms and prophets (vv 26, 27) raise several questions. They are closely interlaced, and they are not literal quotations. Yet in both originals and quotations, the ruling thought is that 'the Deliverer' belongs primarily to 'Zion', and has in store primarily a blessing for her people.

Are we, like some interpreters, to explain the words, 'The Deliverer shall come out of Sion', as predicting a personal and visible return of the ascended Jesus to the literal Zion, for the salvation of Israel, and a glorious outgoing of him from there to the Dispersion, or the world? We will not discuss this and related questions in detail here. All we do now is to express the conviction that the prophetic quotations here cannot be held to predict *unmistakably* a visible and local return of Christ. If we read them correctly, they can be paraphrased like this: 'It stands predicted that to Zion, that is, to Israel, belongs the Deliverer of man, and that for Israel he is to do his work, whenever finally it is done, with a speciality of grace and glory'. Explained in this way, the 'shall come' of verse 26 is the abstract future of divine purpose. In the eternal plan, the Redeemer was, when he first came to earth, to come to, for, and from 'Zion'. And his saving work was to be on lines, and for results, characterized for ever by that fact.

There is no doubt that the Lord Jesus Christ is, personally, literally, visibly, and to his people's eternal joy, coming again; 'this same Jesus, in like manner' (Acts 1.11). And as the ages unfold themselves, undoubtedly the insight of the believing Church into the fullness and, if we may say so, the variety of that great prospect grows. But it still seems to us that a deep and reverent caution is called for before we attempt to treat any detail of that prospect, as regards time, season or mode, as if we quite knew. Across all lines of interpretation of unfulfilled prophecy—to name just one problem—it lies as an unsolved riddle how all the saints of all ages are equally commanded to watch, as those who 'know not what hour their Lord shall come'.

But let us more and more often, however we may differ in detail, recite to one another the glorious essence of our hope. 'To them that look for him will he appear the second time, without sin, unto salvation'; 'We shall meet the Lord in the air'; 'So shall we be ever with the Lord' (Heb. 9.28, 1 Thess. 4.17).

We shall never quite understand the chronology and process of unfulfilled prophecy, till then.

Now briefly and in summary the apostle concludes this 'epistle within the epistle'; this oracle about Israel.

Vv 28–29. *As regards the gospel,* from the point of view of the evangelization of the world apart from Judaism, the 'gospelling' which was, as it were, precipitated by the rebellion of Israel, *they are enemies, on account of you,* permitted, for your sakes, in a certain sense, to take a hostile attitude towards the Lord and his Christ, and to be treated accordingly; *but as regards the election,* from the point of view of the divine choice, *they are beloved, on account of the Fathers; for irrevocable are the gifts and the call of our God.* The 'gifts' of unmerited choice, of a love uncaused by the goodness of its object, but coming from the depth of the Eternal; the 'call' which not only invites the creature, but achieves the purpose of the invitation, these are things which in their nature are not variable with the variations of man and of time. The nation gifted and called in this way, 'not according to its works', is the unalterable object of the eternal affection.

May we not extend the reference of such a sentence to individuals, as well as nations? Here as elsewhere we shall need to remember the rule which tells us, in the heights and depths of all truth, to go to both extremes. Here as elsewhere we must be reverently careful how we apply the prophecy, and to whom.

But does not the oracle say this, that where eternal Love has, without merit, by divine choice, settled upon a person it abides there for ever, not arbitrarily but by a law, which we cannot explain but which we can believe? Still, this is a reflection to be made only in passing here.

Vv 30–31. The immediate matter is a chosen people, not a chosen soul; and so he proceeds: *For as once you obeyed not our God, but now*, in the actual state of things, in his grace, *found mercy, on occasion of their disobedience; so they too now obeyed not, on occasion of your mercy*, in mysterious connection with the compassion which, in your pagan darkness, revealed salvation to you, *that they too may find mercy*. Yes, even their 'disobedience', in the mystery of grace, was permitted for their ultimate blessing; it was to be overruled to that self-discovery which lies deep in all true repentance, and springs up towards eternal life in the saving confidence of self-despair. The pagan (ch. 1) was brought to self-discovery as a rebel against God indicated in nature; the Jew (ch. 2) as a rebel against God revealed in Christ. This latter, if such a comparison is possible, was the more difficult and as it were advanced work in the divine plan. It took place, or rather it is taking and shall take place, later in order, and nearer to the final and universal triumph of redemption.

V 32. *For God shut them all up into disobedience, that he might have mercy upon them all*. He let the Gentile develop his resistance to right into unnatural outrage. He let the Jew develop his into the desperate rejection of his own glorious Messiah. But he gave his permission not as a God who did not care, a mere supreme law, a power sitting unconcerned above the scene of sin. He let the disease burst into the plague-spot in order that the guilty victim might ask at last for his remedy, and might receive it as mercy.

Let us not misuse the passage by reading into it a vain hope of an indiscriminate actual salvation, at the last, of all individuals of the race; a hope for which Scripture not only gives no valid evidence, but speaks against it what at least sound like the most urgent and unequivocal of its warnings. The context here, as we saw in another connection just now, has to do rather with masses than with persons; with Gentiles and Jews in their common characteristics rather than taken as individuals. Yet let us draw from the words, with reverent boldness, reasons to trust wholly the Eternal to be, even in the least understandable of his dealings, true to himself, true to eternal Love, whatever be the action he shall take.

Here Paul's voice, as we seem to listen to it, pauses for a moment, as he passes into unspoken thoughts of awe and faith. He has now given out his prophetic message, telling us Gentiles how great has been the sin of Israel, but how great also is Israel's privilege, and how sure his coming mercy. And behind this great special revelation there still rise on his soul those still more majestic forms of truth which he has led us to consider before; the righteousness of God, the justifying grace, the believing soul's dominion over sin, the fullness of the Spirit, the coming glory of the saints, the emancipated universe, the eternal Love. What remains, after this mighty process of spiritual discoveries, except to adore?

Vv 33–36. *Oh depth of wealth of God's wisdom and knowledge too! How past all searching are his judgments, and past all tracking are his ways! 'For who ever knew the Lord's mind? Or who ever proved his counsellor?' Or who ever first gave to him, and requital shall be made to the giver? Because out of him, and through him, and unto him, are all things: to him be the glory, unto the ages. Amen.*

Even so, Amen. We also fall down before God, with the apostle, with the Roman saints, with the whole Church, will all the company of heaven, and give ourselves to the action of pure worship in which the creature, sinking lowest in his own eyes, yes, out of his own sight altogether, rises highest into the light of his Maker. What a moment that is, what an occasion, for such an approach to him who is the infinite and personal fountain of being and redemption! We have been led from reason to reason, from doctrine to doctrine, from one link to another in a golden chain of redeeming mercies. We have had the dream of human merit expelled from the heart with arrows of light; and the pure glory of a most absolute and merciful grace, has replaced it.

All along we have been reminded, as it were in fragments and radiant glimpses, that these doctrines, these truths, are no mere principles in the abstract, but expressions of the will and of the love of a Person; a fact full of eternal life, but all too easily forgotten by the human mind, when its study of religion is carried away, if only for an hour, from the foot of the cross and the throne. But now all these lines converge upwards to their origin. By the cross they reach the throne. Through the work of the Son—One with the Father, for of the Son too it is written (Col. 1.16) that 'all things are through him, and unto him'—through his work, and in it, we come to the Father's wisdom and knowledge, which drew the plan of blessing, and as it were calculated and provided all its means. We touch the point where the creature reaches its final rest, the vision of the glory of God. We rest, with a deep and rejoicing silence, before the fact of mysteries too bright for our vision. After all the revelations of the apostle we confess with him in faith, with an acceptance as deep as our being, the fact that there is no finding out the final secrets of the ways of God. It becomes to us wonderfully sufficient, in the light of Christ, to know that 'the Lord, the Lord God, merciful and gracious', is also sovereign, ultimate, his own eternal satisfaction; that it is infinitely fit and blessed that, as his will is the true cause of all things, and his presence the secret of their continuation, so he is himself their final cause, end, and goal; they fulfil their idea and blessing, being altogether his: 'all things are unto him'.

'To whom be the glory, unto the ages. Amen.' What do we know about the advancing 'ages', the infinite developments of eternal life? Almost nothing, except the greatest fact of all; that in them the redeemed creature will for ever glorify not itself but the Creator; finding an endless and ever fuller youth, an inexhaustible motive, a rest that is impossible to break, a life in which 'they cannot die any more', in surrendering always all its blissful wealth of being to the will and use of the Blessed One.

We already are, in these 'ages', in Christ. We shall indeed grow for ever with their eternal growth, in him, to the glory of the grace of God. But let us not forget that we are already in them, as regards that life of ours which is hid with Christ in God. With that recollection, let us give ourselves often, and as by the 'second nature' of grace, to adoration. Not necessarily to frequent long withdrawals from the active services of life; we need only read on into the coming passages of the epistle to be reminded that we are set apart, in our Lord, to a life of unselfish contact with all the needs around us. But let that life have for its interior, for its animation, the spirit of worship. Taking by faith our all from God, let us inwardly always give it back to him, as those who not only admit with the simplest gratitude that he has redeemed us from condemnation and from sin, but who have seen with an adoring intuition that we and our all are of the 'all things' which, being 'of him', and 'by him', are also wholly 'unto him', by an absolute right, by the ultimate law of our being, since we are the creatures of the eternal Love.

CHAPTER 25

Christian Conduct and
The Issue of Christian Truth (12.1–8)

Again we may imagine a long and deliberate pause in the work
of Paul and Tertius. We have reached the end, generally speaking, of the dogmatic and so to speak prophetic contents of the
epistle. We have listened to the great argument of righteousness,
sanctification, and final redemption. We have followed the exposition of the mysterious unbelief and the destined restoration of
the chosen nation; a theme which we can see, as we look back
on the perspective of the whole epistle, to have a deep and
suggestive connection with what went before it; for the experience
of Israel, in relation to the sovereign will and grace of God, is
full of light thrown upon the experience of the soul. Now comes
the sequel. Paul brings us the Lord's message of duty, conduct,
and character.

The Christian, filled with the knowledge of an eternal love, is
told how not to dream, but to serve, with all the mercies of God
for his motive.

This is true of the whole New Testament; duty follows doctrine; the divine truths first, and then and therefore the blessed
life. Someone has remarked that everywhere in the Bible, if only
we dig deep enough, we find 'Do right' at the bottom. And we
may add that everywhere also we have only to dig one degree
deeper to find that the command is rooted in eternal underlying
facts of divine truth and love.

Scripture, that is to say, its Lord and Author, does not give
us the terrible gift of a command isolated and in a vacuum. It
supports its commandments on a base of compelling motive; and
it fills the man who is to keep them with the power of a living
Presence in him. But then, on the other hand, the Lord of

Scripture does not leave the motive and the Presence without the clear command. Rather, because they are supplied and assured to the believer, it spreads out a moral directory before his eyes all the more fully and minutely. It tells him, as a man who now rests on God and loves him, and in whom God dwells, not only in general that he is to 'walk and please God' but in particular 'how' to do it (1 Thess. 4.1). It takes his life in detail, and applies the will of the Lord to it. It speaks to him in explicit terms about moral purity, in the name of the Holy One; about patience and kindness, in the name of redeeming Love; about family duties, in the name of the Father and of the Son; about civic duties, in the name of the King Eternal. And so the whole outline and all the details become to the believer things not only of duty but of possibility, of hope, of the strong interest given by the thought that this is how the beloved Master would have us use his divine gift of life. Nothing is more wonderfully free, from one point of view, than love and spiritual power. But if the love is truly given by God and directed towards him in Christ, the man who loves cannot possibly wish to be his own law, and to spend his energy upon his own ideas or preferences. His joy and his conscious aim must be to do, in detail, the will of the Lord who is now so dear to him; and therefore, in detail, to know it.

Let us take deep note of this characteristic of Scripture, its detailed commands, in connection with its revelation of spiritual blessing. If we are called to be teachers of others in any sense, let us follow this example. Richard Cecil, wise Christian counsellor of the eighteenth-century Evangelical Revival, says that if he had to choose between preaching commands and preaching privileges, he would preach privileges; because the privileges of the true gospel tend in their nature to suggest and stimulate right action, while the commands taken by themselves do not reveal the wealth of divine life and power. But Cecil, like his great contemporaries, constantly and diligently preached as a fact both privilege and command; opening with energetic hands the revealed fullness of Christ, and then and therefore teaching 'them which had believed through grace' not only the idea of duty, but its details. Thomas Scott, at Olney, devoted his week-night 'lecture' in the parish church, almost exclusively, to instructions in daily Christian life. Assuming that his hearers 'knew Christ' in personal reality, he told them how to be Christians in the home, in the shop, in the farm; how to be consistent with their renewed life as parents, children, servants, masters, neighbours, subjects. There have been times, perhaps, when such didactic preaching has been too little used in the Church. But the men who, under God, in the eighteenth century and the early years of the nineteenth century, revived the message of Christ crucified and risen as all in all for our salvation, took great care to teach Christian morals. At the present day, in many quarters of Christendom, there is a remarkable revival of the desire to apply saving truth to common life, and to keep the Christian always mindful that he not only has heaven in prospect, but is to travel to it, every step, by the path of practical and watchful holiness. This is a sign of divine mercy in the Church. This is profoundly scriptural.

Meanwhile, God forbid that such teaching on how to live should ever be given, by parent, pastor, schoolmaster, or friend, where it does not first pass through the teachers' own soul into his own life. Alas for us if we show ever so convincingly, and even ever so winningly, the bond between salvation and holiness, and do not 'walk accurately' (Eph. 5.15) ourselves, in the details of our walk.

As we approach the rules of holiness here, let us once more recollect what we have seen all along in the epistle, that holiness is the aim and result of the entire gospel. It is certainly evidence of life, of infinite importance to the question whether a man truly knows God and is on the way to heaven. But it is much more; it is the expression of life; it is the form and action in which life is intended to come out. In an orchard (to use again a parable we have used already) the golden apples are evidences of the tree's species, and of its life. But a wooden label could tell us the species, and leaves can tell the life. The fruit is more than label or leaf; it is the thing for which the tree is here. We who believe are 'chosen' and 'ordained' to 'bring forth fruit' (John 15.16), fruit much and lasting. The eternal Master walks in his garden for the very purpose of seeing if the trees bear fruit. And the fruit he looks for is no visionary thing; it is a life of holy readiness for service to him and to our fellows, in his name.

But now we draw near again and listen:

V 1. *I exhort you therefore, brethren, by means of the compassions of God*; using as my logic and my fulcrum this 'depth of riches' we have explored; this wonderful redemption, with its sovereignty, mercy, acceptance, holiness, glory; and overruling of even sin and rebellion, in Gentile and in Jew, into occasions for salvation; these compassionate indications in the nearer and the eternal future of golden days yet to come;—*I exhort you therefore to present*, to give over, *your bodies as a sacrifice*, an altar-offering, *living, holy, well-pleasing, unto God; for this is your rational devotion*. That is to say, it is the 'devotion', the worship-service, which is done by the reason, mind, thought and will, of the man who has found God in Christ. The Greek word for 'devotion' is tinged with associations of ritual and temple; but it is taken here in a spiritual sense. The individual believer is both priest, sacrifice, and altar; he offers himself to the Lord—living, yet no longer to himself.

But note the significant relationship here of 'the body' with 'the reason'. 'Give over your bodies'; not now your spirit, intelligence, feelings, or aspirations, but 'your bodies', to your Lord. Is this an anti-climax? No more than when the Lord Jesus did, when he walked down from the hill of Transfiguration to the crowd below, and to the sins and miseries it presented. He came from the scene of glory to serve men in its abiding inner light. And even he, when on earth, served men, ordinarily, only through his sacred body; walking to them with his feet; touching them with his hands; meeting their eyes with his; speaking with his lips the words that were spirit and life. As with him so with us. In practice, it is only through the body that we can serve our generation by the will of God. Not without the body but through it, the spirit must tell on the embodied spirits around us. We look, speak, hear, write, nurse, or travel, by means of these physical servants of the will, our living limbs. Without the body, where should we be, in relation to other men? And therefore, without the surrender of the body, where are we, in relation to other men, from the point of view of the will of God?

So there is a true sense in which, while the surrender of the will is all important and primary from one point of view, the surrender of the body, the 'giving over' of the body, to be the instrument of God's will in us, is crucial from another. For many a Christian life it is the most necessary of all things to remember this; it is forgetting or only half-remembering it which keeps that life an almost neutral thing as far as witness and service for the Lord are concerned.

V 2. *And do not grow conformed to this world*, this age, the course and state of things in this scene of sin and death; do not play 'the worldling', assuming a guise which in itself is fleeting, and which for you, members of Christ, must also be hollow; *but grow transfigured*, living out a lasting and genuine change of tone and conduct, in which the figure or appearance truly expresses the essence—*by the renewal of your mind*, by using as an instrument in the holy process the divine light which has cleared your intelligence of the mists of self-love, and taught you to see as with new eyes 'the splendour of the will of God'; *so as that you test*, discerning as by a spiritual touchstone, *what is the will of God, the good, and acceptable, and perfect (will)*.

Such was to be the method, and such the result, in this development of the surrendered life. All is divine in origin and secret. The eternal 'compassions', and the sovereign work of the renewing and illuminating Spirit, are assumed before the believer can move one step. On the other hand the believer, in the full conscious action of his renewed 'intelligence', is to ponder the call to seek 'transfiguration' in a life of unworldly love, and to attain it in detail by using the new insight of a renewed heart. He is to look, with the eyes of the soul, straight through every mist of self-will to the now beloved will of God, as his deliberate choice, seen to be welcome, seen to be perfect, not because all is understood, but because the man is joyfully surrendered to the all-trusted Master. Thus he is to move along the path of an ever brightening transfiguration; at once open-eyed, and in the dark; seeing the Lord, and so with a sure instinct tending towards his will, yet content to let the mists of the unknown always hang over the next step but one.

It is a process, not a crisis: 'grow transfigured'. The origin of the process, the liberation of the movement, is, at least in idea, as definite as possible; 'Give over your bodies'. The Roman Christian, and ourselves, are called here, as they were above (6.13, 19), to a quite definite transaction with the Lord, whether or not something similar has taken place before, or shall be done again. They are called, as if once for all, to look their Lord in the face, and to clasp his gifts in their hands, and then to put themselves and his gifts altogether into his hands, for perpetual use and service. So, from the side of his conscious experience, the Christian is called to a decisive, crucial, instantaneous 'hallowing of himself'. But its outcome is to be a perpetual progression, a growth, not so much 'into' grace as 'in' it (2 Pet. 3.18), in which the surrender in purpose becomes a long series of deepening surrenders in habit and action, and a larger discovery of self, and of the Lord, and of his will, takes effect in the 'shining' of the transfigured life 'more and more, unto the perfect day' (Prov. 4.18).

Let us not distort this truth of progression, and its associated truth of the Christian's continuing imperfection. Let us not profane it into an excuse for a life which at the best is stationary, and must almost certainly be retreating, because not intent upon a genuine advance. Let us not withhold 'our bodies' from the sacred surrender taught here, and yet expect to realize somehow, at some vague date, a 'transfiguration, by the renewal of our mind'. We shall be indeed disappointed of that hope. But let us be both stimulated and sobered by the spiritual facts. As we are yielded to the Lord in sober reality, we are, in his mercy, liberated for growth. But the growth is to come, among other ways, by the careful application of 'the renewal of our mind' to the details of his blessed will.

And it will come, in its true development, only through holy humility. To exalt oneself, even in the spiritual life, is not to grow; it is to wither. So the apostle goes on:

V 3. *For I say, through the grace that has been given me*, 'the grace' of power for apostolic warning, *to every one who is among you, not to be high-minded beyond what his mind should be, but to be minded toward sober-mindedness, as to each God distributed faith's measure.* That is to say, let the individual never, in himself, forget his brothers, and the mutual relation of each to all in Christ. Let him never make himself the centre, or think of his personal salvation as if it could really be taken alone. The Lord, the sovereign giver of faith, the almighty bringer of souls into acceptance and union with Christ by faith, has given your faith to you, and your brother's faith to him; and why? That the individual gifts, the bounty of the One Giver, might join the individuals not only to the Giver but to one another, as recipients of riches that are many yet one, and which are to be spent in service which is one yet many. The One Lord distributes the one faith-power into many hearts, 'measuring' it out to each, so that the many, individually believing in the One, may not collide and fight, but lovingly co-operate in many kinds of service, the result of their 'like precious faith' (2 Pet. 1.2) conditioned by the variety of their lives. This is the point of the parable of the 'body' that follows (an image found only in Paul's writings, see 1 Cor. 12, Col. and Eph.). We may ask if 'parable' is an adequate word. What if the similarity between the human body and the way the exalted Christ unites and animates his saints is much closer?

That union is no mere aggregation or alliance of so many men under the presidency of an invisible Leader. It is a living thing. We are joined, each to the living Head, and so each to all his members, with a tenacity and relation, as genuine, strong, and close as eternal life can make it. The living, breathing man, of many parts yet one, is just the reflection, as it were, of the mystical Christ, the true Body with its heavenly Head.

Vv 4–8. *For just as in one body we have many limbs, but all the limbs have not the same function, so we, the many, are one body in Christ,* in our personal union with him, *but in detail, limbs of one another,* coherent and related not just as neighbours but as complementary parts in the whole. *But having endowments — according to the grace that was given to us — differing, be it prophecy,* inspired utterance, a power from above, yet mysteriously conditioned (1 Cor. 14.32) by the judgment and will of the utterer, *let it follow the proportion of the man's faith,* let it be true to his entire dependence on the revealed Christ, not left at the mercy of his emotions, or as it were played upon by alien unseen powers; *be it active service,* let the man be *in his service,* wholly given to it, not turning aside to covet his brother's more mystic gift; *be it the teacher,* let him likewise be *in his teaching*, whole-hearted in his allotted work, free from ambition; *be it the exhorter*, let him be *in his exhortation; the distributer* of his means, for God, *with open-handedness; the superintend-ent*, of church, or of home, *with earnestness; the pitier* (a broad and unofficial designation!) *with gladness*, doubling his gifts and works of mercy by a heart set free from the aims of self, and therefore wholly at the service of the needy.

This paragraph of eight verses is full of that deep characteristic of gospel life, surrender for service. The call is to a deeply passive inward attitude, with an express view to a richly active outward usefulness. Possessed, and knowing it, of the compassions of God, the man is asked to give himself over to eternal Love for purposes of unworldly and unambitious employment in the path chosen for him, whatever it may be. In this respect above all others he is to be 'not conformed to this world'—that is, he is to make not himself but his Lord his pleasure and ambition. 'By the renewal of his mind' he is to view the will of God from a point inaccessible to the unrenewed, and unjustified, to the man not freed in Christ from the tyranny of sin. He is to see in it his inexhaustible interest, his hope, his ultimate and satisfying aim; because of the identity of the will and the infinitely good and blessed bearer of it. And this more than surrender of his faculties, this happy and restful consecration of them, is to show its reality in one way before all others, in a humble estimate of self as compared with brother Christians, and a watchful willingness to do—not another's work, but the duty that lies next.

This aspect of the life of self-surrender is the theme of this great paragraph of duty. In the following passage we shall find more detailed instructions; but here we have what is to govern all along the whole stream of the obedient life. The man rich in Christ is reverently to remember others, and God's will in them, and for them. He is to avoid the subtle temptation to intrude beyond the Master's allotted work for him. He is to be slow to think, 'I am richly qualified, and could do this thing, and that, and the other, better than the man who does it now.' His chast-ened spiritual instinct will rather go to criticize himself, to watch for the least deficiency in his own doing of the task which at least today is his. He will 'give himself wholly to this', be it more or less attractive to him in itself. For he works as one who does not have to contrive a life as full of success and influence as he can imagine, but to accept a life assigned by the Lord who has first given to him himself.

The passage itself amply implies that he is to use his renewed intelligence actively and honestly. He is to look circumstances and conditions in the face, remembering that in one way or another the will of God is expressed in them. He is to seek to understand not only his duties but his personal resources for them, natural as well as spiritual. But he is to do this as one whose 'mind' is 'renewed' by his living contact and union with his redeeming King, and who has really laid his faculties at the feet of an absolute Master, who is the Lord of order as well as of power.

What peace, energy, and dignity comes into a life which is consciously and deliberately surrendered in this way! The highest range of duties, as man counts highest, is relieved both of its heavy anxieties and of its temptations to a ruinous self-import-ance. And the lowest range, as man counts lowest, is filled with the quiet greatness born of the presence and will of God. In the memoirs of Mme de la Mothe Guyon much is said of her faithful maid-servant, who was imprisoned along with her (in a separate chamber) in the Bastille, and there died, in about 1700. This pious woman, deeply taught in the things of the Spirit, and gifted with an understanding far above the usual, appears never for an hour to have coveted a more ambitious role than that which God assigned her in his obedience. 'She desired to be what God would have her be, and to be nothing more, and nothing less. She included time and place, as well as disposition and action. She had not a doubt that God, who had given remarkable powers to Mme Guyon, had called her to the great work in which she was employed. But knowing that her beloved mistress could not go alone, but must constantly have some female attendant, she had the conviction, equally distinct, that she was called to be her maid-servant.'

A great part of the surface of Christian society would be transfigured if its depth was more fully penetrated with this spirit. And it is to this spirit that the apostle here definitely calls

us, each and every one, not as with a counsel of perfection for
the few, but as the will of God for all who have found out what
is meant by his 'compassions', and have caught even a glimpse
of his will as 'good, and acceptable, and perfect'.

CHAPTER 26

Christian Duty: Details of Personal Conduct (12.9–21)

St Paul has set before us the life of surrender, of the 'giving-over' of ourselves to God, in general terms. The ideal (meant always for a watchful and hopeful realization) has been held up to us. It is a life whose motive is the Lord's 'compassions'; whose law of freedom is his will; whose inmost aim is, without envy or interference towards our fellow-servants, to 'finish the work he hath given *us* to do'. Now follow the details of personal conduct which are to mark the characteristics of the Christian.

As we listen again, we will again remember that the words are for all who are in Christ. The beings indicated here are not the chosen names of a church calendar, nor are they the passionless inhabitants of a utopia. They are all then and now, who 'have peace with God through our Lord Jesus Christ', 'have the Spirit of God dwelling in them', and are living out this wonderful but most practical life in the straight line of their Father's will.

As if he could not heap the golden words too thickly together, St Paul dictates here with even unusual abruptness and terseness of expression, as our translation attempts to show.

Vv 9–14. *Your love, unaffected. Abominating the ill, wedded to the good. For your brotherly-kindness, full of mutual home-affection. For your honour*, your code of precedence, *deferring to one another. For your earnestness, not slothful. For the Spirit*, as regards your possession and use of the divine Indweller, *glowing. For the Lord, bond-serving. For your hope*, that is to say, as to the hope of the Lord's return, *rejoicing. For your affliction, enduring. For your prayer, persevering. For the wants of the saints*, for the poverty of fellow-Christians, *communicating*; 'sharing', is a nobler thing than the mere 'giving' which may ignore the sacred fellowship of the provider and the receiver. *Hospitality—prosecuting* or undertaking with care. *Bless those who persecute you; bless, and do not curse.* This was a solemnly appropriate command, for the community over which, eight years later, the first great persecution was to break. And no doubt there was abundant present occasion for it, even while the scene was comparatively tranquil. Every modern mission-field can illustrate the possibilities of a 'persecution' which may be completely private, or restricted to a small area; which may never reach the point of technical outrage, yet may apply a truly fiery trial to the faithful convert. Even in dignified English society is no such thing known as the 'persecution' of a life 'not conformed to this world', though the assault or torture may take almost invisible and intangible forms, except to the feelings of the object of it? For all such cases, as well as for the confessor on the rack, and the martyr in the fire, this command holds; 'Bless, do not curse.' In Christ find possible the impossible; let the resentment of nature die, at his feet, in the breath of his love.

V 15. *To rejoice with the rejoicing, and to weep with the weeping.* These are holy duties of the surrendered life that are too easily forgotten. Alas, there is such a phenomenon, not altogether rare, as a life whose self-surrender, in some chief aspects, cannot be doubted, but which utterly fails in sympathy. A certain spiritual exaltation is allowed actually to harden, or at least to seem to harden, the consecrated heart; and the person who perhaps witnesses for God with a prophet's ardour is yet not one to whom the mourner would go for tears and prayer in his bereavement, or the child for a perfectly human smile in its play. But this is not as the Lord would have it be. If indeed the Christian has 'given his body over', it is that his eyes, and lips, and hands, may be ready to give loving signs of fellowship in sorrow, and (what is less obvious) in gladness too, to the human hearts around him.

V 16. *Feeling the same thing towards one another*; animated by a happy identity of sympathy and brotherhood. *Not haughty in feeling, but full of lowly sympathies*; accessible, in an unaffected fellowship, to the poor, the social inferior, the weak and the defeated, and again to the smallest and homeliest interests of all. It was the Lord's example; the little child, the wistful parent, the widow with her mites, the poor fallen woman of the street, could 'draw out' his blessed sympathies with a touch, while he responded with an unbroken majesty of gracious power, but with a kindness for which 'condescension' seems a far too cold and distant word.

Do not get to be wise in your own opinion; be ready always to learn; dread the attitude of mind, too possible even for the person of earnest spiritual purpose, which assumes that you have nothing to learn and everything to teach; which makes it easy to criticize and to discredit, and which can prove a completely repellent thing to the observer from outside, who is trying to weigh the gospel by its adherent and advocate.

V 17. *Requiting no one evil for evil*; safe from the spirit of retaliation, in your surrender to him 'who when he was reviled, reviled not again; when he suffered, threatened not'. *Taking forethought for good in the sight of all men*; not letting habits, talk, expenses, drift into inconsistency; watching with open and considerate eyes against what others may fairly think to be unchristian in you. Here is no counsel of cowardice, no recommendation of slavery to a public opinion which may be altogether wrong. It is a command of loyal jealousy for the heavenly Master's honour. His servant is to be nobly indifferent to the world's thought and word where he is sure that God and the world are opposed to each other. But he is to be sensitively attentive to the world's observation where the world, more or less acquainted with the Christian command or principle, and more or less conscious of its truth and right, is watching, maliciously or it may be wistfully, to see if it governs the Christian's practice. In view of this the believer will never be content even with the satisfaction of his own conscience; he will set himself not only to do right, but to be seen to do it. He will not only be true when trusted with money, for example; he will take care that the proofs of his fidelity shall be open. He will not only mean well towards others; he will take care that his manner and bearing, his dealings and conversation, shall unmistakably breathe the Christian air.

V 18. *If possible, as regards your side* (the 'your' is as emphatic as possible in position and in meaning), *living at peace with all men*; yes, even in pagan and hostile Rome. A uniquely Christian principle speaks here. Those who had 'given over their bodies a living sacrifice' might think that their duty was to court the world's opposition, to tilt as it were against its spears, as if the one supreme call was to collide, to fall, and to be glorified. But this would be fanaticism; and the gospel is never fanatical, for it is the law of love. The surrendered Christian is not, as such, one who hopes for even a martyr's fame, but the servant of God and man. If martyrdom crosses his path, it is met as duty; but he does not court it. And what is true of martyrdom is of course true of every lower and milder form of the conflict of the Church, and of the Christian, in the world.

Nothing more nobly proves the divine origin of the gospel than this essential instruction; 'as far as it lies with you, live peaceably with all men'. Such wise and kind forbearance and neighbourliness would never have been bound up with the belief of supernatural powers and hopes, if those powers and hopes had been the mere result of natural enthusiasm. The supernatural of the gospel leads to nothing but moral uprightness and considerateness, in short to nothing but love, between man and man. And why? Because it is truly divine; it is the message and gift of the living Son of God, in all the truth and majesty of his rightfulness. All too early in the history of the Church 'the crown of martyrdom' became an object of enthusiastic ambition. But that was not because of the teaching of the Crucified, nor of his suffering apostles.

Vv 19–21. *Not avenging yourselves, beloved; no, give place to the wrath;* let the angry opponent, the dread persecutor, have his way, so far as your resistance or retaliation is concerned. 'Beloved, let us love' (1 John 4.7); with that strong and conquering love which wins by suffering. And do not fear lest eternal justice should go by default; there is One who will take take of that matter; you may leave it with him. *For it stands written* (Dt. 32.35), '*To me belongs vengeance; I will recompense, saith the Lord*'. '*But if*' (and again he quotes the Old Testament, finding in the Proverbs (25.21, 22) the same prophetic authority as in the Pentateuch), '*but if thy enemy is hungry, give him food; if he is thirsty, give him drink; for so doing thou wilt heap coals of fire on his head*'; taking the best way to the only 'vengeance' which a saint can wish, namely, your 'enemy's' conviction of his wrong, the rising of a burning shame in his soul, and the melting of his spirit in the fire of love. *Be not thou conquered by the evil, but conquer, in the good, the evil.*

'In the good'; as if surrounded by it, moving invulnerable, in its magic circle, through 'the contradiction of sinners', 'the provoking of all men.' The thought is exactly that of Psalm 31.18, 19: 'How great is thy goodness, which thou hast laid up for them that fear thee, which thou has wrought for them that trust in thee before the sons of men! Thou shalt hide them in the secret of thy presence from the pride of man; Thou shalt keep them secretly in a pavilion from the strife of tongues.' 'The good' of this sentence of St Paul's is no vague and abstract thing; it is 'the gift of God' (6.28); it is the life eternal found and possessed in union with Christ, our Righteousness, our Sanctification, our Redemption. Practically, it is 'not it but he'. The Roman convert who should find it more than possible to meet his enemy with love, to do him positive good in his need, with a conquering simplicity of intention, was to do so not so much by an internal conflict between his 'better self' and his worse, as by the living power of Christ received in his whole being; by 'abiding in him'.

It is so now, and for ever. The open secret of divine peace and love is what it was: as necessary, as versatile, as victorious. And its path of victory is as straight and as sure as of old. And the command to tread that path is still as divinely binding as it ever was for the Christian, if indeed he has embraced 'the mercies of God', and is looking to his Lord to be 'transfigured, by the renewing of his mind' for ever.

Several principles are stated in this paragraph. We see first that the sanctity of the gospel is no hushed and cloistered 'indifferentism'. It is a thing intended to be lived out 'before the sons of men'. There is a strong positive element in it. The saint is to 'abominate the evil'; not just to deprecate and deplore it. He is to be energetically 'in earnest'. He is to 'glow' with the Spirit, and to 'rejoice' in the hope of glory. He is to take practical steps to live not only aright, but obviously aright, in ways which 'all men' can recognize. Again, his life is to be essentially social. He is thought of as one who meets other lives at every turn, and he is never to forget or neglect his relation to them. Particularly among Christians, he is to cherish the 'family affection' of the gospel; to defer to fellow Christians in a generous humility; to share his means with the poor among them; to welcome the strangers among them to his house. He is to think it a sacred duty to enter into the joys and the sorrows round him. He is to keep his sympathies open for despised people, and for little matters. Then again, and most prominently after all, he is to be ready to suffer, and to meet suffering with a spirit far greater than that just of resignation. He is to bless his persecutor; he is to serve his enemy in very practical and active ways; he is to conquer him for Christ, in the power of a divine communion.

So the life that is so positive and active in its effects, is to be essentially all the while a passive, bearing, enduring, life. Its strength is to spring not from the energies of nature, which may or may not be vigorous in the man, but from an internal surrender to the claim and government of his Lord. He has 'presented himself to God' (6.13); he has 'presented his body, a living sacrifice' (12.1). He has recognized with a penitent wonder and joy, that he is but the limb of a Body, and that his Head is the Lord. His thought is now not for his personal rights, his individual exaltation, but for the glory of his Head, for the fulfilment of the thought of his Head, and for the health and wealth of the Body, as the great vehicle in the world of the gracious will of the Head.

This passive root below a rich growth and harvest of activity is among the chief and deepest of the characteristics of Christian ethics. All through the New Testament we find it expressed or suggested. The first beatitude uttered by the Lord (Matt. 5.3) is given to 'the poor, the begging, in spirit'. The last (John 20.29) is for the believer, who trusts without seeing. The radiant portrait of holy Love (1 Cor. 13) produces its effect, full of indescribable life as well as beauty, by the combination of almost none but negative touches; the 'total abstinence' of the loving soul from impatience, from envy, from self-display, from self-seeking, from brooding over wrong, from even the faintest pleasure in evil, from the tendency to think ill of others. Everywhere the gospel commands the Christian to take sides against himself. He is to stand ready to forgo even his surest rights, if only he is hurt by so doing; while on the other hand he is watchful to respect even the least obvious rights of others, yes, to consider their weaknesses, and their prejudices, to the furthest just limit. He is 'not to resist evil'; in the sense of never fighting for self as self. He is rather to 'suffer himself to be defrauded' (1 Cor. 6.7) than to bring discredit on his Lord in however due a course of law. The troubles and humiliations of his earthly lot, if such things are the will of God for him, are not to be materials for his discontent, or occasions for his envy, or for his secular ambition. They are to be his opportunities for inward triumph; the theme of a 'song of the Lord', in which he is to sing of strength perfected in weakness, of a power not his own 'overshadowing' him (2 Cor. 12.9, 10).

Such is the passivity of the saints, deep beneath their activity in God's service. The two are in vital connection. The root is essential for the fruit. For the secret and unostentatious surrender of the will, in its Christian sense, is no mere evacuation, leaving the house swept but empty; it is the reception of the Lord of life into the open castle of the City of Mansoul. It is the placing in his hands of all that the walls contain. And placed in his hands, the castle, and the city, will show at once, and continually more and more, that not only order but life has taken possession.

Once more, let us not forget that Paul lays his main emphasis here rather on being than on doing. Nothing is said of great spiritual enterprises; everything has to do with the personal conduct of the men who, if such enterprises are done, must do them. This too is characteristic of the New Testament. Very rarely do the apostles say anything about their converts' duty, for instance, to carry the message of Christ around them in evangelistic aggression, although such evangelism is well recorded (see Acts 7.4; Phil. 1.14, 2.15, 16; Eph. 5.13; 1 Thess. 1.8; 3 John 7).

Yet is it not plain that, when the apostles thought of the life and zeal of their converts, their first care, by far, was that they should be wholly conformed to the will of God in personal and social matters? This was the indispensable condition to their being, as a community, what they must be if they were to prove true witnesses for their Lord.

God forbid that we should draw from this phenomenon the faintest inference to thwart or discredit missionary zeal. But neither in missionary enterprise, nor in any sort of activity for

God and man, is this deep suggestion of the epistles to be forgotten. What the Christian does is even more important than what he says. What he is comes before what he does. He is 'nothing yet as he ought to' be if, amid even innumerable efforts and aggressions, he has not 'presented his body a living sacrifice' for his Lord's purposes, not his own; if he has not learnt, in his Lord, an unaffected love, a holy family affection, a sympathy with griefs and joys around him, a humble esteem of himself, and the blessed art of giving way to wrath, and of overcoming evil in 'the good' of the presence of the Lord.

CHAPTER 27

Christian Duty; in Civil Life and Otherwise: Love
(13. 1–10)

A new distinct but closely connected topic now emerges. We
have been listening to instructions for personal and social life,
all rooted in the inmost characteristic of Christian morals, self-
surrender, self-submission to God. Loyalty to others in the Lord
has been the theme. In the circles of home, of friendship, of
the Church; in relations with men in general, whose personal
opposition or religious persecution was so likely to cross the path
– in all these regions the Christian was to act on the principle
of supernatural submission, as the sure way to spiritual victory.

The same principle is now carried into his relations with the
state. As a Christian, he does not cease to be a citizen. His
deliverance from the death sentence of the law of God only binds
him, in his Lord's name, to a loyal fidelity to human law; limited
only by the case where such law may really contradict the
supreme divine law. The disciple of Christ, as such, while his
whole being has received a freedom unknown elsewhere, is to be
the faithful subject of the Emperor, the orderly inhabitant of his
part of the city, the punctual taxpayer, the ready giver of not a
servile yet a genuine deference to the representatives and ministers of human authority.

He is to do this for both general and special reasons. In
general, it is his Christian duty rather to submit than otherwise,
where conscience toward God is not in the question. Not weakly,
but meekly, he is to yield rather than resist in all his relationships,
purely personal, with men; and therefore with the officials of
order, as men. But in particular also, he is to understand that
civil order is not only a desirable thing, but divine; it is the will
of God for the social race made in his image. In the abstract,

this is absolutely so; civil order is a God-given law, as truly as the most explicit instructions of the ten commandments, in whose second half it is so plainly implied all along. And in the concrete, the civil order under which the Christian finds himself to be is to be regarded as a real instance of this great principle. It is quite sure to be imperfect, because it is necessarily mediated through human minds and wills. Very possibly it may be gravely distorted, into a system seriously oppressive of the individual life. As a matter of fact, the supreme magistrate for the Roman Christians in the AD 58 was a dissolute young man, intoxicated by the discovery that he might do almost entirely as he pleased with the lives around him. But this was not by any defect in the idea and purpose of Roman law, but by fault of the degenerate world of the day. Yet civil authority, even with a Nero at its head, was still in principle a divine thing. And the Christian's attitude to it was to be always that of a willingness, a purpose, to obey; an absence of the resistance whose motive lies in self-assertion. Clearly his attitude was not to be that of the revolutionary, who looks upon the state as a sort of warring power, against which he, alone or in company, openly or in the dark, is free to carry on a campaign. Under even heavy pressure the Christian is still to remember that civil government is, in principle, 'of God'. He is to reverence the institution in its ideal. He is to regard its actual officers, whatever their personal faults, as so far dignified by the institution that their governing work is to be considered always first in its light. The most imperfect, even the most erring, administration of civil order is still a thing to be respected before it is criticized. In principle, it is a 'terror not to good works, but to the evil'.

It hardly needs elaborate remark to show that such a precept, little as it may fit in with many popular political cries of our time, means anything in the Christian but a political servility, or an indifference on his part to political wrong in the actual course of government. The religion which invites every man to stand face to face with God in Christ, to go straight to the Eternal, knowing no intermediary but his Son, and no ultimate authority but his Scripture, for the certainties of the soul, peace of conscience, dominion over evil in himself and in the world, and for more than deliverance from the fear of death, is no friend to the tyrants of mankind. We have seen how, by enthroning Christ in the heart, it teaches a noble inward submissiveness. But from another point of view it equally, and mightily, develops the noblest sort of individualism. It lifts man to a sublime independence of his surroundings, by joining him direct to God in Christ, by making him the friend of God. No wonder then that, in the course of history, Christianity, that is to say the Christianity of the apostles and the Scriptures, has been the invincible ally of personal conscience and political liberty, the liberty which is the opposite of both license and tyranny. It is Christianity which has taught men calmly to die, in face of a persecuting empire, or of whatever other giant human force, rather than do wrong at its command. It is Christianity which has lifted countless souls to stand upright in solitary protest for truth and against falsehood, when every form of governmental authority has been against them. It was, Luther, the student of St Paul, who stood alone but immovable before Pope and Emperor, saying, 'I can not otherwise, so help me God'. We may be sure that if the world shuts the Bible it will only the sooner revert, under whatever type of government, to essential despotism, whether it be the despotism of master, or man.

It is Christianity which has peacefully and securely freed the slave, and has restored woman to her true place by the side of man. But then, Christianity has done all this in a way of its own. It has never flattered the oppressed, nor inflamed them. It has told impartial truth to them, and to their oppressors. The gospel tells uncompromising truth to the rich, but also to the poor. Even in the presence of pagan slavery it laid the law of duty on the slave, as well as on his master. It commanded the slave consider his obligations rather than his rights; while it said the same, precisely, and more at length, and more urgently, to his lord. So it at once avoided revolution and sowed the living seed of immense, salutary, and ever-developing reforms. The doctrine of spiritual equality, and spiritual connection, secured in Christ, came into the world as the guarantee for the whole social and political system of the truest ultimate political liberty. For it equally disciplined and developed the individual, in relation to the life around him.

Serious questions for practical decision-making may be raised, of course, from this passage. Is resistance to a cruel despotism never permissible to the Christian? In a time of revolution, when power wrestles with power, which power is the Christian to regard as 'ordained of God'? It may be sufficient to reply to the former question that, almost self-evidently, the absolute principles of a passage like this take for granted some balance and modification by associated principles. Read without any such reserve, St Paul leaves here no alternative, under any circumstances, to submission. But he certainly did not mean to say that the Christian must submit to an imperial order to sacrifice to the Roman gods. It seems to follow that the letter of the law does not pronounce it inconceivable that a Christian, under circumstances which leave his action unselfish, truthful, the result not of impatience but of conviction, might be justified in positive resistance. But history adds its witness to the warnings of St Paul, and of his Master, that almost inevitably it goes ill in the highest respects with saints who 'take the sword', and that the purest victories for freedom are won by those who 'endure grief, suffering wrongfully', while they witness for right and Christ before their oppressors.

It may also be noted that this passage leaves the Christian not only not bound to aid an oppressive government by active co-operation, but amply free to witness aloud against its wrong; and that his submissive but firm conduct is itself a homage to the inviolability of authority. Experience proves that it is in this way all tyrannies have been morally broken, and all true progress in the history of humanity effected.

What the servant of God should do with his allegiance in a revolutionary crisis is a serious question for any whom it may unhappily concern. Someone has usefully said that 'perhaps nothing involves greater difficulties, in very many instances, than to ascertain to whom the authority justly belongs. . . . Submission in all things lawful to "the existing authorities" is our duty at all times and in all cases; though in civil convulsions . . . there may frequently be a difficulty in determining which are "the existing authorities" '. In such cases, 'the Christian', it has been said, 'will submit to the new power as soon as the resistance of the old shall have ceased. In the actual state of matters he will recognize the manifestation of God's will, and will take no part in any reactionary plot.'

As regards the problem of forms or types of government, it seems clear that the apostle lays no bond of conscience on the Christian. Both in the Old Testament and in the New a just monarchy appears to be the ideal. But our epistle says that 'there is no power but of God'. In St Paul's time the Roman Empire was in theory, as much as ever, a republic, and in fact a personal monarchy. On this question, as in so many others of the outward framework of human life, the gospel is liberal in its applications, while it is, in the noblest sense, conservative in principle.

In summary, then, this paragraph describes the corner-stone of civil order. One side of it is the permanent duty, for the Christian citizen, of reverence for law, of remembrance of the religious aspect of even secular government. The other side is the warning to the ruler, to the authority, that God throws his shield over the claims of the state only because authority was instituted not for selfish but for social ends, so that it fails itself if it is not used for the good of man.

Vv 1–7 *Let every soul*, every person, who has 'presented his body a living sacrifice', *be submissive to the ruling authorities*; clearly, from the context, the authorities of the state. *For there is no authority except by God; but the existing authorities have been appointed by God.* That is, an authority not sanctioned by God is nothing; man is no independent source of power and law. But then, it has pleased God so to order human life and history, that his will in this matter is expressed, from time to time, in and through the actual constitution of the state. *So that the opponent of the authority withstands the ordinance of God*, not merely that of man; *but the withstanders will on themselves bring sentence of judgment*; not only the human crime of treason, but the charge, in the court of God, of rebellion against his will. This is founded on the idea of law and order, which means by its nature the restraint of public mischief and the promotion, or at least protection, of public good. 'Authority', even under its worst distortions, still so far keeps that aim that no human civic power, as a fact, punishes good as good, and rewards evil as evil; and thus for most ordinary people the worst settled authority is infinitely better than real anarchy. *For rulers, as a class, are not a terror to the good deed, but to the evil;* such is always the fact in principle, and such, taking human life as a whole, is the tendency, even at the worst, in practice, where the authority in any degree deserves its name. *Now do you wish not to be afraid of the authority? do what is good, and you shall have praise from it;* the 'praise', at least, of being unmolested and protected. *For God's agent he is to you, for what is good;* through his function God, in providence, carries out his purposes of order. *But if you are doing what is evil, be afraid; for not for nothing,* not without warrant or purpose, *does he wear his sword,* symbol of the ultimate power of life and death; *for God's agent is he, an avenger, unto wrath, for the practiser of the evil. Wherefore,* because God is in the matter, *it is a necessity to submit, not only because of the wrath,* the ruler's wrath in the case concerned, *but because of the conscience too;* because you know, as a Christian, that God speaks through the state and through its minister, and that anarchy is therefore disloyalty to God. *For on this account too you pay taxes;* the same commission which gives the state the right to restrain and punish gives it the right to demand subsidy from its members for its operations; *for God's ministers are they,* his 'minister', a word so frequently used in priestly connections that it may well suggest them here; as if the civil ruler were, in his field, an almost religious instrument of divine order; *God's ministers, to this very end persevering* in their task; working on in the tasks of administration, for the conscious or unconscious execution of the divine plan of social peace.

This is a noble point of view, both for governed and for governors, from which to consider the prosaic problems and necessities of public finance. Understood in this way, the tax is paid not with a cold and compulsory assent to a mechanical exaction, but as an act in tune with the plan of God. And the tax is devised and demanded, not merely as an expedient to adjust a budget, but as a thing which God's law can sanction, in the interests of God's social plan. *Discharge therefore to all men,* to all men in authority, primarily, but not only, *their dues; the tax, to whom* you owe *the tax,* on person and property; *the toll, to whom the toll,* on merchandise; *the fear, to whom the fear*, as to the ordained punisher of wrong; *the honour, to whom the honour*, as to the rightful claimant in general of loyal deference.

Such were the political principles of the new faith, of the mysterious society, which was so soon to perplex Roman statesmen, as well as to supply convenient victims to Roman despots. A Nero was shortly to burn Christians in his gardens as a substitute for lamps, on the charge that they were guilty of secret and horrible orgies. Later, a Trajan, grave and anxious, was to order their execution as members of a secret community dangerous to imperial order. But here is a private message sent to this people by their leader, reminding them of their principles, and prescribing their line of action. He puts them all in immediate spiritual contact with the eternal Sovereign, and so he inspires them with the strongest possible independence, as regards 'the fear of man'. He commands them know, for a certainty, that the Almighty One regards them as accepted in his Beloved, and fills them with his great Presence, and promises them a heaven from which no earthly power or terror can for a moment shut them out. But in the same message, and in the same name, he commands them to pay their taxes to the pagan state, and to do so, not with the contemptuous indifference of the fanatic, who thinks that human life in its temporal order is God-forsaken, but in the spirit of heart-felt loyalty and ungrudging deference, as to an authority representing in its sphere none other than their Lord and Father.

It has been suggested that the first serious opposition of the state towards these mysterious Christians was occasioned by the inevitable interference of the claims of Christ with the stern and rigid order of the Roman family. A power which could assert the right and duty of a son to reject his father's religious worship was taken to be a power which meant the destruction of all social order, a true nihilism. This was a tremendous misunderstanding to encounter. How was it to be met? Not by resistance or passionate protests. The answer was to be that of love, practical and loyal, to God and man, in life and, when occasion came, in death. That path held at least the possibility of martyrdom, but its aim was the peaceful vindication of the glory of God and of the name of Jesus, and the achievement of the best security for human freedom.

Appropriately then, the apostle closes these instructions on civil order with the universal command to love.

Vv 8–10. *Owe nothing to anyone*; avoid absolutely the social disloyalty of debt; pay every creditor in full, with watchful care; *except the loving one another.* Love is to be a perpetual and inexhaustible debt, not to be rejected or neglected, but always due and always paying. It is a debt, not as a forgotten account is owing to the seller, but as interest on capital is continuously owing to the lender. And this, not only because of the fair beauty of love, but because of the legal duty of it: *For the lover of his fellow* ('the other man', be he who he may, with whom the man has to do) *has fulfilled the law*, the law of the second half of the ten commandments. He 'has fulfilled' it; as having at once entered, in principle and will, into its whole requirement; so that all he now needs is not a better attitude but more information. *For the, 'Thou shalt not commit adultery, Thou shalt not murder, Thou shalt not steal, Thou shalt not bear false witness, Thou shalt not covet,' and whatever other commandment there is, all is summed up in this utterance, 'Thou shalt love thy neighbour as thyself'* (Lv. 19.18). *Love works the neighbour no ill; therefore love is the law's fulfilment.*

Is this just a negative command? Is the life of love to be only an abstinence from doing harm, which may avoid thefts, but may also avoid personal sacrifices? Is it a cold and inoperative 'harmlessness', which leaves all things as they are? We see the answer in part in the words, 'as thyself'. Man 'loves himself' (in the sense of nature, not of sin), with a love which instinctively avoids what is repulsive and harmful, but does so because it positively likes and desires the opposite. The man who 'loves his neighbour as himself' will be as considerate of his neighbour's feelings as of his own, in respect of abstinence from injury and annoyance. But he will be more; he will be actively desirous of his neighbour's good. 'Working him no evil', he will reckon it as much 'evil' to be indifferent to his positive true interests as he would reckon it unnatural to be apathetic about his own. 'Working him no evil', as one who 'loves him as himself', he will care, and seek, to work him good.

The true divine commentary on this brief paragraph is the nearly contemporary passage written by the same author, in 1 Corinthians 13. There love is described mainly in negatives, but who fails to feel the wonderful positive of the effect? Its blessed negatives are but a form of unselfish action. It forgets itself, and remembers others, and refrains from the least needless wounding of them, not because it wants merely to live and let live, but because it loves them, finding its happiness in their good.

It has been said that 'love is holiness, spelt short'. Thoughtfully interpreted and applied, the saying is true. The holy man in human life is the man who, with the Scriptures open before him to inform and guide him, while the Lord Christ dwells in his heart by faith as his reason and his power, forgets himself in a work for others which is kept both gentle, wise, and persistent to the end, by the love which, whatever else it does, knows how to sympathize and to serve.

CHAPTER 28

*Christian Duty in the Light of the Lord's Return
And in the Power of His Presence (13.11–14)*

Paul has said much to us about duty, in general and in detail, summing up his message in the duty and joy of love. We have heard him explaining to his disciples how to live as members together of the Body of Christ, and as members also of human society at large, and as citizens of the state. We have been busy latterly with thoughts of taxes, tolls, and private debts, and the obligation of scrupulous rightfulness in all such things. Everything has had relation to the seen and the temporal. The teaching has not strayed into a land of dreams, nor into a desert or a cell; it has had at least as much to do with the market, the shop, and the secular official, as if the writer had been a moralist whose horizon was altogether restricted to this life, and who had no hope for the future.

Yet all the while the teacher and the taught were penetrated and orientated by a perfectly supernatural certainty of the future, commanding the wonder and glad response of their whole being. They carried about with them the promise of their risen Master that he would personally return again in heavenly glory, to their infinite joy, gathering them for ever around him in immortality, bringing heaven with him, and transfiguring them into his own heavenly image.

Across all possible complications and obstacles of the human world around them they beheld 'that blissful hope' (Tit. 2.13). Their Lord, once crucified, but now alive for evermore, was greater than the world; greater in his calm triumphant authority over man and nature, greater in the wonder and joy of himself, his person and his salvation. It was enough that he had said he would come again, and that it would be to their eternal happiness. He had promised; therefore it would surely be.

How and when the promise would take place was a secondary question. Some things, such as the manner, were revealed and certain: 'This same Jesus, in like manner as ye saw him going into heaven' (Acts 1.11). But much more was neither revealed nor imagined. As to the time, Christ's words had left them, as they still leave us, suspended in a reverent sense of mystery, between hints which seem almost equally to promise both speed and delay. 'Watch therefore, for ye know not when the Master of the house cometh' (Mark 13.35); 'After a long time the Lord of the servants cometh, and reckoneth with them' (Matt. 25.19). Paul follows Christ's example in the matter. Here and there he seems to indicate an imminent Advent, as when he speaks of '*us* who are alive and remain' (1 Thess. 4.15). But again, in this very epistle, in his discussion of the future of Israel, he appears to contemplate great developments of time and event yet to come; and very definitely, for his own part, in many places, he records his expectation of death, not of a death-less transfiguration at the Second Coming. Many at least among his converts looked for the coming King with an eagerness which was sometimes restless and unwholesome, as at Thessalonica; and it may have been like this with some of the Roman saints. But St Paul at once warned the Thessalonians of their mistake; and certainly this epistle suggests no such upheaval of expectation at Rome.

Our task here is not to discuss 'the times and the seasons' which now, as much as then, lie in the Father's 'power' (Acts 1.7). It is rather to call attention to the fact that in all ages of the Church this mysterious but definite promise has, with a silent force, made itself present and contemporary to the believing and watching soul. It is not yet fully clear how in the end it shall be seen that 'I come quickly', and 'The day of Christ is not at hand' (Rev. 22.12, 20, 2 Thess. 2.2), were both divinely and harmoniously truthful. But it is certain that both are so; and that in every generation of the now 'long time', 'the hope', as it were imminent, has been calculated for mighty effects on the Christian's will and work.

So we come to this great Advent prophecy, to read it for our own age. Now first let us remember its wonderful illustration of the phenomenon which we have remarked already, the coincidence in Christianity of a faith full of eternity, with a life full of common duty. Here is a community of men called to live under an almost opened heaven; almost to see, as they look around them, the descending Lord of glory coming to bring in the eternal day, making himself present in this visible scene 'with the voice of the archangel and the trump of God', waking his buried saints from the dust, calling the living and the risen to meet him in the air. How can they adjust such an expectation to the demands of 'the daily round'? Will they not fly from Rome to the solitude, to the hill-tops and forests of the Apennines, to wait with awful joy the great lightning-flash of glory? Not so. They somehow, while 'looking for the Saviour from the heavens' (Phil. 3.20), attend to their service and their business, pay their debts and their taxes, offer sympathy to their neighbours in their human sadnesses and joys, and yield honest loyalty to the magistrate and the prince. They are the most stable of all elements in the civic life of the time, if the powers that be would only understand them; while yet, all the while, they are the only people in the city whose home, consciously, is the eternal heavens. What can explain the paradox? Nothing but the fact, person and character of our Lord Jesus Christ. It is not an enthusiasm, however powerful, which governs them, but a Person. And he is both the Lord of immortality and the Ruler of every detail of his servant's life. He is no author of fanaticism, but the divine-human King of truth and order. To know him is to find the secret both of a life eternal and of a patient faithfulness in the life that now is. What was true then, remains true for us now.

Vv 11–12. *And this*, this law of love and duty, let us remember, let us follow, *knowing the season*, the occasion, the growing crisis; *that it is already the hour for our awaking out of sleep*, the sleep of moral inattention, as if the eternal Master were not near. *For nearer now is our salvation*, in that last glorious sense of the word 'salvation' which means the immortal result of the whole saving process, nearer now *than when we believed*, and so by faith entered on our union with the Saviour. (See how Paul delights to associate himself with his disciples in the blessed unity of remembered conversion; 'when we believed'.) *The night*, with its murky silence, the night of trial, temptation and the absence of our Christ, *is far spent, but the day has drawn near*; it has been a long night, but that means a near dawn; the everlasting sunrise of the longed-for Second Coming with its glory, gladness, and unveiling. *Let us put off therefore*, as if they were a foul and entangling night-robe, *the works of the darkness*, the habits and acts of the moral night, things which we can throw off in the name of Christ; *but let us put on the weapons of the light*, arming ourselves, for defence, and for holy war on the realm of evil, with faith, love, and the heavenly hope. So to the Thessalonians five years before (1 Thess. 5.8), and to the Ephesians four years later (6.11–17), he wrote of the holy armour of God, rapidly sketching it in the one place, giving the rich finished picture in the other; suggesting to the saints always the thought of a warfare that was first and mainly defensive, and then aggressive with the drawn sword, and indicating as their true armour not their reason, emotions, or will, taken in themselves, but the eternal facts of their revealed salvation in Christ, grasped and used by faith.

Vv 13–14. *As by day*, for it is already dawn, in the Lord, *let us walk decorously*, becomingly, as we are the hallowed soldiers of our Leader; let our life not only be right in fact; let it show to all men the open 'decorum' of truth, purity, peace, and love; *not in revels and drunken bouts; not in chamberings*, the sins of the secret couch, *and profligacies*, not – to name evils which cling often to the otherwise reputable Christian – *in strife and envy*, things which are pollutions, in the sight of the Holy One, as real as lust itself. *No; put on*, clothe and arm yourselves with, *the Lord Jesus Christ*, himself the living sum and true meaning of all that can arm the soul; *and for the flesh take no forethought lust-ward*. As if, in euphem-ism, he would say, 'Take all possible forethought against the life of self, with its lustful, self-wilful gravitation away from God. And let that forethought be, to arm yourselves, as if never armed before, with Christ.'

How solemnly explicit is Paul about the temptations of the Roman Christian's life! The men who were capable of the appeals and revelations of the first eight chapters yet needed to be told not to drink to intoxication, not to go near the house of ill-fame, not to quarrel, not to grudge. But every modern missionary will tell us that a similar stern plainness is needed now among the newly-converted faithful. And is it not needed among those who have professed the Pauline faith much longer?

It remains a fact of religious life – this necessity to press it home upon the religious that they are called to a practical and detailed holiness; and that they are never to ignore the possibility of even the worst falls. So mysteriously can the subtle 'flesh', in the believing receiver of the gospel, cloud or distort the holy significance of the thing received.

But a glorious method is illustrated here for triumphant resistance to that tendency. What is it? It is not to retreat from spiritual principle to a cold naturalistic programme of activity and conscientiousness. It is to penetrate through the spiritual principle to the crucified and living Lord who is its heart and power; it is to bury self in him, and to arm the will with him. It is to look for him as coming, but also, and yet more urgently, to use him as present. It is as if the Lord Jesus Christ, was laid at our feet in all he is, in all he has done, in his indissoluble union with us in it all, as we are one with him by the Holy Spirit. It is for us to see in him our power and victory, and to 'put him on', in a personal act which, while all by grace, is yet in itself our own. And how is this done? It is by the 'committal of the keeping of our souls unto him' (1 Pet. 4.19), not vaguely, but definitely and with purpose, in view of each and every temptation. It is by 'living our life in the flesh by faith in the Son of God' (Gal. 2.20); that is to say, in effect, by perpetually making use of the crucified and living Saviour, one with us by the Holy Spirit; by using him as our living deliverer, peace and power, amid all that the dark hosts of evil can do against us.

If we would truly 'arm ourselves with the Lord Jesus Christ' we must wake up and stir ourselves to 'know whom we have trusted' (2 Tim. 1.12). We must explore his Word about himself. We must ponder it, above all in prayer about his promises, till they live to us in his light. We must watch and pray, that we may be alert to employ our armour. The Christian who steps out into life light-heartedly, thinking superficially of his weakness, and of his enemies, is only too likely also to think of his

Lord superficially, and to find of even this heavenly armour that 'he cannot go with it, for he hath not proved it' (1 Sa. 17.39). But all this leaves absolutely untouched the divine simplicity of the matter. It leaves it wonderfully true that the decisive, satisfying, and thorough moral victory and deliverance comes to the Christian not by trampling about with his own resolves, but by committing himself to his Saviour and Keeper, who has conquered him, that now his Saviour may conquer 'his strong enemy' for him. Experience shows that this is no romantic daydream.

Let us, writer and reader, address ourselves afresh in practice to this wonderful secret. Let us, as if we had never done it before, 'put on the Lord Jesus Christ'. Our interpretation of the holy Word, which not only 'abideth, but liveth for ever' (1 Pet. 1.23), is useless if it does not somehow come home. For that word was written on purpose to come home; to touch and move the conscience and the will, in the realities of our inmost, and also or our most outward, life. Never for one moment do we stand as merely interested students and spectators, outside the field of temptation. Never for one moment therefore can we dispense with the great secret of victory and safety.

Full in face of the realities of sin, St Paul here writes down, across them all, these words, this spell, this name; '*Put ye on the Lord Jesus Christ.*' He seems to say, take first a steady look at your need, in the light of God; but then, at once, look off, look here. Here is that by which you can be 'more than conqueror'. Take your sins at the worst; this can subdue them. Take your surroundings at the worst; this can free you from their power. It is 'the Lord Jesus Christ', and the 'putting on' of him.

Let us remember, as if it were a new thing, that Christ is a Fact. Then let us remember that it is a fact that man, in the mercy of God, can 'put him on'. He is not far off. He presents himself to our touch, our possession. He says to us, 'Come to me'. He unveils himself as literal sharer of our nature; as our sacrifice; our righteousness, 'through faith in his blood'; as the Head and Life-spring, in an indescribable union, of a deep calm tide of spiritual and eternal life, ready to circulate through our being. He invites himself to 'make his abode with us' (John 14.23); indeed more, 'I will come in to him'; 'I will dwell in his heart by faith' (Rev. 3.20; Eph. 3.17). He will be the permanent occupant and master of our ungovernable and self-deceptive heart (Je. 17.9).

Yes, we can 'put him on' as our 'armour of light'. We can put him on as 'the Lord', surrendering ourselves to his absolute while most generous sovereignty and will, the deep secret of rest. We can put him on as 'Jesus', clasping the truth that he, our human brother, yet divine, 'saves his people from their sins' (Matt. 1.21). We can put him on as 'Christ', our Head, anointed without measure by the eternal Spirit, and now sending that same Spirit into his happy members, so that we are indeed one with him, and receive into our whole being the resources of his life.

Such is the armour and the arms. As has been said of a related passage (Eph. 6.13), 'by the "weapons of God" the Lord our Saviour is to be understood'. The Holy Spirit will say to us about Romans 13:13–14, as the voice said on the occasion of Augustine's conversion, 'Take and read, take and read'. We will 'put on', never to take off. Then we shall step out of the old path in a strength that is new and to be renewed for ever, armed against evil, armed for the will of God, with Jesus Christ our Lord.

CHAPTER 29

Christian Duty: Mutual Tenderness and Tolerance: The Sacredness of Example (14.1–23)

Vv 1–6. *But him who is weak*—we might almost say, *him who suffers from weakness, in his faith* (in the sense here not of creed, a meaning of 'faith' rare in St Paul, but of reliance on his Lord; reliance not only for justification but, in this case, for holy freedom), *welcome into fellowship—not for criticisms of his scruples*, of the anxious internal debates of conscience. *One man believes*, has faith, issuing in a conviction of liberty, in such a mode and degree *as to eat all kinds of food; but the man in weakness eats vegetables only*; an extreme case, but doubtless not uncommon, where a convert, tired out by his own scruples between food and food, cut the knot by rejecting meat altogether. *The eater—let him not despise the non-eater; while the non-eater—let him not judge the eater; for our God welcomed him to fellowship*, when he came to the feet of his Son for acceptance. *You—who are you, thus judging Another's servant? To his own Lord*, his own Master, *he stands*, in approval—*or, if that must be, falls*, under displeasure; *but he shall be upheld* in approval; *for able is that Lord to set him so*, to bid him 'stand'. *One man distinguishes day above day; while another distinguishes every day;* a paradoxical but intelligible phrase, it describes the thought of the man who, less anxious than his neighbour about stated 'holy-days', still aims not to 'level down' but to 'level up' his use of time; to count every day 'holy', equally dedicated to the will and work of God. *Let each be quite assured in his own mind*; using the thinking-power given him by his Master, let him reverently work the question out, and then live up to his convictions, while (this is conveyed by the emphatic 'his own mind') he respects the convictions of his neighbour. *The man who 'minds' the day*, the 'holy-day' in question, in any given instance, *to the Lord he 'minds' it; [and the*

man who 'minds' not the day, to the Lord he does not 'mind' it]; both
parties, as Christians, in their convictions and their practice,
stand related and responsible, directly and primarily, to the
Lord; that fact must always govern and qualify their mutual
judgments. *And the eater*, the man who takes food indifferently
without scruple, *to the Lord he eats, for he gives thanks* at his meal
to God; and the non-eater, to the Lord he does not eat the food he is
scrupulous over, *and gives thanks to God* for that of which his
conscience allows him to partake.

The connection of this paragraph with what went before it is
suggestive and instructive. There is a close connection between
the two; it is clearly marked by the 'but' of verse 1, a link
strangely missed in the Authorized Version. The 'but' indicates
a difference of thought, however slight, between the two passages.
And the difference seems to be this. The close of the thirteenth
chapter emphasized Christian wakefulness, decision, and the
battlefield of conquering faith. The Roman convert, roused by
its trumpet-call, will be eager to be up and doing, against the
enemy and for his Lord, armed from head to foot with Christ,
devoted to a life of open and active holiness. He will be filled
with a new sense both of the seriousness and of the freedom of
the Gospel.

But then, some 'weak brother' will cross his path. It will be
some recent convert, perhaps from Judaism itself, perhaps an ex-
pagan, but influenced by the Jewish ideas so prevalent at the
time in many Roman circles. This Christian, not distrustful, at
least in theory, of the Lord alone for pardon and acceptance, is
however quite full of scruples which, to the man fully 'armed
with Christ', may and do seem really serious mistakes and hin-
drances. The 'weak brother' spends much time in studying the
traditional rules of eating and fasting, and the code of permitted
food. He is sure that the God who has accepted him will hide
his face from him if he lets the new moon pass like an ordinary
day; or if the Sabbath is not kept by the rule, not of Scripture,
but of the Rabbis. Every social meal gives him painful and
frequent occasion for troubling himself, and others; he takes
refuge perhaps in an anxious vegetarianism, in despair of otherwise being undefiled. And inevitably such scruples do not end

in themselves. They infect the man's whole tone of thinking and action. He questions and discusses everything, with himself, if not with others. He is on the way to let his view of acceptance in Christ grow fainter and more confused. He walks, he lives; but he moves like a chained and imprisoned man.

Such a case as this would be a severe temptation to the 'strong' Christian. He would be greatly inclined, of himself, first to make a vigorous protest, and then, if the difficulty proved obstinate, to think hard thoughts of his narrow-minded friend; to doubt his right to the Christian name at all; to reproach him, or (worst of all) to satirize him. Meanwhile the 'weak' Christian would have his harsh thoughts too. He would not, by any means for certain, show as much meekness as weakness. He would let his neighbour see, in one way or other, that he thought him little better than a worldling, who made Christ an excuse for personal indulgence.

How does Paul meet this problem, which must have crossed his own path so often, and sometimes in the form of a bitter opposition from those who were 'suffering from weakness in their faith'? It is quite plain that his own convictions lay with 'the strong', so far as principle was concerned. He 'knew that nothing was unclean' (v 14). He knew that the Lord was not saddened, but pleased, by the temperate and thankful use, untroubled by morbid fears, of his natural gifts. He knew that the Jewish festival system had found its goal and end in the perpetual 'let us keep the feast' (1 Cor. 5.3) of the true believer's happy and holy life. So he does, in passing, rebuke 'the weak' for their harsh criticisms of 'the strong'. But then, he throws all the more weight, the main weight, on his rebukes and warnings to 'the strong'. Their principle might be right on this great detail. But this left untouched the yet more stringent overruling principle; to 'walk in love'; to take part against themselves; to live in this matter, as in everything else, for others. They were not to be at all ashamed of their special principles. But they were to be deeply ashamed of one hour's unloving conduct. They were to be quietly convinced, in respect of private judgment. They were to be more than tolerant—they were to be loving—in respect of common life in the Lord.

Their 'strength' in Christ was never to be ungentle; never to be used like a giant. It was to be shown, first and most, by patience. It was to take the form of the calm, strong readiness to understand another's point of view. It was to appear as reverence for another's conscience, even when the conscience went astray for lack of better light.

Let us take this apostolic principle into modern religious life. There are, of course, times when we shall be specially bound to put it carefully in relation to other principles. When St Paul, some months earlier, wrote to Galatia, and had to deal with an error which darkened the whole truth of the sinner's way to God through Christ, he did not say, 'Let every man be quite assured in his own mind.' He said (1.8), 'If an angel from heaven preach any other gospel, which is not another, let him be cursed.' The question there was, 'Is Christ all, or is he not? Is faith all, or is it not, for our laying hold of him?' Even in Galatia, Paul warned the converts of the miserable and fatal mistake of 'biting and devouring one another' (5.15). But he commanded them not to wreck their peace with God upon a fundamental error. Here, at Rome, the question was different; it was secondary. It concerned certain details of Christian practice. Was an outworn and exaggerated ceremonialism a part of the will of God, in the justified believer's life? No. Yet it was a matter on which the Lord, by his apostle, counselled rather than commanded. It was not of the foundation. And the always overruling law was the tolerance born of love. Let us in our day remember this, whether our inner sympathies are with 'the strong' or with 'the weak'. In Jesus Christ, it is possible to realize the ideal of this paragraph even in divided Christendom. It is possible to be convinced, yet sympathetic. It is possible to see the Lord for ourselves with glorious clearness, yet to understand the practical difficulties felt by others, and to love, and to respect, where there are even great divergences. No one works more for a final spiritual consensus than the one who, in Christ, lives like this.

Incidentally, meantime, Paul, in this passage which so curbs 'the strong' lets fall maxims which protect for ever all that is good and true in that well-worn and often misused phrase, 'the right of private judgment'. No spiritual despot, no claimant to be the autocratic director of a conscience, could have written

those words, 'Let every man be quite certain in his own mind';
'Who art thou that judgest Another's servant?' Such sentences
assert not the right so much as the duty, for the individual
Christian, of a reverent 'thinking for himself'. They maintain a
true and noble individualism. And there is a special need just
now in the Church to remember, in its place, the value of Christian individualism. The idea of the community, the society, is just
now so widely prevalent (doubtless not without the providence
of God) in human life, and also in the Church, that an assertion
of the individual, which was once disproportionate, is now often
necessary, lest the social idea in its turn should be exaggerated
into a dangerous mistake. Coherence, mutuality, the truth of the
Body and the Members; all this, in its place, is not only important
but divine. The individual must inevitably lose where individualism is his whole idea. But it is ill for the community, above all
for the Church, where the individual tends really to be merged
and lost in the total. The Church can be perfectly strong only
where individual consciences are tender, and enlightened; where
individual souls personally know God in Christ; where individual
wills are ready, if the Lord call, to stand alone for known truth
even against the religious community; if there also the individualism is not self-will, but Christian personal responsibility; if
the man 'thinks for himself' on his knees; if he reverences the
individualism of others, and the relations of each to all.

The individualism of Romans 14, asserted in an argument full
of the deepest secrets of cohesion, is the holy and healthful thing
it is because it is Christian. It is developed not by the assertion
of self, but by individual communion with Christ.

Now Paul goes on to further and still fuller statements in the
same direction:

Vv 7–9. *For none of us to himself lives, and none of us to himself dies.*
Is it merely that we live lives always, necessarily, related to one
another? He certainly has this in his thoughts, but he reaches it
through the greater, deeper, previous truth of our relation to the
Lord. The Christian is related to his brother-Christian through
Christ, not to Christ through his brother, or through the common
organism in which the brethren are 'each other's limbs'. Each
individual Christian is first related 'to the Lord', with absolute

directness, and with a perfect and wonderful immediateness. His life and his death are 'to others', but through Christ. The Master's claim is eternally first; for it is based direct upon the redeeming work in which he bought us for himself.

For whether we live, to the Lord we live; and whether we be dead, to the Lord we are dead; in the state of the departed, as before, 'relation stands'. *Alike therefore whether we be dead, or whether we live, the Lord's we are*; his property, bound first and in everything to his possession. *For to this end Christ both died and lived again that he might become Lord of us both dead and living.*

Here is the deep truth seen already in earlier passages in the epistle. We have had it reasoned out, above all in the sixth chapter, in its revelation of the way of holiness, that our only possible right relations with the Lord are governed by the fact that we rightly and everlastingly belong to him. There, however, the thought was more of our surrender under his rights. Here it is of the mighty preceding fact, under which our most absolute surrender is nothing more than the recognition of his irrevocable claim. What the apostle says here, in this wonderful passage of mingled doctrine and duty, is that, whether or not we admit our slavery to Christ, we are nothing if not his slaves by right. He has not only rescued us, but rescued us so as to buy us for his own. We may be true to the fact in our internal attitude; we may be oblivious of it; but we cannot get away from it. It looks us every hour in the face, whether we respond or not. It will still look us in the face through the endless life to come.

For clearly it is this objective aspect of our 'belonging' which is here in point. St Paul is not reasoning with the 'weak' and the 'strong' from their experience, from their conscious loyalty to the Lord. Rather, he is calling them to a new realization of what such loyalty should be. This is why he reminds them of the eternal claim of the Lord, made good in his death and resurrection; his claim to be their Master, individually and altogether, in such a way that every thought about one other was to be governed by his claim on them all. This passage also has something to say about the present state of the dead.

The apostle mentions death and the dead four times over in this short paragraph. 'No one of us dieth to himself'; 'Whether we die, we die unto the Lord'; 'Whether we die, we are the Lord's'; 'That he might be Lord of the dead'. And this last sentence, with its mention not of the dying but of the dead, reminds us that the reference in them all is to the Christian's relation to his Lord, not only at death, but in the state after death. It is not only that Jesus Christ, as the slain One risen, is absolute disposer of the time and manner of our dying. It is not only that when our death comes we are to accept it as an opportunity for the 'glorifying of God' (John 21.19; Phil. 1.20) in the sight and in the memory of those who know of it. It is that when we have 'passed through death', our relation to the slain One risen, to him who, as such, 'hath the keys of Hades and of death' (Rev. 1.18), is perfectly continuous and the same. He is our absolute Master, there as well as here.

Here is a truth which must richly repay the Christian's repeated remembrance and reflection; not only in asserting the eternal rights of our blessed Redeemer over us, but in shedding light and peace, and the sense of reality and expectation, on both the prospect of our own passage into eternity and the thoughts we hold about the present life of our holy beloved ones who have entered into it before us.

Everything which really assists the soul in such thoughts, and at the same time keeps it fully and practically alive to the realities of faith, patience, and obedience here below is precious. While the indulgence of unauthorized imagination in that direction is almost always weakening and disturbing to the present action of scriptural faith, the least help to a solid realization and anticipation, supplied by the Word that cannot lie, is in its nature both hallowing and strengthening. Such a help we have here.

He who died and rose again is the Lord of the blessed dead, the blessed dead are his slaves and servants. And all our thought of them, as they are now, gains indefinitely in life, in reality, in strength and glory, as we see them, through this narrow but bright 'door in heaven' (Rev. 5.1), not just resting but serving before their Lord, who has bought them for his use, and who holds them in his use quite as truly now as when we had the joy of their presence with us, and he was seen by us living and working in them and through them here.

It is true that the primary and essential character of their present state is rest, as that of their resurrection state will be action. But the two states overflow into each other. In one glorious passage the apostle describes the resurrection bliss as also 'rest' (2 Thess. 1.7). And here we have it indicated that the heavenly intermediate rest is also service. What the precise nature of that service is we cannot tell. This is part of our normal and God-chosen lot here, which is to 'walk by faith, not by sight' (2 Cor. 5.7). But it is of great spiritual help to us to remember, as we draw nearer to that happy assembly above, that, whatever be the manner and exercise of their holy life, it is true life; power, not weakness; service, not inaction. He who died and revived is Lord, not just of us, but of them.

But we must return from this detour to Paul's concern with this life.

Vv 10–12. *But you — why do you judge your brother?* (he takes up the verb used in his former appeal to the 'weak', v 3). *Or you too* (he turns to the 'strong', see again v 3) — *why do you despise your brother? For we shall stand*, all of us, on one level, whatever were our feelings about each other on earth, whatever claim we made here to sit as judges on our brethren, *before the tribunal of our God. For it stands written* (Is. 45.23), *'As I live, saith the Lord*, sure it is as my eternal being, *that to me*, not to another, *shall bend every knee; and every tongue shall confess*, shall ascribe all sovereignty, *to God'*, not to the creature. *So then each of us about himself*, not about the faults or errors of his brother, *shall give account to God.*

We have here, as in 1 Corinthians 3.11–15 and 2 Corinthians 5.10, a glimpse of that heart-searching prospect for the Christian, his summons in the next life, *as a Christian*, to the tribunal of his Lord. In all the three passages, and now particularly in this, the language, though it lends itself freely to the general judgment, is limited by context, to the Master's scrutiny of his own servants. The question to be tried and decided (speaking humanly) at his 'tribunal', in this context, is not that of glory or damnation; the people being examined are accepted; the enquiry is in the domestic court of the palace, so to speak; it concerns the award of the King regarding the results and value of his accepted servants' labour and conduct, as his representatives, in their earthly life.

'The Lord of the servants cometh, and reckoneth with them' (Matt. 25.19). They have been justified by faith. They have been united to their glorious Head. They shall be saved whatever be the fate of their work. But what will their Lord say of their work? What have they done for him, in labour, in witness, and above all in character? He will tell them what he thinks. He will be infinitely kind; but he will not flatter. And somehow, surely — 'it doth not yet appear' how, but somehow — eternity, even the eternity of salvation, will bear the imprint of that award. 'What shall the harvest be?'

And all this shall take place (this is the special emphasis here) on an individual basis. 'Every one of us — for himself — shall give account.' We reflected, a little above, on the true place of 'individualism' in the life of grace. We see here that there will indeed be a place for it in the experiences of eternity. The scrutiny of the tribunal will concern not society, the total, but the member, the individual. Each will stand in a solemn solitude there, before his divine examiner. The question will be, what he was, as the Lord's member. The result will be, what he shall be in eternity.

Let us not be troubled over this with the trouble of the worldling, as if we did not know him who will scrutinize us, and did not love him. Around the thought of his tribunal, from that point of view, there are cast no deadly terrors. But it is a prospect fit to make the life which 'is hid with Christ in God', and which is life indeed through grace, full of serious purpose. It is a deep reminder that the beloved Saviour is also, and in no figure of speech, the Master too. We would not have him not to be this. He would not be all he is to us as Saviour, were he not this also, and for ever.

After this solemn forecast St Paul quickly moves to further appeals. And now all his stress is laid on the duty of the 'strong' to use their 'strength' not for self-assertion, not for even spiritual selfishness, but all for Christ, all for others, all in love.

Vv 13–14. *No more therefore let us judge one another; but judge*, decide, *this rather — not to set stumblingblock for our brother, or trap. I know —* he instances his own experience and principle — *and am sure, in the Lord Jesus*, as one who is in union and communion with him, seeing truth and life from that viewpoint, *that nothing*, nothing of the sort in question, no food, no time, *is 'unclean' of itself;* literally 'by means of itself', by any inherent mischief; *only, to the man who counts anything 'unclean', to him it is unclean.* And therefore you, because you are not his conscience, must not tamper with his conscience. It is, in this case, mistaken; mistaken to his own loss, and to the loss of the Church. Yes, but what it needs is not your compulsion, but the Lord's light. If you can do so, bring that light to bear, in a testimony made impressive by holy love and unselfish considerateness. But dare not, for Christ's sake, compel a conscience. For conscience means the man's best actual sight of the law of right and wrong. It may be a dim and distorted sight; but it is his best at this moment. He cannot violate it without sin, nor can you bid him do so without yourself sinning. Conscience may not always see correctly. But to sin against conscience is always wrong.

V 15. *For*—the word takes up the argument in general, rather than the last detail of it—*if for food's sake your brother suffers pain,* the pain of a moral struggle between his present convictions and your commanding example, *you have given up walking love-wise. Do not, with your food* (there is a searching point in the 'your', touching to the heart the deep selfishness of the action), *work his ruin for whom Christ died.*

Such sentences are too intensely and tenderly in earnest to be called sarcastic; otherwise, how sharp an edge they carry! 'For food's sake!' 'With your food!' The man is shaken out of the sleep of what seemed an assertion of freedom, but was after all much rather a dull indulgence of—that is, a mere slavery to—himself. 'I like this meat; I like this drink; I don't like the worry of these scruples; they interrupt me, they annoy me.' Unhappy man! It is better to be the slave of scruples, than of self. In order to allow yourself another dish you would disregard an anxious friend's conscience, and, so far as your conduct is concerned, push him to a violation of it. But that means a push on the slope which leans toward spiritual ruin. The way to damnation is paved with violated consciences. The Lord may counteract your action, and save your injured brother from himself—and you. But your action is, none the less, calculated for his damnation. And all the while this soul, for which, in comparison with your

dull and narrow 'freedom', you care so little, was so much cared
for by the Lord that he died for it.

Vv 16–19. *Do not therefore let your good*, your glorious creed of holy
freedom in Christ, *be railed at*, as only a thinly veiled self-indulgence after all; *for the kingdom of our God is not feeding and drinking;*
He does not claim a throne in your soul just to make it your
sacred privilege, as an end in itself, to take what you please at
table; *but righteousness*, surely here, in Romans, the 'righteousness'
of our divine acceptance, *and peace*, the peace of perfect relations
with him in Christ, *and joy in the Holy Spirit*, the pure strong
gladness of the justified, as in their sanctuary of salvation they
drink the 'living water', and 'rejoice always in the Lord'. *For he
who in this way lives as bondservant to Christ* spending his spiritual
talents not for himself but for his Master, *is pleasing to his God,
and is genuine to his fellow-men.* Yes, he stands the test of their keen
scrutiny. They can soon detect the counterfeit under spiritual
assertions which really assert self. But their conscience affirms
the genuineness of a life of unselfish and happy holiness.

Accordingly therefore let us pursue the interests *of peace, and the*
interests *of an edification which is mutual*; the 'building up' which
looks beyond the man to his brothers, and modifies by that look
even his plans for his own spiritual life.

Vv 20–21. Again he returns to the sad and distorted state of
preferring personal comforts, and even the assertion of the principle of personal liberty, to the good of others. *Do not for food's
sake be undoing the work of our God. 'All things are pure';* he doubtless
quotes a frequently heard slogan; and it was truth itself in the
abstract, but capable of becoming a fatal fallacy in practice; *but*
anything *is bad to the man who is brought by a stumblingblock to eat it.*
Yes, this is bad. What is good in contrast?

Good it is not to eat flesh, and not to drink wine (a word for our
time and its conditions), *and not to do anything in which your brother
is stumbled, or entrapped, or weakened.* Yes, this is Christian freedom;
a liberation from the strong and subtle law of self; a freedom to
live for others, independent of their evil, but the servant of their
souls.

Vv 22–23. *You—the faith you have, have it by yourself, in the presence
of your God.* You have believed; you are therefore in Christ; in

Christ you are therefore free, by faith, from the preparatory restrictions of the past. Yes; but all this is not given you for personal display, but for divine communion. Its right result is in a holy intimacy with your God, as in the confidence of your acceptance you know Him as your Father. But as regards human relationships, you are emancipated not that you may disturb the neighbours with shouts of freedom and acts of license, but that you may be at leisure to serve them in love. *Happy the man who does not judge himself*, who does not, in effect, decide against his own soul, *in that which he approves*, pronounces satisfactory to conscience. Unhappy he who says to himself, 'This is lawful', when the verdict is all the while purchased by self-love, or otherwise by the fear of man, and the soul knows in its depths that the thing is not as it should be. *And the man who is doubtful*, whose conscience is not really satisfied between the right and wrong of the matter, *if he does eat, stands condemned*, in the court of his own heart, and of his aggrieved Lord's opinion, *because it* was *not the result of faith*; the action had not, for its basis, the holy conviction of the freedom of the justified. *Now anything which is not the result of faith, is sin;* that is to say, clearly, 'anything' in such a case as this; any indulgence, any obedience to example, which the man, in a state of inward ambiguity, decides for on a principle other than that of his union with Christ by faith.

Thus the apostle of justification, and of the Holy Spirit, is the apostle of conscience too. He is as insistent upon the awful sacredness of our sense of right and wrong, as upon the offer and the security, in Christ, of peace with God, and the holy Indwelling, and the hope of glory. Let our steps reverently follow his, as we walk with God, and with men. Let us 'rejoice in Christ Jesus', with a 'joy' which is 'in the Holy Spirit'. Let us reverence duty and conscience in our own life, and also in the lives around us.

CHAPTER 30

Christian Duty: The Lord's Example: His Relation to Us All (15.1–13)

The wide and searching treatment which the apostle has already given to the right use of Christian freedom is insufficient. He must go on to put it into more explicit contact with the Lord himself.

We gather without doubt that the state of the Roman mission, as it was reported to St Paul, gave special occasion for such full discussion. It is more than likely, as we have seen from the first, that the bulk of the disciples were ex-pagans; probably of very various nationalities, many of them Asian, and as such not more favourable to distinctive Jewish claims and beliefs. It is also likely that they found amongst them, or beside them, many Christian Jews, or Christian Jewish proselytes, of a type more or less like them; the school whose less worthy members supplied the men to whom St Paul, a few years later, writing from Rome to Philippi, refers as 'preaching Christ of envy and strife' (Phil. 1.15). The temptation of a religious (as of a secular) majority is always to tyrannize, more or less, in matters of thought and practice. A dominant school, in any age or region, too easily comes to talk and act as if all decided expression on the other side were an instance of 'intolerance', while it allows itself severe and censorious actions of its own. This mischief was very probably in action at Rome. The 'strong', with whose principle, in its true form, St Paul agreed, were disposed to domineer in spirit over the 'weak', because the weak were comparatively few. Thus they were guilty of a double fault; they were presenting a miserable parody of holy freedom, and they were acting outside the unselfish fairness which is essential in the gospel character. For the sake not only of the peace of the great mission church, but of the honour of the truth, and of the Lord, the apostle therefore dwells on mutual duties, and returns to them again and again after apparently completing what he has to say. Let us listen as he now returns to the subject, to set it more fully than ever in the light of Christ.

Vv 1–2. *But* (it is the 'but' of resumption, and of new material) *we are bound, we the able* (perhaps a sort of nickname for themselves among the school of 'liberty', 'the capables') — *to bear the weaknesses of the unable* (again, possibly, an unkind nickname for a group) *and not to please ourselves. Each one of us, let him please* not himself but *his neighbour, as regards what is good, with a view to edification.*

In classical literature the word 'please' tends to mean the 'pleasing' which fawns and flatters; the complaisance of the parasite. But it is lifted by Christian usage to a noble level. The cowardly and interested element drops out of it; the thought of willingness to do anything to please remains; but limited by the law of right, and aimed only at the other's good. Here, it is the unselfish and watchful aim to meet half way, if possible, the thought and feeling of a fellow-disciple, to conciliate by sympathetic attentions, to be considerate in the smallest matters of opinion and conduct; a genuine exercise of inward liberty.

There is a gulf of difference between interested timidity and disinterested considerateness. In flight from the former, the ardent Christian sometimes breaks the rule of the latter. St Paul is at hand to warn him not to forget the great law of love. And the Lord is at his hand too, with his own supreme example.

V 3. *For even our Christ did not please himself; but, as it stands written,* Ps. 69.9, *'The reproaches of those who reproached thee, fell upon me.'*

It is the first mention in the epistle of the Lord's example. We have seen his person, the atoning work, the resurrection power, and the great return. The holy example can never take the place of any one of these facts of eternal life. But when they are secure, then the reverent study of the example is of urgent and immeasurable importance.

'He did not please himself'. 'Not my will, but thine, be done.' Perhaps the thought of the apostle is dwelling on the time those words were spoken in Gethsemane out of a depth of inward conflict and surrender which 'it hath not entered into the heart of man'—except the heart of the Man of men himself—'to conceive'. Then indeed 'he did not please himself'. Every living being naturally and necessarily shrinks from pain as pain, from grief as grief, it 'pleases itself' in escape or in relief. The Son of Man was no exception to this law of universal nature; and now he was called to greater pain and grief than ever before experienced by one person. We read the record of Gethsemane, and its sacred horror is always new; the disciple passes in thought from the garden to the cruel tribunal of the High Priest with a sense of relief; his Lord has risen from the unfathomable to the fathomable depth of his woes—till he goes down again, at noon next day, on the cross. 'He pleased not himself.' He who soon after, by the lake-side, said to Peter, in view of his glorious and God-glorifying end, 'They shall carry thee whither thou wouldest not'—along a path from which all thy manhood shall shrink—He too, as to his human feelings did not wish to go to his own unknown agonies. But then, blessed be his name, he did wish to go to them, from the side of the infinite harmony of his purpose with the purpose of his Father, in his immeasurable desire for his Father's glory. So he 'drank that cup', which shall never now pass on to his people. And then he went into the house of Caiaphas, to be 'reproached', during some six or seven terrible hours, by men who, professing zeal for God, were all the while blaspheming him by every act and word of malice and untruth against his Son; and from Caiaphas he went to Pilate, and to Herod, and to the cross, 'bearing that reproach'.

We are called in these words not necessarily to any agony of body or spirit; not necessarily even to an act of severe moral courage; only to patience, largeness of heart, brotherly love. Shall we not answer 'Amen'? Shall not even one thought of 'the fellowship of his sufferings' kill in us the miserable 'self-pleasing' which shows itself in religious bitterness, in the refusal to pay attention and to understand, in a censoriousness which has nothing to do with firmness, in a personal attitude exactly opposite to love?

He has cited Psalm 69 as a scripture which, with all the problems of its condemnatory paragraph, yet lives and moves with Christ, the Christ of love. And now—not to confirm his application of the Psalm, for he takes that for granted—but to affirm the positive Christian use of the Old Testament as a whole, he goes on to speak at large of 'the things fore-written'. He does so with the special thought that the Old Testament is full of truth relevant to the Roman church just now; full of the bright, and uniting, hope of glory; full of examples as well as commands for patience, that is to say, holy perseverance under trial; full finally of the Lord's equally gracious relation to the nations and to Israel.

V 4. *For all the things fore-written*, written in the earlier Scriptures, in the age that both preceded the gospel and prepared for it, *for our instruction were written*—with an emphasis upon 'our'—*that through the patience and through the encouragement of the Scriptures we might hold our hope*, the sure and steadfast hope of glorification in the glory of our conquering Lord. That is to say, the true 'Author behind the authors' of this mysterious Book watched, guided, effected its construction, from end to end, with the unwavering purpose of instructing for all time the developed Church of Christ. And in particular, he adjusted the Old Testament records and commands of 'patience', the patience which 'suffers and is strong', suffers and goes forward, and of 'encouragement', the word which is more than 'consolation', while it includes it; for it means the voice of positive and revitalizing appeal. All parts of the Old Testament are rich in commands to persevere and be of good courage, and in examples of men who were made brave and patient by the power of God in them, as they took him at his word. And all this, says the apostle, was on purpose, on God's purpose. That varied Book is indeed in this sense one. Not only is it, in its Author's intention, full of Christ; in the same intention it is full of him for us. We may confidently explore its pages, looking in them first for Christ, then for ourselves, in our need of peace, and strength, and hope.

Let us add one word, in view of the anxious controversy of our day, within the Church, over the structure and nature of those 'divine Scriptures', as the Christian fathers love to call them. The use of the Bible in the spirit of this verse, the persistent searching of it for the instructing mind of God in it, with the belief that it was 'written for our instruction', will be the surest and deepest means to give us 'perseverance' and 'encouragement' about the Bible itself. The more we really know the Bible, at first hand, before God, with the knowledge both of acquaintance and reverent sympathy, the more shall we be able with intelligent spiritual conviction, to 'persist' and 'be of good cheer' in the conviction that it is indeed not of man (though through man), but of God. The more shall we use it as the Lord and the apostles used it, as being not only of God, but of God for us; his word, and for us. The more shall we make it our divine daily manual for a life of patient and cheerful sympathies, holy fidelity, and 'that blessed hope'—which draws 'nearer now than when we believed'.

V 5. *But may the God of the patience and the encouragement*, he who is author and giver of the graces unfolded in his word, he without whom even that word is but a sound without significance in the soul, *grant you*, in his own sovereign way of acting on and in human wills and affections, *to be of one mind mutually, according to Christ Jesus;* 'Christwise', in his steps, in his attitude, under his commands; having towards one another, not necessarily an identity of opinion on all details, but a community of sympathetic kindness, as in Philippians 2.2–5.

V 6. And all this, not only for the comfort of the community, but for the glory of God: *that unanimously, with one mouth, you may glorify the God and Father of our Lord Jesus Christ;* turning from the sorrowful friction worked by self-will when it intrudes into spiritual matters, to a holy and effective antidote, found in adoring him who is equally near to all his true people, in his Son.

V 7. *Wherefore welcome one another into fellowship, even as our Christ welcomed you*, all the individuals of your company, and all the groups of it, *to our God's glory*. These last words may mean either that the Lord's welcome of 'you' 'glorified' his Father's grace; or that that grace will be 'glorified' by the holy victory of love over prejudice among the Roman saints. Perhaps this latter explanation is to be preferred, as it echoes and enforces the last words of the previous verse. But why should not both references be present in the one phrase, where the actions of the Lord and his disciples are seen in their deep harmony?

Vv 8–13. *For I say that Christ stands constituted servant of the circumcision,* minister of divine blessings to Israel, *on behalf of God's truth, so as to ratify* in act *the promises belonging to the fathers,* so as to secure and vindicate their fulfilment, by his coming as Son of David, Son of Abraham; *but* (a 'but' which, by its slight correction, reminds the Jew that the promise, given wholly through him, was not given wholly for him) *so that the nations, on mercy's behalf, should glorify God,* blessing and adoring him on account of a salvation which, in their case, was less of 'truth' than of 'mercy', because it was less explicitly and immediately of covenant; *as it stands written* (Ps. 18.49), '*For this I will confess to thee,* will own thee, *among the nations, and will strike the harp to thy name*'; Messiah confessing his eternal Father's glory in the midst of his redeemed Gentile subjects, who sing their 'lower part' with him. *And again it,* the Scripture, *says* (Dt. 32.43), '*Be jubilant, nations, with his people.*' *And again* (Ps. 107.1), *Praise the Lord, all the nations, and let all the peoples praise him again*'. *And again Isaiah says* (11.10), '*There shall come* (literally 'shall be') *the Root of Jesse, and he who rises up*— 'rises', in the present tense of the divine decree—*to rule (the) nations; on him (the) nations shall hope;* with the hope which is in fact faith, looking from the sure present to the promised future. *Now may the God of that hope,* 'the hope' just cited from the prophet, the expectation of all blessing, up to its crown and flower in glory, on the basis of Messiah's work, *fill you with all joy and peace in your believing, so that you may overflow in that hope, in the Holy Spirit's power;* 'in his power', as if clasped in his divine embrace, and so energized to look upward, heavenward, away from embittering and dividing temptations to the unifying as well as blessed prospect of your Lord's return.

Paul closes here his long, wise, tender appeal and counsel about the unhappy divisions of the Roman mission. He has led his readers all round the subject. With the utmost tact, and also candour, he has given them his own mind, 'in the Lord', on the matter in dispute. He has pointed out to the scrupulous and restrictive the fallacy of claiming the function of Christ, and asserting a divine rule where he has not imposed one. He has addressed the 'strong' (with whom he agrees in a certain sense) at much greater length, reminding them of the moral error of making more of any given application of their principle than of the law of love in which the principle was rooted. He has brought both parties to the feet of Jesus Christ as absolute Master. He has led them to gaze on him as their blessed example, in his infinite self-oblivion for the cause of God, and of love. He has poured out before them the prophecies, which tell at once the Christian Judaist and the ex-pagan convert that in the eternal purpose Christ was given equally to both, in truth and mercy. Now he prays for both sides, and for all the individuals involved, a wonderful fullness of those blessings in which the spirit of their strife would rapidly expire. Let that prayer be granted, and how could 'the weak brother' look with quite his old anxiety on the problems suggested by the dishes at a meal, and by the dates of the rabbinic calendar? And how could 'the capable' bear any longer to lose his joy in God by an assertion, full of self, of his own insight and 'freedom'? Profoundly happy and at rest in their Lord, whom they embraced by faith as their righteousness and life, and whom they anticipated in hope as their coming glory; filled through their whole consciousness, by the indwelling Spirit, with a new insight into Christ; they would fall into each other's embrace, in him. They would be much more ready, when they met, to speak 'concerning the King' than to begin a new stage of their not very elevating discussion.

How many a church controversy, now as then, would fade away, leaving room for a living truth, if the disputants could only turn to the praises and glories of their redeeming Lord himself! It is at his feet, and in his arms, that we best understand both his truth, and the true or mistaken thoughts of our fellows.

Meanwhile, let us take this prayer and apply it to our own lives. What the apostle prayed for the Romans, in view of their controversies, he prays for us, as for them, in view of everything. Let us stand back and look at the picture. Here—conveyed in this strong petition—is St Paul's idea of the true Christian's true life, and the true life of the true Church. What are the elements, and what is the result? Six points may be made.

1. It is a life lived in direct contact with God. 'Now the God of hope fill you'. He sends them here (as above, v 5) from even

himself to the living God. In a sense, he sends them even from 'the things forewritten', to the living God; not in the least to disparage the Scriptures, but because the great function of the divine word, as of the divine ordinances, is to guide the soul into an immediate relationship with the Lord God in his Son. God is to deal direct with the Romans. He is to manipulate, and to fill, their being.

2. It is a life not starved or restricted, but full. 'The God of hope *fill you*'. The disciple, and the Church, is not to live as if grace were like a nearly dried-up stream. The believer, and the institution, are to live and work in tranquil but moving strength, 'rich' in the fruits of their Lord's 'poverty' (2 Cor. 8.9); filled out of His fullness; never, spiritually, at a loss for him; never, practically, having to act or bear except in his great and gracious power.

3. It is a life that is bright and beautiful; 'filled with all joy and peace' in Christ present, and Christ to come. A sacred while open happiness and a pure internal rest is to be there, born of 'his presence, in which is fullness of joy', and of the sure hope of his return, bringing with it 'pleasures for evermore'. This joy, this peace, found and maintained 'in the Lord', is to pervade all the contents of the Christian life, its periods of duty or trial, its intervals of rest or silence. It is not always demonstrative but always underlying, and always a living power.

4. It is a life of faith; 'all joy and peace in your believing'. That is to say, it is a life dependent for its all upon a Person and his promises. Its glad certainty of peace with God, of the possession of his righteousness, is not through feelings and experiences, but of believing; it comes, and stays, by taking Christ at his word. Its power over temptation, its 'victory and triumph against the devil, the world, and the flesh', is by the same means. The believer, the Church, takes the Lord at his word:—'I am with you always'; 'Through me thou shalt do valiantly'; and faith, that is to say, Christ trusted in practice, is 'more than conqueror'.

5. It is a life overflowing with the heavenly hope; 'that ye may abound in the hope'. Sure of the past, and of the present, it is—what out of Christ no life can be—sure of the future. The golden

age, for this happy life, is in front, and is no utopia. 'Now is our salvation nearer'; 'We look for that blissful hope, the appearing of our great God and Saviour'; 'Them which sleep in him God will bring with him'; 'We shall be caught up together with them; we shall ever be with the Lord'; 'They shall see his face; thine eyes shall see the King in his beauty'.

6. And all this it is as a life lived 'in the power of the Holy Spirit'. Not by enthusiasm, not by any stimulus which self applies to self; not by resources for gladness and permanence found in independent reason or affection; but by the almighty, all-tender power of the Comforter. 'The Lord, the Life-Giver', giving life by bringing us to the Son of God, and uniting us to him, is the giver and strong sustainer of the faith, and so of the peace, joy, and hope, of this blessed life.

'Now it was not written for their sakes only, but for us also', in our circumstances of personal and of common experience. The application of this one statement to the problems perpetually raised by the divided state of organization and opinion in modern Christendom is vast and significant. It gives us one vital secret as the sure remedy, if it may but be allowed to work, for this deplorable state of affairs. That secret is 'the secret of the Lord, which is with them that fear him' (Ps 25.14). It is a fuller life in the individual, and so in the community, of the peace and joy of believing; a larger abundance of 'that blessed hope', given by that power for which numberless hearts are learning to thirst with a new intensity, 'the power of the Holy Spirit'.

It was in that direction above all that the apostle gazed as he yearned for the practical and spiritual unity of the Roman saints. This great master of order, this man made for government, alive to the sacred importance, in its true place, of the external institution of Christianity, yet makes no mention of it here, no, scarcely gives one allusion to it in the whole epistle. The word 'Church' is not heard till the final chapter; and then it is used only, or almost only, of the scattered mission-stations, or even mission-groups, in their individuality. The ordered ministry is mentioned only twice, in passing (Rom. 12.6–8, 16.1). He is addressing the saints of the great city which was later to develop into even terrific exaggerations the idea of church order. But he has practically nothing to say to them about unification and cohesion beyond this appeal to hold fast together by drawing nearer each and all to the Lord, and so filling each individual's soul and life with Christ.

Our modern problems must be met with attention, with firmness, with practical purpose, with due regard to history, and with submission to revealed truth. But if they are to be truly solved they must be met outside the spirit of self, and in the communion of the Christian with Christ, by the power of the Spirit of God.

CHAPTER 31

Roman Christianity: Paul's Commission: his Intended Itinerary: He Asks for Prayer (15.14–33)

The epistle is now almost complete, apart from Paul's last words about people and plans.

He will say a warm, gracious word about the spiritual state of the Roman believers. He will justify, with a noble courtesy, his own authoritative attitude as their counsellor. He will talk a little of his hoped for and now seemingly approaching visit, and matters connected with it. He will greet the individuals whom he knows, and commend the bearer of the letter, and add last messages from his friends. Then Phoebe may receive her charge, and go on her way.

V 14. *But I am sure, my brethren, quite on my own part, about you, that you are, yourselves,* irrespective of my influence, *brimming with goodness,* with high Christian qualities in general, *filled with all knowledge, competent in fact to admonish one another.* Is this insincere flattery, or weakness, easily persuaded into a false optimism? Surely not; for the speaker here is the man who has spoken straight to the hearts of these same people about sin, judgment, and holiness; about the holiness of these daily duties which some of them (so he has said plainly enough) had been violating. But a truly great heart always loves to praise where it can, and, discerningly, to think and say the best. Christ himself said of his imperfect and disappointing followers, as he spoke of them in their hearing to his Father, 'They have kept thy word'; 'I am glorified in them' (John 6. 10). So here his servant does not give the Romans a formal certificate of perfection, but he does rejoice to know, and to say, that their community is Christian in a high degree, and that in a certain sense they have not needed information about justification by faith, nor about principles of love and liberty in their conduct. In essence, all has been known to them already; an assurance which could certainly not have been entertained in regard to every mission. He has written not as to children, giving them an alphabet, but as to men, developing facts into science.

Vv 15–16. *But with a certain boldness I have written to you, here and there, just as reminding you; because of the grace,* the free gift of his commission and of the equipment for it, *given me by our God,* given in order to *my being Christ Jesus' minister* sent *to the nations, doing priest-work with the gospel of God, that the oblation of the nations,* the offering which is in fact the nations self-laid upon the spiritual altar, *may be acceptable, consecrated in the Holy Spirit.* It is a startling and splendid passage of metaphor. Here alone (unless we except the few and affecting words of Phil. 2.17), the apostle presents himself to his converts as a sacrificial minister, or 'priest' in the sense in which it is usually used in English. Neither Christ nor any of the great founders of the Church use the word 'priest' to describe the Christian minister. In Hebrews it refers to the finished and on-going work of Christ. In 1 Peter it refers to all Christians and to their spiritual sacrifices, 'the praises of him who called them into his wonderful light' (1 Pet. 2.5, 9). In the Christian Church, the pre-Levitical idea of the old Israel reappears in its sacred reality. He who offered to the Church of Moses (Ex. 19.6) to be one great priesthood, 'a kingdom of priests, and a holy nation', found his favoured nation unready for the privilege, and so Levi took the place alone as its representative. But now, in his new Israel, as all are sons in the Son, so all are priest in the Priest. And the ministry which is his own divine institution, the gift (Eph. 4.11) of the ascended Lord to his Church, is never once designated, as such, by the term which would have marked it as the parallel to Levi, or to Aaron.

Is this passage in any degree an exception? No, for it contains its own full inner evidence of its metaphorical nature. The 'priest-working' here refers not to a ritual, but to 'the gospel' 'The oblation' is the nations. The sanctifying element, shed as it were upon the victims, is the Holy Spirit. Not in a material temple, and serving at no tangible altar, the apostle brings his many converts as his offering to the Lord. The Spirit, at his preaching

and on their believing, descends upon them; and they offer themselves 'a living sacrifice' where the fire of love shall consume
them, to his glory.

V 17. *I have therefore my* right *to exultatation, in Christ Jesus,* as his
member and instrument, *as to what regards God*; not in any respect
as regards myself, apart from him. And then Paul proceeds as if
about to say, in evidence of that assertion, that he always declines
to intrude on a brother apostle's ground, and to claim as his own
experience what was in the least degree another's; but that indeed
through him, in sovereign grace, God has done great things, far
and wide.

Vv 18–19a. *For I will not dare to talk at all of things which Christ did
not work out through me* (there is an emphasis on 'me'), *to effect
obedience of (the) nations* to his gospel, *by word and deed, in power of
signs and wonders, in power of God's Spirit*; a reference, strangely
impressive by its incidental nature, to the exercise of miracle-
working gifts by the writer. This man, who was so strong in
thought, so practical in counsel, and so extremely unlikely to
have been under an illusion about a large factor in his adult and
intensely conscious experience, speaks direct from himself about
his wonder-works. And the allusion, dropped like this in passing,
is itself evidence of the perfect mental balance of the witness;
this was no enthusiast, intoxicated with ambitious spiritual
visions, but a man entrusted with a mysterious yet sober treasure.

V 19b. *So that from Jerusalem, and round about it* (Acts 26.20), *as far
as the Illyrian* region, the highland seaboard which looks across
the Adriatic to the long eastern side of Italy, *I have fulfilled the
gospel of Christ*, carried it practically everywhere, satisfied the idea
of distributing it that it shall be accessible everywhere to the
local people.

Vv 20–24. *But* this I have done *with this ambition, to preach the
gospel not where Christ was already named, that I might not build on
another man's foundation; but* to act on the divine word, *as it stands
written* (Is. 52.15), '*They to whom no news was carried about him, shall
see; and those who have not heard, shall understand.*' Here was an
'ambition' that was as far-sighted as it was noble. Would that
the principle of it could have been better remembered in the
history of Christendom, and not least in our own age; so that it

would not be so necessary to deplore the wasteful overlapping of efforts and systems.

Thus as a fact I was hindered for the most part – obstacles were the rule, signals of opportunity the exception – *in coming to you*; you, whose city is no untrodden ground to messengers of Christ, and therefore not the ground which had a first claim on me. *But now, as no longer having place in these regions*, eastern Roman Europe no longer an unattempted and accessible district to enter, *and having a home-sick feeling* (see above, 1.11) *for coming to you, these many years – whenever I may be journeying to Spain, [I will come to you]. For I hope on my journey through, to see the sight of you* (as if the view of so important a church would be a real spectacle), *and by you to be escorted there, if first I may have my fill of you, however imperfectly*.

As always, in the courtesy of pastoral love (see 1.11, 12), he says more, and thinks more, of his own expected gain of refreshment and encouragement from them, than even of what he may have to impart to them.

How little did he realize how that 'home-sick feeling' would be met. He was indeed to see Rome, and not just as a visitor. He was to live there in his own hired lodgings for two long years of sorrows and joys, restraints and wonderful occasions, innumerable discussions, and the writing of great Scriptures. But he did not see what lay between.

For St Paul ordinarily, as always for us, it was true that we know not what awaits us. For us, as for him, it is better to walk with God in the dark, than to go alone in the light.

Did he ultimately visit Spain? We shall never know until we are permitted to ask him in heaven. It is not at all impossible that, released from his Roman prison, he first went westward and then – as at some time he certainly did – travelled to the eastern Mediterranean. But no tradition, however, faint, connects St Paul with Spain. Yet is it irrelevant to remember that in his gospel of justification by faith he has visited Spain in later ages, at the time of the Reformation, and more recently?

Vv 25–29. *But now I am journeying to Jerusalem*, the journey whose course we know so well from Acts 20 and 21, *ministering to the saints*, serving the poor converts of the holy city as the collector and conveyer of alms for their needs. *For Macedonia and Achaia,* the northern and southern provinces of Roman Greece, finely personified in this vivid passage, *thought good to make something of a communication*, a certain gift to be shared among the recipients, *for the poor of the saints who live at Jerusalem*; the place where poverty seemed specially, for whatever reason, to haunt the converts. '*For they thought good!*' – yes; but there is a different side to the matter. Macedonia and Achaia are generous friends, but they have an obligation too: *And debtors they are to them*, to these poor people of Jerusalem. *For if in their spiritual things the nations shared, they*, these nations, *are in debt, as a fact, in things carnal*, things belonging to our 'life in the flesh', *to minister to them*; to do them public and religious service.

When I have finished this then, and sealed this fruit to them, put them into ratified ownership of this 'proceed' of Christian love, *I will come away by your road to Spain*. (He means, 'if the Lord will'; it is instructive to note that even St Paul does not make it a duty, with an almost superstitious repetition, always to say so.) *Now I know that, coming to you, in the fulness of Christ's benediction I shall come.* He will come with his Lord's blessing on him, as his messenger to the Roman disciples; Christ will send him charged with heavenly messages, and attended with his own prospering presence. And this will be 'in fulness' with a rich overflow of saving truth, and heavenly power, and blissful fellowship.

Here he pauses, to ask them for that gift which he covets so much – intercessory prayer. He has been speaking with a kind and even sprightly pleasantry (there is no irreverence in the recognition) of Macedonia and Achaia, and their gift, which is also their debt. He has spoken also of what we know from elsewhere (1 Cor. 16.1–4) to have been his own scrupulous purpose not only to collect the alms but to see them punctually delivered, above all suspicion of misuse. He has talked with cheerful confidence of the road by Rome to Spain. But now he realizes what the visit to Jerusalem involves for himself. He has tasted in many places, and at many times, the bitter hatred felt for him in unbelieving Israel; a hatred the more bitter, probably, the more his astonishing activity and influence were felt in region after region. Now he is going to the central focus of the opposition, to the city of the Sanhedrin and the Zealots. And St Paul is no Stoic, indifferent to fear, lifted in an unnatural exaltation above circumstances, though he is ready to walk through them in the power of Christ. His heart anticipates the experiences of outrage and revilings, and the possible breaking up of all his missionary plans. He thinks too of prejudice within the Church, as well as of hatred from outside; he is not at all sure that his cherished collection will not be coldly received, or even rejected, by the Judaists of the mother-church; whom yet he must and will call 'saints'. So he tells all to the Romans, with a generous and winning confidence in their sympathy, and begs their prayers, and above all sets them praying that he may not be disappointed over his longed-for visit to them.

All was granted. He was welcomed by the church. He was delivered from the fanatics, by the strong arm of the Roman empire. He did reach Rome, and he had holy joy there. Only, the Lord took his own way, a way they did not know, to answer Paul and his friends.

Vv 30–33. *But I appeal to you, brethren,* – the 'but' carries an implication that something lay in the way of the happy prospect just mentioned – *by our Lord Jesus Christ, and by the love of the Spirit,* by that holy family affection inspired by the Holy One into the hearts which he has renewed, *to wrestle along with me in your prayers on my behalf to our God; that I may be rescued from those who disobey* the gospel *in Judea, and that my ministration which takes me to Jerusalem may prove acceptable to the saints,* may be taken by the Christians there without prejudice, and in love; *that I may with joy come to you, through the will of God, and may share refreshing rest with you,* the rest of holy fellowship where the tension of discussion and opposition is broken, and the two parties perfectly understand one another in their Lord. *But the God of our peace be with you all.* Yes, so be it, whether or not the longed-for 'joy' and 'refreshing rest' is granted in his providence to the apostle. With Paul's beloved Romans, anywise, let there be 'peace'; peace in their community, and in their souls; peace with God, and peace in Christ. And so it will be, whether their human friend is or is not permitted to see them, if only the eternal Friend is there.

As we have seen above, there is a deep and attractive tenderness in this paragraph, where the writer's heart tells the readers quite freely of its personal misgivings and longings. One of the most pathetic, sometimes one of the most beautiful, phenomena of human life is the strong man in his weak hour, or rather in his feeling hour, when he is glad of the support of those who may be so much weaker than himself. There is a sort of strength which prides itself upon never showing such symptoms; to which it is a point of honour to act and speak always as if the individual were self-contained and self-sufficient. But this is a narrow type of strength, not a great one. The truly great strong man is not afraid, when appropriate, to let himself go; he is well able to recover. An underlying power leaves him at leisure to show upon the surface very much of what he feels. The breadth of his insight puts him into varied contact with others, and keeps him open to their sympathies, however humble and inadequate these sympathies may be. The Lord himself, 'mighty to save', cared more than we can fully know for human fellow-feeling, as we know from texts like 'Will ye also go away?' 'Ye are they that have continued with me in my temptations'; 'Tarry ye here, and watch with me'; 'Lovest thou me?'

No false spiritual pride tempts St Paul to conceal his anxieties from the Romans. It is a temptation sometimes to those who have been called to help and strengthen others, to affect for themselves a strength which perhaps they do not quite feel. It is well meant. Such a person is afraid that if he admits to having a burden he may seem to be false to the gospel of 'perfect peace'; that if he even lets it be suspected that he is not always in the ideal Christian state of mind, his warmest exhortations and testimonies may lose their power. But whatever the risks let him, about such things as about all others, tell the truth. It is a sacred duty in itself; there is no place in the heavenly gospel for spiritual evasion. And he will undoubtedly find that truthfulness, transparent honesty, will not really take away from his witness to the promises of his Lord. It may humiliate him, but it will not discredit Jesus Christ. It will indicate the imperfection of the recipient, but not any defect in the thing received. And the fact that the witness has been found quite candid against himself, where there is occasion, will give a double weight to all his direct testimony to the possibility of a life lived in the hourly peace of God.

It is no part of our Christian duty to feel doubts and fears! And the more we act upon our Lord's promises as they stand, the more we shall rejoice to find that misgivings tend to vanish where once they were always falling thick and fast upon us. Only, it is our duty always to be transparently honest.

However, we must not treat this theme here too much as if St Paul had given us an unmistakable text for it. His words now before us express no anxious care about his intended visit to Jerusalem. They only indicate a deep sense of the seriousness of the prospect, and of its dangers. And we know from elsewhere (see especially Acts 21.13) that that sense did sometimes amount to a feeling of agony, in the course of the very journey which he now contemplates. And we see him here quite without the wish to conceal his heart in the matter.

In closing we note, for our learning, his example as a man who desires to be prayed for. Prayer was indeed vital to St Paul. He is always praying himself; he is always asking other people to pray for him. He 'has seen Jesus Christ our Lord'; he is his Lord's inspired minister and delegate; he has been 'caught up into the third heaven'; he has had a thousand proofs that 'all things', infallibly, 'work together for his good'. But he is left by this as certain as ever, with a persuasion as simple as a child's, and also as deep as his own life-worn spirit, that it is immensely well worth his while to secure the intercessory prayers of those who know the way to God in Christ.

CHAPTER 32

A Commendation: Greetings: A Warning: A Doxology
(16. 1–27)

We may imagine ourselves once more to be watching the scene in the house of Gaius. Hour upon hour has passed over Paul and his scribe as the wonderful message has developed itself, simultaneously and everywhere the word of man and the Word of God. They began in the morning, and the themes of sin, righteousness, glory, the present and the future of Israel, the duties of the Christian life, and the special problems of the Roman mission, have carried the hours along to noon, to afternoon. Now, the sun is setting.

The apostle, pacing the room, as people often do when dictating, is aware that his message is at an end, as to doctrine and counsel. But before he tells his secretary to stop, he has to express the personal thoughts and affections in his heart, which his last words about his coming visit to Rome have stirred up. And now Paul and Tertius are no longer alone; others have found their way to the room – Timotheus, Lucius, Jason, Sosipater; Gaius himself; Quartus; and no less a neighbour than Erastus, Treasurer of Corinth. A page of personal messages is still to be dictated, from St Paul, and from his friends.

Now first he must not forget the pious woman who is – so we may assume – to take charge of this packet, and to deliver it at Rome. We know nothing of Phoebe but from this brief mention. We cannot perhaps be formally certain that she is here described as a female church-official, a 'deaconess' in a sense of that word familiar in later developments of church order – a woman set apart by the laying-on of hands, appointed to enquire into and relieve temporal distress, and to be the teacher of female enquirers in the mission. But there is at least a great likelihood that something like this was her position; for she was not merely an active Christian, she was 'a ministrant of the church'. And she was certainly, as a person, worthy of reliance and praise, now that some cause unknown to us took her from Achaia to Italy. She had been a devoted and it would seem particularly a brave friend of converts in trouble, and of St Paul himself. Perhaps in the course of her visits to the desolate she had fought difficult battles of protest, where she found harshness and oppression. Perhaps she had pleaded the forgotten cause of the poor, with a woman's courage, before some neglectful richer 'brother'.

Then Rome itself, as he sees Phoebe reaching it, comes into his mind. And there, moving up and down in that strange and almost awful world, he sees one by one the members of a large group of his personal Christian friends, and his beloved Aquila and Prisca are most visible of all. These must be individually greeted.

What the nature of these friendships was we know in some instances, for we are told here. But why the persons were at Rome, in the place which Paul himself had never reached, we do not know, nor ever shall. Many students of the epistle, it is well known, find a serious difficulty in this list of friends placed here; and they would have us see this sixteenth chapter as a fragment inserted from some other letter. But no ancient copy of the epistle gives us, by its condition, any real ground for such conjectures. And all that we have to do to realize possibilities in the actual features of the case, is to assume that many at least of this large Roman group, as surely Aquila and Prisca (see 1 Cor. 16.19), had recently migrated from the Eastern Mediterranean to Rome; a migration as common and almost as easy then as is the modern influx of foreigners to London.

It has been suggested that some of the people named here may have been members of the 'household of Caesar' mentioned in Philippians 4. 22. We have only to suppose that among St Paul's converts and friends in Asia and Eastern Europe many either belonged already to Caesar's 'household', or entered it after conversion, as purchased slaves or otherwise; and that some time before our epistle was written there was a large draft from the provincial to the metropolitan department; so that, when St Paul thought of personal Christian friends at Rome, he would happen to think, mainly, of 'saints of Caesar's household'. Such a theory would also, by the way, help to explain the emphasis with which just these 'saints' sent their greeting, later, to Philippi (see Phil. 4.22). Many of them might have lived in Macedonia, and particularly in the Roman colony of Philippi, before the time of their supposed transference to Rome.

We may add a word about 'the households', or 'people' – of Aristobulus and Narcissus – mentioned in these greetings. It seems at least likely that the Aristobulus of the epistle was a grandson of Herod the Great, and brother of Agrippa of Judea; a prince who lived and died at Rome. At his death it would be no improbable thing that his 'household' should pass by legacy to the Emperor, while they would still, as a sort of clan, keep their old master's name. Aristobulus' servants, probably many of them Jews (Herodion, St Paul's kinsman, may have been a retainer of this Herod), would thus now be a part of 'the household of Caesar', and the Christians among them would be a group of 'the household saints'. As to the Narcissus of the epistle, he may well have been the all-powerful freedman of Claudius, put to death early in Nero's time. On his death, his retainers would become, by confiscation, part of 'the household'; and its Christian members would be thought of by St Paul as among 'the household saints'.

Thus it is at least possible that the holy lives which here pass in such rapid succession before us were lived not only in Rome, but in a more or less close connection with the service and business of the Court of Nero. So freely does grace make light of circumstance.

Now we must come to the text.

Vv 1–5a. *But* – the word may mark the movement of thought from his own delay in reaching them to Phoebe's immediate coming – *I commend to you Phoebe, our sister* (this Christian woman bore, without change, and without reproach, the name of the Moon-Goddess of the Greeks), *being a ministrant of the church which is in Cenchreae*, the Aegean port of Corinth; *that you may welcome her, in the Lord,* as a fellow-member of his Body, *in a way worthy of the saints,* with all the respect and the affection of the gospel, *and that you may stand by her in any matter in which she may need you,* stranger as she will be at Rome. *For she on her part has proved a stand-by* (almost a champion, one who stands up for others) *of many,* yes, *and of me* among them.

Greet Prisca and Aquila, my co-workers in Christ Jesus; the friends *who for my life's sake submitted their own throat* to the knife (it was at some crisis otherwise utterly unknown to us, but well known in heaven); *to whom not only I give thanks, but also all the churches of the nations;* for they saved the man whom the Lord consecrated to the service of the Gentile world. *And the church at their house* greet with them; that is, the Christians of their neighbourhood, who used Aquila's great room as their house of prayer; the embryo of our parish or district church. This provision of a place of worship was something Prisca and Aquila had been accustomed to do. They had gathered 'a domestic church' at Corinth, not many months before (1 Cor. 16.19). And earlier still, at Ephesus (Acts 18.26), they wielded such a Christian influence that they must have been a central point of influence and gathering there also. In Prisca, or Priscilla, as it has been remarked, we have 'an example of what a married woman may do, for the general service of the church, in conjunction with home-duties, just as Phoebe is the type of the unmarried servant of the church, or deaconess.'

Vv 5b–16. *Greet Epaenĕtus, my beloved, who is the first-fruits of Asia,* that is of the Ephesian province, *unto Christ;* doubtless one who 'owed his soul' to St Paul in that three years' missionary pastorate at Ephesus, and who was now bound to him by the indescribable tie which makes the converter and converted one.

Greet Mary – a Jewess probably, Miriam or Maria – *for she toiled hard for you;* when and how we cannot know.

Greet Andronicus and Junias, Junianus, *my kinsmen, and my fellow-captives* in Christ's *war;* a loving and memorable reference to the human relationships which so freely, but not lightly, he had sacrificed for Christ, and to some persecution (was it at Philippi?) when these good men had shared his prison; *men who are distinguished among the apostles;* either as being themselves, in a secondary sense, devoted 'apostles', Christ's missionary delegates, though not of the apostolate proper, or as being honoured above ordinary Christians, for their work and their character, by the apostolic brotherhood; *who also before me came to be*, as they are, *in Christ*. Not improbably these two early converts helped to 'goad' (Acts 26.14) the conscience of Paul while he was still persecuting them, and to prepare the way of Christ in his heart.

Greet Amplias, Ampliatus, *my beloved in the Lord*; surely a personal convert of his own.

Greet Urbanus, my co-worker in Christ, and Stachys – another masculine name – *my beloved*.

Greet Apelles, that tested man in Christ; the Lord knows, not we, the tests he stood. *Greet those who belong to Aristobulus' people*.

Greet Herodion, my kinsman.

Greet those who belong to Narcissus' people those who are in the Lord.

Greet Tryphaena and Tryphosa (almost certainly, by their names, female slaves), *who toil* in the Lord, perhaps as 'servants of the church', so far as earthly service would allow them.

Greet Persis, the beloved woman (with faultless delicacy he does not here say 'my beloved', as he had said of the Christian men mentioned just above), *for she toiled hard in the Lord*; perhaps at some time when St Paul had watched her in a former and more Eastern home.

Greet Rufus – just possibly the Rufus of Mark 15.21, brother of Alexander, and son of cross-carrying Simon; the family was evidently known to St Mark, and we have good cause to think that St Mark wrote primarily for Roman readers – Rufus, *the chosen man in the Lord*, a saint of the élite; *and his mother – and mine!* This nameless woman had done a mother's part, somehow and somewhere, to the motherless missionary, and her love is now recorded for posterity.

Greet Asyncrĭtus, Phlegon, Hermas, Patrŏbas, Hermes, and the brethren who are with them; perhaps dwellers in some isolated and distant quarter of Rome, a little church by themselves.

Greet Philologus and Julia, Nereus and his sister, and all the saints who are with them, in their assembly.

Greet one another with a sacred kiss; the Eastern pledge of friendship and respect. *All the churches of Christ greet you*; Corinth, Cenchreae, 'with all the saints in the whole of Achaia' (2 Cor. 1.1.).

We know little or nothing about the people listed here, but we do know that they were Christ's and are now with him.

So we watch this unknown yet well-beloved company, with a sense of fellowship and expectation impossible out of Christ. This page is no mere relic of the past; it is a list of friendships to be made in heaven, and to be possessed for ever, in the endless life where personality indeed shall be eternal, but where also the union of personalities, in Christ, shall be beyond our utmost present thought.

Vv 17–21 But Paul cannot close with these messages of love. He remembers another and pressing need, a serious spiritual peril in the Roman community. He has not even alluded to it before, but it must be handled, however briefly, now:

But I appeal to you, brethren, to watch the persons who make the divisions and the stumbling blocks you know of, *alien to the teaching which you learnt* (there is an emphasis on 'you', as if to differentiate the true-hearted converts from these troublers); – *and do turn away from them*; go, and keep, out of their way; wise counsel for a peaceable but effective resistance. *For such people are not bondservants of our Lord Jesus Christ, but they are bondservants of their own belly.* They talk much of a mystic freedom; and free indeed they are from the accepted dominion of the Redeemer – but all the more they are enslaved to themselves; *and by their pious language and their specious pleas they quite beguile the hearts of the simple*, the unsuspicious. And they may perhaps have special hopes of deceiving you, because of your well-known readiness to submit, with the submission of faith, to sublime truths; a noble character, but calling inevitably for the safeguards of intelligent caution: *For your obedience*, 'the obedience of faith', shown when the gospel reached you, *was carried* by report *to all men*, and so to these deceivers, who hope now to entice your faith astray. *As regards you, therefore*, looking only at your personal condition, *I rejoice. Only I wish you to be wise as to what is good, but uncontaminated* (by defiling knowledge) *as to what is evil.* He would not have their holy readiness to believe distorted into an unholy and falsely tolerant curiosity. He would have their faith not only submissive but spiritually intelligent; then they would be alive to the risks of a counterfeited and illusory 'gospel'. They would feel, as with an educated Christian instinct, where decisively to hold back, where to refuse attention to unwholesome teaching. *But the God of our peace will crush Satan down beneath your feet speedily.* This spiritual mischief, writhing like the serpent of Paradise into your happy surroundings, is nothing less than a stratagem of Satan; a movement of his mysterious personal antagonism to your Lord, and to you his people. But Christ, the enemy's conqueror, working in you, will make the struggle short and decisive. Meet the inroad in the name of him who has made peace for you, and works peace in you, and it will soon be over. *The grace of our Lord Jesus Christ be* (or may we not render *is?*) *with you.*

What precisely was the mischief, who precisely were the dangerous teachers, spoken of here so abruptly and so urgently by St Paul? It is easier to ask the question than to answer it. Some commentators have identified them with the 'strong' of Romans 14 and 15, but this seems impossible. Paul criticizes that group for their actions, while accepting their principles. He will have nothing to do with the evil teaching mentioned here, which seems to be early Gnosticism.

The Romans, so we take it, were troubled by teachers who used the language of Christianity, saying much of 'redemption', and of 'emancipation', and something of 'Christ', and of 'the Spirit'; but all the while they meant a thing totally different from the gospel of the cross. By redemption and freedom, they meant liberation of spirit from matter. By Christ and the Spirit, they meant mere links in a chain of phantom beings, supposed to span the gulf between the Absolute Unknowable Existence and the finite world. And their morality too often tended to the belief that as matter was hopelessly evil, and spirit the unfortunate prisoner in matter, the material body had nothing to do with its unwilling, and pure, inhabitant: let the body go its own evil way, and work out its base desires.

Our sketch is taken from developed Gnosticism, such as it is known to have been a generation or two later than St Paul. But it is more than likely that such errors were present, in essence, all through the apostolic age. And it is easy to see how they could from the first disguise themselves in the special terminology of the gospel of freedom and of the Spirit.

Such things may look to us, after so many hundreds of years, only like fossils of the old rocks. They are indeed fossil specimens, but of existing species. The atmosphere of the Christian world is still infected, from time to time with unwholesome subtleties, in which the purest forms of truth are indescribably manipulated into the deadliest related error; a mischief sure to betray itself, however (where the person tempted to get involved with it is both wakeful and humble), by some fatal flaw of pride, or of untruthfulness, or of an uncleanness however subtle. And for the believer tempted like this, there is still, as of old, no advice more important than St Paul's advice here. If he would deal with such snares in the right way, he must 'turn away from them'. He must turn away to the Christ of history. He must occupy himself once more with the old gospel of pardon, holiness, and heaven.

Is the letter to be ended here at last? Not quite yet; not until Paul's colleagues have added their greetings. And first comes up the dear Timotheus, the man nearest of all to Paul's heart. Timotheus repays the affection of Paul with unwavering fidelity. And he will be true to the end to his Lord and Redeemer, through whatever tears and agonies of feeling. Then Lucius will speak, perhaps the Cyrenian of Antioch (Acts 13.1); and Jason, perhaps the convert of Thessalonica (Acts 17.5); and Sosipater, perhaps the Berean Sopater of Acts 20.4; three blood-relations of Paul, who was not left completely without human relationships, though he had laid them all at his Master's feet. Then the faithful Tertius claims the well-earned privilege of writing one sentence for himself. And Gaius modestly requests his greeting, and Erastus, the man of civic dignity and wide affairs. He has found no discord between holding a great secular office and the life of Christ; but today he is just a brother with brethren, named side by side with the Quartus whose only title is that beautiful one, 'the brother', 'our fellow in the family of God'. So the gathered friends speak each in his turn to the Christians of Rome; we listen as the names are given:

Vv 21–23. *There greets you Timotheus my fellow-worker, and Lucius,
and Jason, and Sosipatrus, my kinsmen.*

There greets you I, Tertius, who wrote the epistle in the Lord; he had
been simply Paul's conscious pen, but also he had willingly
written as being one with Christ, and as working in his cause.

There greets you Gaius, host of me and of the whole church; universal
welcomer to his door of all who love his beloved Lord, and now
particularly of all at Corinth who need his Lord's apostle.

*There greets you Erastus, the treasurer of the city, and Quartus (Kouar-
tos), the brother.* (V 24 is probably to be omitted, as a later
insertion.)

Here, as we imagine the scene, there is indeed a pause, and what
might look like an end. Tertius lays down the pen. The circle of
friends breaks up, and Paul is left alone – alone with his unseen
Lord, and with that long, silent letter; his own, yet not his own.
He takes it in his hands, to read, to ponder, to believe, to call
up again the Roman converts, so dear, so far away, and to
commit them again for faith, and for life, to Christ and to his
Father. He sees them troubled by the encircling masses of pagan
idolatry and vice, and by the embittered Judaism which meets
them at every turn. He sees them hindered by their own mutual
prejudices and mistakes; for they are still sinners. Lastly, he
sees them approached by the dangerous delusion of an unholy
mysticism, which would substitute matter for sin, and dreams
for faith, and an unknowable Somewhat, inaccessible to the finite,
for the God and Father of our Lord Jesus Christ. And then he
sees this astonishing gospel, whose glorious outline and argument
he has been caused to draw, as it was never drawn before, on
those papyrus pages; the truth of God, not of man; hidden so
long, promised so long, known at last; the gospel which displays
the sinner's peace, the believer's life, the radiant boundless future
of the saints, and, in all and above all, the eternal love of the
Father and the Son.

In this gospel, 'his gospel', he sees his God revealed afresh.
And he adores him afresh, and commits to him afresh these dear
ones of the Roman mission.

He must give them one word more, to express his overflowing

heart. He must speak to them of the One who is Almighty for them against the complex might of evil. He must speak of the gospel in whose lines the almighty grace will run. It is the gospel of Paul, but also and first the 'proclamation made by Jesus Christ' of himself as our salvation. It is the secret 'hushed' throughout the long ages of the past, but now spoken out; the message which the Lord of Ages now commands to be announced to the nations, that they may submit to it and live. It is the vast fulfilment of those mysterious Scriptures which are now the credentials, and the watchword, of its preachers. It is the supreme expression of the sole and eternal Wisdom; clear to the intellect of the heaven-taught child; more unfathomable, even to the angels, than creation itself. To the God of this gospel he must now entrust the Romans, in the glowing words in which he worships him through the Son in whom he is seen and praised. To this God – while the very language is broken by its own force – he must give everlasting glory, for his gospel, and for himself.

Paul takes the papers, and the pen. With dim eyes, and in large, laborious letters (see Gal. 6.11), and forgetting at the close, in the intensity of his soul, to make perfect the grammatical connection, he inscribes, in the twilight, this most wonderful of doxologies. Let us watch him to its close, and then in silence leave him before his Lord, and ours:

Vv 25–27. *But to him who is able to establish you, according to my Gospel, and the proclamation of, made by Jesus Christ, true to (the) unveiling of (the) secret hushed in silence during ages of times, but manifested now, and through (the) prophetic Scriptures, according to the edict of the God of Ages, for faith's obedience, published among all the nations – to God Only Wise, through Jesus Christ – to whom be the glory unto the ages of the ages. Amen.*